How to p... SPECIAL SITUATIONS in the STOCK MARKET

by Maurece Schiller

Martino Publishing
Mansfield Centre, CT
2016

Martino Publishing
P.O. Box 373,
Mansfield Centre, CT 06250 USA

ISBN 978-1-61427-959-4

© 2016 Martino Publishing

All rights reserved. No new contribution to this publication may be reproduced, stored in a retrieval system, or transmitted, in any form or by any means, electronic, mechanical, photocopying, recording, or otherwise, without the prior permission of the Publisher.

Cover Design Tiziana Matarazzo

Printed in the United States of America On 100% Acid-Free Paper

How to profit from

SPECIAL SITUATIONS

in the STOCK MARKET

by Maurece Schiller

American Research Council • Larchmont, N. Y.

COPYRIGHT, 1959, BY AMERICAN RESEARCH COUNCIL, INC.

LARCHMONT, NEW YORK

ALL RIGHTS RESERVED, INCLUDING THE RIGHT TO REPRODUCE

THIS BOOK OR PORTIONS THEREOF IN ANY FORM

LIBRARY OF CONGRESS CATALOG CARD NUMBER 59-11646

Printed in The United States of America

PREFACE

The special situation investment methods described in this book bring to the investor the "know-how" from which large fortunes can be made out of a relatively small investment.

Actually, the field of special situation investing holds a number of very timely and significant advantages for the investor. Among these are:

1. The profits are for the most part capital gains. This is a virtual necessity today in view of the high level of taxes on regular income and the favorable tax treatment of capital gains.

2. In addition to expected capital gains, there is the unique advantage of frequent "windfalls" which often bring profits to levels substantially above the original calculations. These "windfalls" may develop in many ways, one being cash payments made periodically to the investor after he has been repaid his initial capital investment plus capital gain.

3. The special situation medium very often provides an anti-inflation shelter through capitalizing the values underlying assets of securities of companies where a "corporate action" is developing.

4. Over and above all these advantages, many special situations have the tremendous attraction of reducing risk to the minimum. Many special situations are virtually riskless. In addition, by

removing the mystery from such technical activities as "arbitrage" "short selling" "discount" and "undervalue", the way has been opened to participate in an investment field which offers relatively high profits and safety of principal. Through the special situation method you determine how much profit you desire, then, let the investment do the work.

This is a "how to do it" book that discloses the investing procedure to assured profits. It shows you: (a) where to look for the investments; (b) how to recognize a special situation investment; (c) how to put the investments to work for your benefit. The book will be of value to the informed investor, as well as the newcomer to investing. The latter will find the precise step by step procedure a direct and helpful guide to investments of his own finding having characteristics similar to those situations discussed here. The experienced investor will find the analytical and investigatory procedures opening new vistas in his present range of investment areas.

A major objective of this book is to provide the large and small investors <u>with the investing procedures used by successful professionals</u>. These highly skilled investors are the buyers and sellers of the investments handled by your insurance company, bank or investment fund when working with your money. Heretofore, special situation methods were known to a mere handful of investors. Now that financial data is plentiful, the procedures can be applied by the investing public.

The availability of financial information has opened to all investors new investment channels as well as a new investment concept. This new approach is the core of special situation investing. Briefly it can be described as <u>"having a profit that will be available within an anticipated length of time."</u> The newness of this investing concept can be readily seen when compared with the familiar formula of first purchasing, which is then followed by a wait and hope period for a profit to materialize.

One of the most interesting features of this book for the investor is the extensive use of examples of specific special situations, past and present, which are used to illustrate the various types of situation and technique of profiting from them. More than 100 examples are given, including over 35 which are to a great extent currently live or significant.

With the market in general at so high a level, this book comes at an especially timely period. It is at just such a moment as this that the most advantageous investment opportunities may be found in the special situation area. This book will provide the investor with the informed "know how" to guide him to profits in special situations.

Maurece Schiller

April, 1959

CONTENTS

	Page
1. WHAT MAKES A SPECIAL SITUATION?	1
Corporate action making a Special Situation	2
Basic Requirements of a Special Situation	3
Significance of "duration" of a corporation action	4
When to buy	5
How to determine existence of "undervalue"	6
How to calculate the Special Situation	6
Minimum Risk	7
Dividends	7
Sources of information	8
2. MERGERS & ACQUISITIONS	11
Mergers and acquisitions defined	11
Relative values are the keys to profit potentials	12
Example: AMER. WOOLEN-TEXTRON-ROBBINS MILLS	13
Example: MERRITT-CHAPMAN & SCOTT	14
Casting more light on relative values	15
Self-liquidating features establish profits in mergers	17
Example: McCRORY STORES-McLELLAN STORES	18
The kernel of an acquisition is price	19

Alertness to opportunity 19
       Example: FOREMOST DAIRIES-GOLDEN STATE merger 20
How to determine probabilities of profit 21
Analytical approach; 12 basic questions and answers 22
       Example: HUDSON-NASH-AMERICAN MOTORS............. 23
The importance of voting. What is a proxy? 24
How to obtain the profits... 27
       Example: STERLING DRUG-HILTON DAVIS 27
Choice of procedure 28
Another choice - "hedge" 30
How to sell short 30
Expenses 31
Findings of the analysis - the decision 32
Origin of mergers/acquisitions................................... 32
Merger based on soundness 32
       Example: MERCK-SHARP & DOHME 33
       Example: LIQUID CARBONIC-GENERAL DYNAMICS 33
Acquisitions in response to economic necessity 34
       Example: CHRYSLER-BRIGGS MFG. 34
Merger as a result of "family sell-out" 36
       Example: HICKOCK OIL-PURE OIL 36
Where does opposition breed?.................................... 37
       Example: AMERICAN WOOLEN 37
Why external opposition should be evaluated 38
       Example: FOLLANSBEE STEEL 38
Where to look for merger/acquisitions 40
       Example: PORTER CO.-THERMOID 40
14 companies with other stock interest 41

3. LIQUIDATIONS   42

Definition of liquidations 42
       Example: SOUTHERN PRODUCTION..................... 43
Something for Nothing... 43
       Example: CONTINENTAL FDY & MACHINE 43
Types of liquidations 44
Investor's profit margins in liquidations 45
       Example: AMERICAN REPUBLICS CORP.................. 45
Partial liquidations 46
Optional liquidation 46
       Example: WILLYS-OVERLAND CORP. 47
Significance of voting control.................................. 47
Why the plan was unattractive 48
Values in residual corporate shells 48
       Example: SERVEL.................................... 48
Procedure for investing in "liquidations" 49

What to look for in a liquidation	49
Where to find the tax status	50
Example: BOSTON ELEVATED	50
Progress procedure	51
Legal aspects	52
Timing schedule of liquidations	52
Methods of distribution of assets	53
Distribution in kind	53
Example: ASSOCIATED GENERAL UTILITIES	54
Piecemeal liquidation	55
Example: KALAMAZOO STOVE & FURNACE	55
Why are liquidations available?	58

4. SPIN-OFFS   60

What is a spin-off?	60
Example: TRANSAMERICA	60
Example: ACF BRILL MOTORS	62
Spin-off as a dividend	63
Example: GRAHAM-PAIGE-ROYAL AMERICAN	63
Undervalue in spin-offs	63
Background of spin-offs	64

5. STUBS   65

What is a stub?	65
How to invest in a stub	66
Classification: 8 types and companies	66
How to approach a stub	67
Stubs representing undesignated claims	68
Example: OWENS-ILLINOIS GLASS	68
Stubs representing accrued-dividend claim	68
Example: CONSOLIDATED RETAIL STORES	68
Reversionary certificates	68
Example: WESTERN RAILWAY OF ALABAMA	69
A tax-suit stub: STANDARD GAS & ELECTRIC	70
A residual asset: RIDGEWAY CORP.	71
Certificates of contingent interest: INTERNAT'L PAPER	71
Reclaimed assets and tax windfall	72
Example: AMERICAN POWER & LIGHT	72
NEW YORK, NEW HAVEN & HARTFORD RR (CBI's)	73
Guaranteed stock with assured appreciation	74
Example: GOLD & STOCK TELEGRAPH	74

6. TENDERS

How are tenders used? Where to find them 76
    Example: TEXTRON 77
How are tenders processed? 77
    Example: PARMELEE 78
Additional profit possibilities 79
Windfall profits from tenders 79
Sinking-fund tenders 81
    Example: AMERICAN BANK NOTE 82
Anticipating the use of a tender 83
    Example: EASTERN STEAMSHIP LINES 84
Analysis of the situation 85
How to calculate probable tender price 85
Tender invitation used to acquire all shares of a company 86
    Example: COMMODORE HOTEL 86

7. REORGANIZATIONS   87

The profit play 87
Where can I find reorganizations? 88
How to get the profit 89
The significance of the opposition 89
Protective committees 89
    Example: MISSOURI PACIFIC RR 90
How to establish an investment position 91
Summary of step-by-step procedure 92
Approach to analysis of the plan 94
Hedge position 95
EQUITABLE OFFICE BUILDING 95
Surprise ruling 96

8. RAILROAD REORGANIZATIONS   98

The three-step approach 98
DENVER & RIO GRANDE, WESTERN RY arbitrage 99
How to own preferred stock at low cost 101
How to establish a low-cost income bond 101
How to establish a low-cost first-mortgage bond 101
Investment in when-issued securities 102
Case History: DENVER & RIO GRANDE 103
HUDSON & MANHATTAN RR reorganization 105
An epic case history: MISSOURI PACIFIC RR 109

9. PUBLIC UTILITY HOLDING COMPANY REORGANIZATIONS — 113

- Where to look for the investment opportunities 113
- Investor approach to a divestment 115
- How to locate the profit....................................... 115
- The "parts" and the "whole" 116
    - Example: AMERICAN POWER & LIGHT..................... 116
- Why the public utility divestment period offered many profit opportunities 116
- Procedure for setting up a divestment situation 118
    - Example: COMMONWEALTH & SOUTHERN CORP........... 119
- INTERNAT'L HYDRO-ELECTRIC SYSTEM 120
- STANDARD POWER & LIGHT 124
- STANDARD GAS & ELECTRIC 127

10. RECAPITALIZATIONS — 131

- Where to look for recapitalizations 132
- Who approves a recapitalization 132
- Establishing an investment position 132
- Objectives of financial study 133
- Case history CHICAGO EASTERN ILLINOIS 133
- Recapitalization to eliminate high-cost nonredeemable preferred stock 136
    - Example: AMERICAN CAR & FDY......................... 136
- The importance of voting on a plan............................ 138
- Symptoms of a recapitalization 138
- What to look for before you buy............................... 139
- Working aides 140
- Types of recapitalizations 140
    - Example: PENN DIXIE CEMENT CO........................ 141
    - Example: R. HOE & CO................................... 142
- Corporate action in recapitalization plan 142
- By-product beneficiaries of a recapitalization 145
- Summary of important points to be considered 145

11. APPRAISALS — 147

- Who creates an appraisal 148
- How to profit from an appraisal 148
- Importance of placing right value on a security................ 149
- Types of appraisals 150
- What every dissenter should know 150
- Who creates the stockholder's rights........................... 150
- Importance of knowing your rights 151
    - Example: HUDSON MOTOR-NASH KELVINATOR 151

Birthplace of an appraisal 154
How to evaluate a security for appraisal.................................. 155
Pitfalls 155
The "lone wolf" approach 156
    Example: MAXSON FOOD SYSTEM-FOREMOST DAIRY...... 156
How to establish the right to request an appraisal 156

12. OVERSUBSCRIPTIONS 158

The three phases of subscription "rights" 158
What are rights and warrants? 159
The preemptive privilege 160
How to locate the profit 160
How to calculate the value of a right 161
Quality analysis 162
SOUTH CAROLINA ELECTRIC & GAS............................... 162
BARIUM STEEL 163
Information and publicity sources.. 164
Summary of important points in oversubscriptions............... 164
Recent oversubscription opportunities................................ 166
  GENERAL PUBLIC SERVICE & SOUTHWESTERN PUBLIC
  SERVICE 166

13. "SOMETHING DOING" SITUATIONS 167

Characteristics... 167
Where can "something doing" situations be found?............. 168
Carry-forward tax credit table 170
MOTOR PRODUCTS CORP... 171
Analytical procedure 173
Disclosure of the shell game 174
How to get the profit 175

INDEX 177

CHAPTER 1

What Makes a Special Situation?

Special situations are investments in stocks or bonds that reflect "corporate action." Corporate action may be defined as activities which occur within the administrative scope of the corporation rather than at the business level.

Special-situation investments are attractive because they offer (1) safety of principal, the foundation upon which all true special situations are built, and (2) assured profits.

In addition, special-situation investments frequently have a dash of "great hopes and expectations" known as "romance," or "windfall."

In ordinary investments the romance expectation may provide the buying impulse; but it is speculative; the experience may prove a costly one. In special-situation investments, however, there is romance without risk. It lies in hidden values which quite unexpectedly come into being. These assets often develop substantially larger profits than had originally been estimated. Unanticipated profits may result from newly found values coming to light in: (1) obscure assets, (2) tax adjustments, (3) acceleration of the consummation of the corporate action, and (4) new ideas injected into a special situation while it is in the development period.

A special situation is not difficult to appraise because practically all the needed information is readily available. If you are an informed investor you can quickly determine the profit potential of the situation. All you need is pencil, paper, curiosity, and a desire to make money.

A characteristic of special situations, generally not present in other investments, is the prior knowledge of the aggregate profit. Because the expected profit is known beforehand, the cross currents which could affect that profit are anticipated and analyzed partly through such questions as:

Is the particular situation limited to the calculated profit?

Does the situation have more than one corporate action which may benefit it?

Will the profit be a fixed amount established only at consummation of the corporate action?

Will the profit accumulate progressively and be reflected marketwise as the situation develops?

Can the situation be terminated with a profit before consummation of the corporate action?

What percentage of the profit would be lost if the duration period is protracted?

Could an extended duration period result in additional profits?

Corporate Action Makes a Special Situation

An appealing quality of a special situation is its minimal risk. Moreover, profit possibilities frequently exceed conventional speculations. Because minimum risk and large-profit potentials are present, these situations appeal to conservative as well as speculatively minded investors, since profits arise from corporate action which is ultimately reflected in the value of the securities. This differs from ordinary investments which depend upon the quality of the security along with market action to create a profit. Corporate action, then, is the fundamental characteristic which distinguishes special situations from ordinary investments.

To assist you in obtaining a clear picture of corporate action, we shall divide a corporation into two identities. The corporate identity we are interested in here is concerned with finances that represent money invested in the company, i.e., the capital structure. A corporate action is an administrative move affecting the capital structure.

A special situation's existence is limited to the life of the corporate action. Completion of the corporate action should automatically terminate the special situation. This self-liquidating characteristic eliminates guesswork as to when to dispose of an investment.

The corporation's other activity is concerned with the business for which the corporation was organized -- manufacturing a commodity or rendering a service. Corporate actions are not directly concerned with profits or losses from operations of the business.

It follows, then, that a corporate action which creates a special situation pertains to a specific corporate activity, and the investment would not be influenced importantly by prevailing economic conditions; nor would the attainment of the profit objective be dependent upon the movement of the securities market. It is the corporate action which creates the profit. Therefore, the completion of the corporate action would, at the same time, establish the profit.

Profits from special-situation investments lie in the intrinsic value of the corporation's securities. This value ultimately is reflected in greater worth of the special-situation vehicle.

The investor's objective in a special-situation investment is capital gains. This differs from the usual investment objective of a return (income) for the use of money. The special-situation investor thinks in terms of dollar increases (or decreases) in the principal used in a transaction. The money invested is the capital, and the profits are recognized as "capital gains."

Having broadly defined the nature of special-situation investments, it would be helpful, at this point, to discuss the structure of this profitable investment medium. Special-situation investments have specific basic characteristics. The absence of a single characteristic detracts from the securities' qualifications as a special situation.

Basic Requirements of a Special Situation

Four elements should be present in a special-situation investment: Foremost is the corporate action that is occurring. Next, the market price of the stock or bond should be below the expected worth. This is known as "undervalue." The third factor is the availability of facts so the investment can be calculated, i.e., figured mathmatically. The fourth is the investment's minimum-risk status. In a special situation, then:

1. A specific "corporate action" occurs.
2. The security in undervalued.
3. The investment is calculable.
4. The security is at a minimum-risk level.

When the above elements are combined in one security a special situation exists.

Which Corporate Actions Lead to Special Situations?

As the mining prospector knows his geologic formations, so the securities investor is sensitive to the fields in which special situations germinate. There are ten places where corporate actions originate. A brief comment about each follows.

<u>Mergers and Acquisitions</u>. These corporate actions bring to light special-situation investment opportunities almost daily.

<u>Liquidations</u>. This profitable field is given wide publicity, which makes this category a readily available medium for investors' use.

<u>Tenders</u>. Tenders are used for the purchase and sale of blocks of securities. The procedure is well known to investors through offers to purchase securities by an acquiring corporation.

<u>Reorganizations and/or Recapitalizations</u>. These offer varied opportunities for profit in view of the numerous corporate activities involved in such developments.

<u>Spin-offs and Divestment of Assets</u>. These corporate actions may result from voluntary decisions or from governmental mandatory directives. The public utility holding company divestments during the 1940's and the more recent separations, in the moving-picture industry, of producers from theatre operators, illustrate compulsory corporate action.

<u>Tax Contingencies</u>. Investment opportunities may exist in tax refunds expected to accrue from established operational losses of a business.

<u>Appraisals</u>. Request for an appraisal is a professional province not often frequented by the average investor. The subject, nevertheless, is discussed in detail, since merely knowing the procedure can be put to profitable use.

<u>Residual Stubs</u>. These, generally, are low-priced shares which offer a percentage play in the winding up of a corporation's affairs.

<u>Oversubscriptions</u>: This category is a recent development in the corporate-action orbit. It is an offering of additional shares to stockholders. In the privilege of subscribing to shares remaining at the expiration of the subscription lies the special-situation profit potential.

<u>Significance of "Duration" of a Corporate Action</u>

A paramount decision confronting investors is <u>when</u> to purchase and how long to stay with a specific investment. After having discovered a special situation it is essential to estimate the length of time that will be required to complete the corporate action. This phase is known as the duration period. Profits in special situations are, to a major degree, determined by the length of time one's capital is employed. Therefore duration is an important element. This is so since the main return upon the money placed in a special situation is in the form of capital gains. The effect of duration can be seen when we amortize the estimated capital gain over the duration period. Should the investment be held for a protracted period the profit is subject to the law of diminishing returns.

Obviously, a 20% return which takes two years for fulfillment is better than a 20% return allocated over four years. In the first instance the rate of return would be 10% per annum, while in the latter case it would be only 5%. Thus the shorter the duration period, the greater the percentage return.

The longevity of a special-situation investment is significant since income frequently is not obtained, nor is it of prime importance. Furthermore, under the present tax law it is more advantageous to have long-term (over six months) periods, than to receive a current yield in the form of capital gains.

Uncertainties in duration arise from the character structure of an investment. Conspicuous contingencies causing duration delays are legal and tax differences. While some special situations come into being because of legal and tax disputes, other situations may be impaired if such contingencies develop unexpectedly. The decision whether or not to participate frequently is determined by the duration factor.

The following illustration demonstrates the importance of duration. A mathematically calculated appreciation of 40% over a two-year period would be dissipated if the situation became protracted. This would occur where a fixed value is to be obtained when the corporate action is completed. Each subsequent year's delay would depreciate the annual rate of return so that only 10% would be realized if consummation required four years, while further extension could wipe out any gain or reduce it to an unprofitable level.

A further example of the importance of duration can be seen where a capital appreciation of 40% is indicated on a two-year time factor. This is equal to 20% gain on an annual basis. That investment would not be as inviting as a situation offering 10% with six months to go, or 5% with only three months to go. While the percentage of profit on an annual basis is the same in each case, i.e., 20%, the margin for possible upset of the duration is considerably smaller in the latter instance. Too frequently "duration" has changed the complexion of many attractive special-situation candidates.

When to Buy - Why Timing Is Not a Special-situation Problem

To know when to buy is often difficult in ordinary investing. However, in special situations much of the uncertainty is removed by the status of the situation. In the first place, to warrant consideration the expected corporate action should be beyond the vague, wishful-hoping stage. The corporate action should be sufficiently advanced toward consummation so that its occurrence can be expected within some definite period.

Ergo, since the corporate action does exist, it is then a matter of calculation whether the situation meets your profit requirements. You would refrain from purchasing if the profit is too small. You would wait to invest until the profit spread improved.

How to Determine the Existence of "undervalue"

The profit-potential factor is known as "undervalue," sometimes referred to as "discount." Undervalue means that a stock or bond is available at a price below its expected worth upon completion of the corporate action. The difference between the market price of a security and an expected higher value resulting from a corporate action is known as discount. A stock that has an estimated worth or tangible value of $20 per share and is priced in the market at $15 per share would be considered to be selling at a discount of $5 per share. This is equivalent to 25% of the $20 value (5 ÷ 20 = 25%).

The security is considered undervalued in terms of the estimated value resulting from the corporate action creating the special situation. A corporation in liquidation may have assets worth $10 per share, while the shares may be available in the market at $9 per share. Thus the situation would be undervalued to the extent of 10%. When the liquidation has been completed it is expected that the shareholder will have received $10 for each of his shares.

How to Calculate the Special Situation

Having established the prerequisites of corporate action and undervalue, we next want to know whether it can be calculated to determine its desirability as a special-situation investment. The first step is to figure the amount of expected profit. (Anticipated price less costs equals the profit.) If the ultimate profit is satisfactory (investor's objectives differ), then you should proceed with the investigation. The procedure is discussed in detail later. However, particular attention should be given to: (1) opposition to the corporate action, (2) legal claims, and (3) tax contingencies. While these three factors may not be exactly measurable in dollars and cents, consideration should be given to the full effect of adverse decisions. The amount of potential loss you could incur in the event the anticipated corporate action does not materialize should be carefully figured.

The thinking at this stage is that, should this corporate action fail to materialize, the security would return to its former price. Thus the potential loss would be the difference between the market price of the security at a date preceding the corporate action's influence on the market and the price the investor paid for the security. The example; let us take a stock which has been selling around the 25 level prior to any influence of a prospective corporate action. Subsequently the shares advanced to the 30 range, reflecting anticipation of something doing in the corporation. You then purchased the shares. Should the anticipated action fail to materialize, the stock would recede to the 25 price. At that level you would have a 5=point loss.

Favorable influences also should be investigated. For illustrative purposes consider a corporation that is in liquidation. To know that a definite date has been set for the distribution of the corporation's cash funds or assets would only be of value if verified. Then such specific information would permit calculation of the potential of the investment. The percentage of profit could then be obtained by applying the known asset value and the duration period against the amount to be invested. For application of this procedure see page 71, Southern Production. Furthermore, by verifying the favorable influences, in this case the duration, you would contribute to the safety of the situation.

During the life of a special situation it is expected that the calculated worth will remain comparatively constant because the underlying assets are based on sound values not subject to broad fluctuations. An example of the calculation procedure is clearly seen in the sale of Briggs Manufacturing Corporation's assets to the Chrysler Corporation (see page 35.)

Minimum Risk

An element which endears special situations to investors is the characteristic of "minimum risk." Their high level of safety places special-situation investments among the most riskless of undertakings. It is indeed comforting to own a security which gives one a feeling of confidence as to the amount of profit and/or loss that could occur. The monetary risks in a true special situation can be reduced to a calculated minimum through mathematical computations and the application of available pertinent data. Because of this many special situations offer safety of principal equivalent to high-grade, triple-A loans or bonds.

Special situations germinate when the available information discloses all the essential material. Acting on such information, the possibility of loss in relation to the probability of successful completion will be negligible since, through prudent selection, we can discard those securities where data remain unverified, or which are excessively speculative in character. The procedure for estimating the risk potential is to calculate first the amount of loss that would be incurred in the event the corporate action failed to materialize. If the price paid for the shares reflected an increase because of the pending corporate action, then that additional amount would be the major portion of the calculated loss.

The estimated loss potential should be related to the amount of capital to be invested. If the calculated loss amounts to a substantial part of the capital required, then the transaction is not considered a true special situation.

A special situation showing a capital gain of 10% on an annual basis should have a probability of 9 to 1 in favor of success. While the percentage gain could be considerably higher in numerous instances, the risk probability should not increase in the same ratio. Should that occur, then the situation would be a speculation rather than a special-situation investment.

Dividends

We have not touched on dividends and interest because these play a minor role when appraising a special-situation investment. However, since the presence of dividends and interest may exert an influence upon the quality of the situation, they become a contributing factor. Where dividends and/or interest are sufficient to pay for the cost of the capital invested, the situation would arouse a more spontaneous enthusiasm for further analysis. The significance of income is measured solely by the amount it contributes to the possible profit. Thus dividends and interest are viewed differently here than in ordinary long-term investment where the stability of income may be the deciding factor.

Sources of Information

We have discussed the various elements which, when combined in one investment, create a special situation in a stock or bond. Besides locating a special situation and classifying it for easy analysis, it is helpful to verify the pertinent data. The sources which may disclose, add to, or validate information about these investments are numerous. While all sources cannot be used at one time for a single special situation, knowledge of "where to go to find out" is essential when working with special situations.

The prime sources for information concerning corporate actions are: (1) The metropolitan newspapers and the nationally distributed financial publications such as the Wall Street Journal and the Journal of Commerce. (2) Financial news, advisory and statistical services, such as Barron's, Standard & Poor's, Inc., and Moody's Inc. (3) Trade publications specializing in a specific industry such as Iron Age, Oil and Gas Journal, the Fairchild Publications, and Missiles & Rockets. (4) The libraries of banks, exchanges, public libraries, and the Securities Exchange Commission (SEC) have many financial reports that can be used as reference for valuable corporate information. (5) SEC recently has initiated, for public use, a new publication, Securities & Exchange News Digest. It contains a summary of financial proposals filed with and actions by SEC. This may be one of your most valuable sources of corporate-action information. (6) A most comprehensive source is the corporation itself. Corporate public releases often comprise the following:

The annual report contains valuable statistical facts, highlights of the year, business activities, product developments, and future plans.

Interim reports generally review quarterly earnings and business progress.

Company organ is a publication prepared for employees, stockholders, and interested individuals. It contains general corporate news.

Public relations department is frequently an excellent source for immediate data.

Footnotes, that is, the small-print segment of company reports, frequently include information which offers clues to values of properties and securities holdings.

Corporation officers' speeches and published articles are generally available upon request. The public relations department of most corporations will be glad to see that you receive copies of their releases.

Notices of annual meeting and proxy statements generally include data relating to such corporate activities as mergers, acquisitions, and interrelated directors.

Prospectuses published at the time of issuance of securities contain a complete record of the corporation. This reveals much valuable information. Prospectuses are available from SEC and at offices of the issuers of the securities.

Reports prepared by corporations for SEC and the Commission's findings and orders reveal the following data:

    The complete history of the corporation
    Stock and bond holdings of management and large holders
    Interrelated securities holdings of officers with other corporations
    Contracts with officials
    Stock options
    Securities transactions by officers, directors, large holders, and the corporation itself
    Capitalization details
    Loan agreements and restrictive clauses

Persons involved with the corporations' activities constitute an excellent source of authoritative data. This would include (1) those concerned with: issuance of securities, (2) banking affiliates, (3) committees representing groups of shareholders, (4) engineers, (5) legal associates, and (6) officers of the corporation.

A unique feature of "Wall Street" is the accessibility of information. An esprit de corps for mutual exchange of information, which is not found in other industries or professions, characterizes Wall Street. Another singular feature is that it pays to investigate all rumors. Notwithstanding the general opinion to the contrary, there is more truth than fabrication in most hearsay stories relating to mergers, acquisition, and liquidations.

A Special Situation Has No Secret Life

A special-situation security is one of the common variety of stocks and bonds traded on national exchanges or the unlisted markets. The procedure for participation, that is, purchase and sale, is the same as in other securities transactions. These are generally arranged through an investment broker. There are no secret markets or unknown securities in special-situation investments.

Special-situation investments, by their very existence, eliminate guessing. All the information one needs can generally be obtained. We have seen that the special situation can be figured on a money basis. An additional but not essential aid would be for the investor to have a "sense for dollars" similar to that extrasensory perception that characterize the reporter with a "nose for news" or the gardener's "green thumb."

Unlike ordinary investments, special situations must be sought. They do not present themselves with a label like a stock classified as preferred or a bond designated as a first mortgage. Therefore it would be helpful if you learned to identify special situations within the scope of the categories mentioned earlier. Proper classification puts you on the right track and eases the way for further investigation. Special-situation investments offer challenges to deductive thinking combined with investigatory plodding inherent in detective work. The clues are there. This book locates their nesting places.

The following chapters will take you through the step-by-step procedure of each special-situation category. We shall work mainly through examples, discussing situations which conform and those which veer from the basic rules. We shall show where the four basic elements of <u>corporate action</u>, <u>undervalue</u>, and <u>calculable</u> and <u>minimum risk</u> are present in specific examples. You will see how these are applied to make profits.

Each chapter is a self-contained unit describing a specific category of special situation. Since our fundamental principles of securities analysis and investigation are continually used throughout this book, you will meet frequent references to the analytical procedures. These are discussed in detail in Chapter 2.

The examples used in this book are typical in that similar conditions recur. In order to illustrate the completed step-by-step procedure in a typical case, certain of the investment examples are such as have previously consummated their particular corporate actions. However, where available, a most recent, pending, or prospective case has been used to demonstrate the specific point. Consequently, instances are present where the situations are currently alive. This means they may still have profit possibilities and therefore are worth investigating.

CHAPTER 2

Mergers and Acquisitions

This chapter treats with the principles of investigation and analysis as applied to special situations. Because of the broad scope of this subject, the material has been divided into three parts. The first explores profit possibilities and how they can be recognized. This is followed by a section dealing with the analytical methods for determining whether the profits can be obtained. The third part is devoted to the technical procedures used to obtain the profits.

Mergers and acquisitions are the common garden varieties of special situations. Since most business enterprises are receptive to a merger/acquisition, announcements of actual, prospective, and pending situations are plentiful. Newspapers and financial publications follow their progress with daily reports. Many of the nation's larger corporations were created by and continue to grow through the merger/acquisition procedure. The drug, chemical, food, electrical, petroleum, automotive, and steel industries present interesting cases of such growth.

Mergers and Acquisitions Defined

The words "merger" and "acquisition" frequently are used interchangeably. Here are definitions of the terms as used in this book.

A merger is a combination of two or more business enterprises into a single unit through the transfer of their properties to one surviving corporation. A merger permits pooling of the assets and operations of the combining corporations.

An acquisition is the procurement of a majority of the controlling interest of an enterprise, which then is at the sole disposition of the acquiring company.

For special-situation investors mergers and acquisitions differ in two fundamental characteristics. Recognition of these differences enables you to classify the investment opportunities and, in turn, to select the procedures to be used.

One difference is that two or more companies must actively participate in order to consummate a merger, while an acquisition can be completed through the sole activities of one corporation. The second difference is that corporate mergers require the approval of stockholders of all the corporations involved, while an acquisition may not require stockholder approval. In the latter case, the "fait accompli" (the acquisition) can be achieved through the purchase of control of a corporation in the securities market or via private negotiation.

With these differences in mind we will begin our trip through investment opportunities via special situations by first studying mergers.

The end result of a merger is that one of the combining companies becomes the dominant operating corporation. When this status has been established the profit opportunities exist in the securities of the corporation to be absorbed. To illustrate, this circumstance prevailed in the Merck & Co.-Sharp & Dohme merger, in which, as is characteristic of this type of merger, there was an exchange of shares, 2 1/4 shares of Merck common for each share of Sharp & Dohme. Merck continued as the surviving corporation.

Profit possibilities in this instance were available at the time the plan was announced since Merck common stock was priced around $23 per share and Sharp & Dohme common stock around $45 per share. A purchaser of 100 shares of Sharp & Dohme at a cost of $4,500 could sell at $23 per share the 225 shares of Merck to be received in exchange for the 100 shares of Sharp & Dohme. Proceeds from such a sale would amount to $5,175 (23 x 225). This would establish a gross profit of $675. The procedure for obtaining the profit is discussed on page 33.

Relative Values Are the Keys to Profit Potentials

Mergers are often consummated through the creation of a new corporation formed to expedite the desired combination. In such cases each class of security of the combining corporations may contain opportunities for special-situation investment. The opportunities arise in the relationship between the outstanding securities and those to be issued by the new corporation. Thus the fusing corporations should be viewed as though the merger had become effective and the resulting securities examined in relation to the new corporation. The examination would disclose the relative values of the securities involved, which in turn would disclose the differences in their market worth. The presence of such differences makes it possible to obtain a profit.

As an illustration of <u>relative values</u> we have selected the closing phase of the classic three-cornered merger of American Woolen Co., Textron, Inc., and Robbins Mills. This presents a situation where a new corporation was created to consummate the merger. Here we see three relationships of securities involved in a merger, namely:

1. Relationship to the outstanding securities
2. Relationship to the securities to be outstanding of the new corporation
3. Relationship to the securities of its own corporation

Under the plan, Textron would be the surviving corporation, with its name changed to Textron American, Inc. The capitalization comprised:

Insurance loans	$10,598,000	
15-year (5%) debentures	20,438,080	
Convertible preferred stock		625,219 shares
4% preferred stock, Series A		26,635 shares
4% preferred stock, Series B		88,558 shares
Common stock		2,889,014 shares

The exchange ratios, the prices of the various securities around the time of the public announcement of the amended plan, and the indicated values in relation to the proposed merger were as follows:

Textron, Inc.

Price 12/7/54		Indicated Value
$10.62	Common stock, to remain unchanged	$10.62
$18.75	Common stock, to remain unchanged	$18.75

American Woolen Co.

$76.00	$4 prior preferred, to receive $105 of 15 year debentures	$84.00
$85.62	7% preferred, to receive $120 of 15 year debentures	$96.00
$20.50	Common stock, to receive: 2 shares of Textron Amer. common (2 x 10.62)	$21.25

Robbin Mills

$33.00	4.50% preferred, to receive: 2 shares of Textron Amer. pf. (18 3/4 x 2)	$37.50
	Plus cash for accrued dividend	$ 2.06
	Total	$39.56
$10.62	Common stock, share for share	$10.62

- 13 -

Textron common and preferred shares would be unchanged, being the surviving company. Therefore it is possible to value American Woolen common and Robbins Mills common and preferred stocks in relation to the respective Textron securities. If we use the prices of December 7, 1954, the date on which the plan (with the minor changes) was announced, we can spot the following value "differences":

American Woolen common which was priced at 20 1/2 had a value of 21 1/4 in relation to the new corporation. Robbins Mills common which was priced at 10 5/8 had the equivalent value under the proposed plan. However, Robbins Mills preferred, when related to the similar Textron preferred, had a value of 37.50, (plus the $2.06 for accrued dividends) as compared with the market price of 33. In the foregoing instances we were able to relate the prices to existing securities and so could spot profit opportunities.

Another security relationship existed in the above merger. Here American Woolen preferred stock would be exchangeable for 15-year debentures, a newly created security of the merged companies. Since these debentures could not be related to outstanding securities they could be valued in relation to the new corporation. Therefore the market value would be determined by the position of the new debentures in relation to assets and participation in earnings. In this instance a fair price seemed to be around 80, which would offer a return of 6% on the debentures. This yield would be in line with the market values of similar-quality securities and the new company's comparative rating. On the basis of the adjusted plan*, the estimated values for the debentures to be received offered profit possibilities in American Woolen Preferred.

This example of value relationships illustrates the practical approach for recognizing relative values and their profit possibilities.

Merritt-Chapman & Scott Corp.'s seven-way merger presents an excellent example of relative values. The company had gathered, over a period of time, substantial stock interest in the six companies which comprised the ultimate merger. These holdings had been revealed in SEC releases, financial publications, and newspapers and company reports. This information was followed by the election to the Boards of Directors of persons known to be associated with the Merritt-Chapman interests. Specifically, this occurred in the Newport Steel Corp. as well as in DeVoe & Raynolds Co. and Marion Power Shovel Co.

---

*The previous allocations of American Woolen preferred stocks were $5.00 less of debentures for each class of preferred. The increased offer suggested the probability that the preferreds warranted better treatment in view of the strong position they maintained in their own company. The dollar value of the debentures received gave full recognition to the strong position of the preferreds in relation to its own capitalization.

The existence of interrelated directorships gave the clue to the subsequent moves. One was the acquisition of a substantial equity interest in each of the companies. The merger proposal followed.

The seven-way merger offered opportunities for special-situation profit though the price level of some of the component companies rose after the initial acquisitions.

The tabulation which follows shows the six companies to be merged into M.C. & S., the ratio of exchange, the price of the shares as of December 16, the aggregate value in shares of M.C. & S., and the spread or potential profit per share. The table discloses that on a single share basis the gross profit potential for Devoe & Raynolds amounts to $2.84, equivalent to a return on an annual basis of 7.7%, while the net, after costs incurred for both purchasing and selling, would be about 5.5%. However, should the merger consummate within the expected time of three months, then the rate of return would be 22%. The Tennessee Products & Chemical Corp. offers the greatest potential profit, 11% before costs, or a net of 9% after commission and taxes. In both Newport Steel and Marion Power Shovel, where M.C. & S. controls over 90% of the shares, the gross spread ranges from 4% in Newport to no spread at all in the Marion Power shares. The market in the Osgood Co. shares is too thin for consideration. The New York Shipbuilding spread amounted to only 4.3% gross. However, it is interesting because the share-for-share exchange ratio can be used as a guide from which to estimate the value of M.C. & S. common stock.

The accompanying tabulation shows the relative values of the shares of the participating companies in relation to M.C. & S. the dominant company. (See p. 16)

Under the terms of the merger the company would accept all shares deposited for exchange if 80% or more of the stock (of the three companies named first in the table) is presented. However, the company reserves the right, in the event that the 80% stipulation is not met, to accept all shares not recalled. The terms would not apply to the companies wherein M.C. & S. now has over 90% equity interest. In the latter instances the question of approval of the merger is of course academic, since the management has the necessary voting strength to make the consolidation effective.

Casting More Light on Relative Values

To further clarify the concept of relative values in mergers, it might be helpful to create a simple corporate structure which can show the various relationships in their elementary stage. For example, let us assume that the Acme Corp. and the Brown Corp. contemplate merging. The basic relationship follows:

The Acme Corp.'s capital consists of, 1,000 shares of common stock. The book value is $100,000. Thus each share has a value of $100,000 ÷ 1,000 = $100.) Mr. X, a stockholder of the Acme Corporation, owns 100 shares, which is equal to $10,000, or a 10% interest.

- 15 -

M. C. & S. SEVEN-WAY MERGER

Company	Exchange Ratio	Market Price of Co. to be Merged	Market Price of M C & S	Aggregate Value in Shares of M C & S	Per share Spread
Devoe & Raynolds	1.66 shares of M.C.& S. for each Class A	$37	$24	$39.84	$2.84
New York Ship Bldg.	1 share M.C.& S. for each common share	23	24	24.00	1.00
Tenn. Products & Chem.	1.25 shares M.C.& S. for each share	27	24	30.00	3.00
Newport Steel	1 share M.C.& S. for each 2-1 shares. (cost: $23.10)	11	24	24.00	0.90
Marion Power Shovel	3 shares of M.C.& S. for each 2 shares	36	24	36.00	nil
Osgood Co.	3 shares M.C.& S. for each 2 shares				

The Brown Corp.'s capital consists of, 1,000 shares of common stock. The book value is $10,000. Thus each share has a value of $10,000 ÷ 1,000 = $10). Mr. Y, a stockholder of the Brown Corp., owns 200 shares, which equals $2,000, or a 20% interest.

In the above example the Acme stock is worth ten times as much as the Brown stock. Thus in a merger Mr. X's stock should receive ten times as much interest in the new corporation as would be allocated to Mr. Y of the Brown Corp.

Another value to be recognized when considering merger special situations, is market value. Share prices most frequently reflect earning power and dividend policy rather than net worth (book value). Furthermore, the stock market prices fluctuate in response to supply and demand. These influences frequently cause share prices of pending merging corporations to be at varying levels in relation to the book values and/or indicated merger valuations. Under such conditions, when the merger plan is in the process of being concluded, an opportunity for special-situation investment may well be present in the securities. Here again "a difference" in price of values exists.

A third approach to recognizing values is to compare the true worth of the merging Corporations in relation to each other. Deviation in such relationships presents profit possibilities. In the aforementioned example, we valued Acme's in relation to Brown's worth. We will now value Acme and Brown individually in relation to a new corporation to be formed to expedite the merger.

The new corporation's capitalization consists of Acme's $100,000 plus Brown's $10,000, or $110,000. The equity interest could still be represented by 1,000 shares of new capital stock. The new stock would then have a per share value of $110. ($110,000 ÷ 1,000 = 110).

Based on the same financial relationship that existed prior to the merger, Acme stockholders would be entitled to 90.9% of the new capitalization, or 909 shares, while Brown stockholders would receive the balance of 91 shares, which represents 9.1% of the total capitalization.

Mr. X, stockholder of Acme owned 100 shares, or 10% of the outstanding shares. Therefore, he would be entitled to receive 90.9 shares, or 10% of the 909 shares allocated to Acme under the merger terms. This would have a value of 90.9 shares x 110, equal to $10,000, which is equivalent to the value of Mr. X's shares prior to the merger.

Self-liquidating Features Establish Profits in Mergers

The profit possibilities in merger situations arise in corporate change. As a matter of fact, fulfillment of the merger-plan provisions could automatically remove you as a security holder from the situation. This would occur where you have used the arbitrage procedure described below and illustrated by the McCrory-McLellan merger.

All special situations are in a sense liquidations. When the corporate change for which you have entered the situation has occurred, there is no further reason to remain with it. In consequence the special-situation investment either terminates according to plan or should be liquidated as a matter of routine.

A basic approach, proved by years of success, is to direct your thinking to the end that your ultimate position will be cash. The exchange medium for consummation of the merger should be cash or securities readily convertible into cash. It is the cash value of the exchanged securities which determines the profit and the success of the transaction.

To profit, one must purchase for less and sell for more. Proposed or pending mergers frequently hold this inviting possibility. Often the purchase and sale can be accomplished simultaneously, though the transaction cannot be terminated until the merger has been consummated. This, in effect, is known as a simple arbitrage. The following hypothetical case describes typical arbitrage opportunities in merger situations, while the McCrory-McLellan merger demonstrates the procedure in practice.

Company A shares are exchangeable for Company B shares on a share-for-share basis. Company A shares have a market price of $16 while Company B shares are priced at $14. A gross profit of $2 per share could be created through purchase of Company B shares at $14 and sale of Company A shares at $16. When the merger has been declared effective, the investor could deposit his Company B shares in exchange for Company A shares and deliver them to the broker to whom the shares had been sold earlier.

Arbitrage - Hedge Situation. McCrory Stores-McLellan Stores Merger
---

This merger proposal offered an opportunity for a hedge-arbitrage position. Both companies' shares are listed on the New York Stock Exchange. At the time of the public announcement that the "Boards" had approved the merger of the two variety-store chains, the spread in favor of McLellan Stores common stock amounted to 4.4% on an annual basis.

The risk of the merger not being consummated was insignificant since both companies are controlled by United Stores Corp., which owns 35% of McCrory and 47% of McLellan common, enough to assure completion of the proposed plan. Under the agreement McLellan stockholders would receive 1 1/4 shares of McCrory in exchange for each McLellan share. McCrory was priced around 13 3/8, and McLellan at 16--1 1/4 x 13 3/8 amounts to $16.71. Thus a gross profit of $71 could be established on an investment of $1,600. This equals 4.4% on an annual basis. Since the merger was expected to be completed in three months, by January 31, 1959, the rate of return would then equal 17.6%. The dividend rates of both companies would be about equal based on the rate of exchange.

A hedge position would require purchase of McLellan common stock and borrowing and selling short,* 1 1/4 times the amount of McCrory common. It should be kept in mind that quite often, after the first flush of the public awareness of a situation, a better spread may develop than was present in the beginning. Thus it may be worth following the progress of a plan and the price movements of the shares during the waiting period.

---

*Short-selling procedure is discussed on page 30.

The Kernel of an Acquisition Is Price

The technical procedures for establishing an investment position in an acquisition or merger are similar in many respects. The end result, from the special-situation investor's point of view, is the same in either category; namely, the satisfactory completion of the proposed plan brings to a termination the special-situation investor's activity.

The word "acquisition," when used in reference to a special situation, implies securing operating control of the acquired corporation. An acquisition differs from outright sale of properties in that the acquired corporation's identity may continue though the physical properties are controlled by the acquiring company.

The value of the securities of the corporation to be acquired would not be influenced by the use made of its facilities by the acquiring company. The price offered for the property is the sole determinant of the value in an acquisition. It is that specific price with which we are concerned for profit potentials.

Acquisitions are usually processed in one of the three following ways:

1. Purchase of shares in the open market
2. An offer to exchange securities of the principals
3. An offer of a cash payment for the securities

Where an acquisition is being considered, it is of the utmost importance to know the medium for payment and the disposition of such proceeds. It is also important to know whether the acquired corporation intends to continue its corporate identity or distribute the assets and liquidate.

Where liquidation is planned, it makes a significant difference whether the exchange "terms" specify cash or securities of the acquiring corporation. Cash has a known value, while securities must be appraised and are subject to market fluctuations.

Alertness to Opportunity

The investor seldom has exclusive or advance knowledge of corporation's intent to "acquire" or merge. Nevertheless, opportunity frequently is present to enter an acquisition or merger situation around the time the proposed plan is released in the press. This arises from lingering doubts until the proposed plan is consummated.

The degree of uncertainty determines the size of the discount in a situation. Discount is the money difference between the expected price at the time the "plan" has been consummated, and the market price at which the security may be purchased. The size of the discount is the vital clue to the probabilities of completion of the plan. The securities market is sensitive and, through the prices of the securities, reflects the concensus of opinions regarding the consummation of the plan. A substantial discount sounds the alarm of trouble ahead, while a small or banking discount indicates the probability of completion of the plan.

One cause for uncertainty may be traced to the provisions of the proposed plan. Generally the provisions must be satisfied at a not-too-distant date from the time of the formal announcement. The contingent terms of a merger plan include, among other requisites, approval by the stockholders in accordance with charter requirements. These stipulations often differ in the percentage of assents needed (in relation to the number of outstanding shares) to consummate the deal. Unlike mergers, such conditions do not exist in acquisitions since the decision pertaining to minimum number of shares or percentage of capitalization needed to complete the deal rests with the acquirer.

Doubt as to consummation of a play may arise where the proposed plan appears inequitable to a class of security. Doubt also could exist due to divergent objectives of security holders and members of the Board of Directors, as in the case of the Foremost Dairies - Golden State Co. merger.

Opposition was present at the time the merger proposal was announced. The objective of the opposition was to obtain a tax-free ruling for Golden State stockholders. Revision of the plan eliminated the objections and accomplished the objective. This is shown in the following comparative table of the initial and final plans. Since time was needed to work out the adjustments, investors could take advantage of the delay, which gave ample opportunity to study the situation for profit possibilities. We stress at this point that delays can be used to advantage.

FOREMOST DAIRIES, INC. - GOLDEN STATE CO. LTD. MERGER

Company	Issue	First Offer	Approved Exchange
Golden State Co. One share of:	4% Preferred	1 share 4 1/2% pf. ($50) plus $50 of 4% conv. deb.	1 share 4% pf. ($100 par)
One share of:	Common	.65 of com. plus $15 of 4% conv. deb.	1 share com. plus 4/50 of 4 1/2% pf. ($50 par)
Foremost Dairies One share of:	6% Preferred	.5 of 4 1/2% pf. .5 of com. $25 of 4% conv. deb.	To be redeemed at $52.50 per share
One share of:	4 1/2% Pf.	No change	No change 1 share 4 1/2% pf.
One share of:	Common	No change	1 share common

The first offer proposed creation of convertible debentures, issuance of additional preferred stock, and a change in the par value of the common. The approved plan simplified the exchange of shares so that stockholders of each company would receive the same amount of preferred and common shares as they held, except that Golden State common stockholders would also receive for each share 4/50 of a share of 4 1/2% preferred stock. The other notable change in plan was the redemption of the 6% preferred stock of Foremost.

Golden State common stock was priced around $25.75 per share at the time the revised plan was announced. Foremost common was priced around $26, and the preferred at $44 per share. Consequently, a share of Golden State would, after approval of the plan, be worth $26 plus $3.50 (value of the preferred stock) equal to $29.50.

This situation offered a discount of 16% from the prospective worth. Another way of expressing this is: Based on the money invested, this situation shows a gross profit of 13% computed on an annual rate of return. Should the transaction be completed in six months the percentage return would be 26%, while a three months' period to consummation would show a return of 52%. The special-situation investment was successfully terminated, and profits showed a return at the rate of 75% for those who entered the situation at the time the revised plan was released.

Opposition

The understanding and evaluating of opposition to a proposed plan cannot be overstressed.* You will find it helpful to investigate all opposing claims, weigh the merits of such contentions, and ferret out intentions. Additional areas of opposition are discussed in the closing pages of this chapter. Frequently the basis of dissent is price. When that is the case, analysis of the financial balance sheet is suggested, including careful reading of the notes in fine print, along with the earnings report. The source of the opposition's disagreement may be found in financial statements. Close contact with the negotiating parties and the corporation's officers, plus alertness to news releases can be valuable aids.

PART 2 - HOW TO DETERMINE THE PROBABILITIES OF A POTENTIAL PROFIT

We have shown by the use of hypothetical examples, by definition, and through illustrations the existence of potential profits. The next step is to determine the probabilities of establishing such profits. This is the middle step and the heart of the analytical approach to many special situations. The sources for data and methods for locating them are fundamental. Hence much of the following procedure has permanent value for application in Mergers and Acquisitions, and in other special-situation classifications.

---

*To paraphrase a well-known advertising slogan, "Never underestimate the power of the opposition."

The Analytical Approach

The order of investigation presented here is the routine usually followed by the author. However, the investor may follow his own inclinations as to where to begin, since it is the conclusions drawn from the data as a whole, rather than the order of in which they are assembled, that are important.

To analyze an acquisition or merger one can begin by seeking the answers to the following questions:

1. What is the risk in this situation?
2. What percentage of the capitalization of the subject corporations is controlled by the directors who have approved the proposed plan?
3. What portion of the undesignated shares are closely held? What percentage of the outstanding shares is held by unrelated stockholders?
4. Is there opposition to the plan?
5. What is the basis for opposition? What is the intent of the opponents?
6. What percentage of the outstanding shares is needed for assent to result in consummation of the proposed plan?
7. What is the length of time during which the plan will be considered?
8. Are dividends to be paid by either or both corporations during the waiting period?
9. What is the relationship of both corporations' shares in respect to past and current market prices?
10. What is the estimated worth of each corporation's shares as viewed from the financial aspect?
11. Does the geographical location of plants, distribution facilities, and the product classification enhance the desirability of the proposed plan?
12. Has the Internal Revenue, the Department of Justice, or other government agencies evidenced an interest in the proposed plan?

How to Begin

The search for the answers might start with examination of a recent balance-sheet statement and earnings report of the corporations involved. Always ascertain the market prices of their securities. Then compare the relative size of the corporations in regard to the following:

Dollar amount of sales (gross)
Dollar amount of sales per share of stock
Percentage of profit on sales (profit margin)
Taxes paid (gross) and per share
Depreciation and depletion charges
Reserves
Net earnings, and per share earnings
Percentage of earnings paid out in dividends

Dividend record
Cash position
Inventory position
Book value (per share)
Working capital (per share)
The value placed on patents, goodwill and intangibles
Capitalization - with reference to ratios of outstanding securities

Comparison of the foregoing financial statistics will show the relative values of the corporations. Study of these relative values will give clues to the potential pressure of "requests for appraisal."* The restraining influence of appraisal requests could result in abandonment of an approved merger.

Should a wide divergence in the estimated values of the corporations involved receive inadequate recognition in the "terms" of agreement, excessive dissents to the "plan" might occur. This could be unfavorable since "too many objectors may spoil the deal," as in the case of the Hudson-Nash merger. Existence of such dissent should restrain a prudent investor from participating in the situation.

The merger of Hudson Motors-Nash Kelvinator into American Motors, Inc., did not qualify as a special-situation investment. However, it has considerable practical interest because of the confusion and loss of use of rights which some stockholders experienced. The highlights are presented to demonstrate the value of knowing one's rights as a stockholder when a corporate action is under consideration. Hudson Motor shares declined continually from 13 1/4 (January, 1954) reflecting rumors of a pending merger which were being voiced in the newspapers. On March 23, the day before the special meeting for considering adoption of an agreement of merger with Nash Kelvinator Corporation, the shares sold at 9 5/8. Subsequently, the shares declined to $8 per share.

On the first day of trading in the newly formed American Motors, Inc., the equivalent value for Hudson shares was $7.33. This low price undoubtedly brought to mind a news report which many stockholders had read in the early days of April. This stated in part: "Hudson stockholders who had voted against the merger with Nash Kelvinator and who seek cash for their shares were informed that the price would be 9 5/8 per share. This was based on the market value as of March 23, 1954, the day prior to the special meeting."

This piece of advice had been released by the Hudson Motor Co. It was misleading in that it indicated a specific price would be the settlement price for Hudson Motors stockholders who voted against the merger. The announcement did not state that the price of 9 5/8 was merely an offer by the company, nor did it further disclose who specifically would be entitled to accept this price. Furthermore, it did not disclose that qualified dissenters could sue for "a fair cash value."

---

*Chapter 11 of this book is devoted to the study of "appraisal."

In view of the lowered price ($8.00) for Hudson at the time the merger became effective, many stockholders requested the published price of 9 5/8, believing they were entitled to that price from the Hudson Company or the merged corporation.

Some stockholders who had voted against the merger, but had not complied with the subsequent requisites for obtaining a "fair cash value" for their shares, found it difficult to understand their inability to obtain the 9 5/8 price.

Knowledge of their stockholder rights could have been obtained by reading the prospectus sent to each stockholder. This would have revealed that the first step required objecting in writing within twenty days after the merger was authorized, to obtain the "fair cash value" for his shares. For further details and excerpts from the prospectus see chapter 11 on Appraisals.

The Importance of Voting

One of the most important contingencies of any "plan" is the minimum number of affirmative votes needed for the proposed plan to be declared effective. This can range from a mere majority, to 80-90% or even 100% assent requirement. Therefore it is important to know the position of the voting securities in relation to the proposed plan.

The voting strength of the larger holders of voting securities who are in favor of the proposed plan is generally obtainable. In numerous instances the proponents of a plan have the voting control, and consequently consummation is reasonably assured. The Merritt-Chapman & Scott seven-way merger has three such voting controls in the ownership of more than 90% of the equity interest in Newport Steel, Marion Power Shovel, and The Osgood Co.

Voting strength as well as other vital data often can be ascertained from the "Notice of Meeting and Proxy Statement" which must be forwarded to all security holders entitled to vote on the plan. It is a good idea to obtain (from the company or through an investment broker) a recent copy of the previous Notice of Meeting and Proxy Statement. Both communications may be viewed at the main offices of brokerage firms, financial-statistical publishing companies, financial libraries at the exchanges, various banks, and at the SEC offices.

What is a Proxy?

A proxy is a power of attorney to act on behalf of the stockholder. It generally is limited to a specific meeting and for specific purposes. See the following page for an actual proxy.

The solicitation of a proxy is the request (by the incumbent management or the opposition) for authorization to exercise the shareholder's vote at the designated meeting. The use of the vote is defined in the notice of meeting and proxy statement.

> CONSOLIDATED PAPER COMPANY
>
> # PROXY
>
> This proxy is solicited on behalf of the Management for Annual Meeting of Stockholders, Tuesday, February 24, 1959.
>
> The undersigned hereby appoints C. H. R. Johnson, S. J. Newcomer, and G. L. Bronson, and each of them, proxies of the undersigned, with power of substitution, who may act by a majority of such of said proxies or their substitutes as shall be present at the meeting or, if only one be present, then that one shall have all of the powers hereunder, to vote and act with respect to all shares of common stock of the Corporation which the undersigned would be entitled to vote, as fully as the undersigned could vote and act if personally present, at the Annual Meeting of Stockholders to be held on February 24, 1959, at 10:00 A.M. Eastern Standard Time at the principal office of the Corporation, 921 East Elm Avenue, Monroe, Michigan, or at any adjournment thereof:
>
> 1. On the proposal to amend the third paragraph of Article III, Section 1 of the By-Laws to read:
>
>   "Members of the Board of Directors, who are not employees of the Corporation, personally attending any duly constituted meeting of the board, shall receive a fee for attendance and shall receive reimbursement for necessary travel expenses, the amounts thereof to be determined by a majority vote of the Board of Directors."
>
>   FOR ☐   AGAINST ☐
>
>   THE MANAGEMENT FAVORS A VOTE "FOR".
>
>   (Please specify your choice by placing a check in the appropriate square above. The proxy will be voted in accordance with the specification so made. If no choice is specified the proxy will be voted FOR the proposal.)
>
> 2. Upon the election of 12 directors each for the term of one year.
>
> 3. In their discretion upon all other matters brought before the meeting.
>
> The undersigned hereby acknowledges receipt of the Annual Report for the year 1958, Notice of Annual Meeting, and Proxy Statement, each dated February 3, 1959, ratifies all that said proxies, or their substitutes, may lawfully do by virtue hereof, and revokes all former proxies.
>
> Dated: _____ 1959   Signature: _____(L.S.)
>
> On stock held in joint ownership all owners should sign. In signing as Attorney, Administrator, Executor, Guardian or Trustee, please add your title as such. Please sign and date this proxy and return in enclosed prepaid envelope.

A proxy requested in a communication from the corporation would generally be in favor of the management. An opposition's request for a shareholders' proxies might supply valuable information about its voting strength.

What to Look For

The proxy statement will disclose the equity (stock ownership) and other security holdings of the management, officers, directors, and those with substantial interest in the company. Look for interrelated stock interest or interlocking management. Their presence would favor consummation of the plan.

The Marion Power Shovel Company acquisition by Merritt-Chapman & Scott was preceded by considerably market activity. The cause of this activity was not publicized until the annual meeting held the following April. A news release stated

- 25 -

that three Merritt-Chapman directors had been elected to the Board of Marion Power. However, the intent to place directors on the Board and acquire an interest in the company was first revealed in the proxy statement which preceded the meeting. After obtaining representation on the Board of Directors, an offer was made to exchange Merritt-Chapman shares for Marion Power shares in the ratio of three to two. At that time Merritt-Chapman shares were priced around 24 and Marion Power at 35. The opportunity for a profit did not exist as the price differential was too small.

The context of a Notice of Meeting and Proxy Statement contains valuable facts relating to corporate activities. Present and future plans described therein often give a clue to possible course of a proposed plan. The Hudson Motor Company - Nash Kelvinator merger meeting communication comprised 78 pages of valuable information pertaining to the proposed merger and the financial state of both corporations. The table of contents is presented to show the comprehensiveness of this source of information.

- The date of meeting
- Purposes of meeting
- Capitalization entitled to vote
- Description of the merger plans
- Comparison of earnings of both companies for past five years
- Comparison of book values
- Comparison of units of production
- Comparison of market prices of shares of both corporations
- Description of the products produced
- Assets, facilities, and properties described exhaustively
- Business developments of recent interest
- Competition
- Labor relations, pension and insurance, and social insurance programs
- Government contracts
- Pending litigation
- Capitalization changes in the new formation
- Manner of exchanging shares for the new corporation
- By-laws of surviving corporation
- Abandonment of agreement of merger and conditions pertaining therein
- Board of Directors, of surviving corporation
- Board of Directors, present occupation; date of election to board and number of shares beneficially owned of the participating corporations
- Remuneration of directors and officers
- Employment contracts with individuals
- Rights of dissenting stockholders
- Articles of incorporation of surviving corporation
- Financial statements of a recent date with comprehensive notes
- Federal Tax status

The Willys Overland Motors proxy statement used at the time of the proposed sale of automotive facilities had additional valuable data pertaining to their partial liquidation. The reasons for the sale of the automotive facilities were stated along with the use of proceeds of the sale. Such broad disclosure has become quite usual today.

Keep in mind when a corporate change is being considered, to "See your proxy statement before you buy." All the data are not essential. It is somewhat like panning for gold or separating the wheat from the chaff; but that which you can use is "golden."

Part 2 has outlined the analytical approach. By use of questions and answers the ways to find the information needed to estimate the potential of a situation have been made clear. We have also seen that knowing the relative financial condition of companies involved in a corporate action can give the investor an advantage in appraising the proposed plan's consummation possibilities. We have shown what to look for and where to find it. Extensive use of the sources of information and careful application of the data will aid materially in giving the situation a minimum-risk status.

PART 3 - HOW TO OBTAIN THE PROFITS

We know that profit possibilities exist where a merger or acquisition is contemplated. We have discussed the steps to be taken to determine the possibility of establishing the profit. Should our analysis show favorable prospects of consummation of the proposed plan, we may proceed to the third and final step--the procedure to be followed to secure the profit. Experience has shown that the following investigatory processes reveal the data needed to substantiate an investment position in a particular situation.

Sterling's Acquisition of Hilton-Davis Chemical, Step-by-step Procedure

We present the acquisition of Hilton-Davis Chemical Co. by Sterling Drug, Inc., at this point, to show the precise step-by-step procedure and the thinking that leads to each step. This comprehensive analysis covers the acquisition from inception through consummation. The procedure is recommended as the approach to all special-situation investments.

Background information, available to all investors, disclosed that Sterling Drug's growth was being furthered through mergers and acquisitions. This policy focused attention on Sterling's activities. As a result, special-situation investors were alert to investment opportunities that developed.

Existence of Profit Potential

A news release announced an offer to exchange one share of Sterling Drug common stock for 3 1/4 shares of Hilton-Davis Chemical Corporation. It was

possible at that time to purchase Hilton Davis shares at $17 per share, which for
3 1/4 shares amounted to $55.25. Sterling Drug shares were priced at $64.25 per
share. Thus a spread (the difference in market value) of 9 points, equal to $2.75 per
share of Hilton-Davis, prevailed. The $2.75 is obtained by dividing the 9-points
spread by the number of shares required to obtain one share of Sterling, which in
this case was 3 1/4 shares. This computation indicated that the equivalent of $19.75
could be obtained for Hilton-Davis shares.

Choice of Procedure

This special-situation investor had the choice of two procedures by which to
establish the above profit. One was to purchase Hilton-Davis shares at the then-
available price with the intention of retaining the shares until consummation of the
acquisition. Then, when the acquisition would be declared effective, dispose of the
Sterling Drug shares which would be received upon exchange for the Hilton-Davis
shares.

The weak link here would be the investor's vulnerability to potential loss in the
event the proposed acquisition were abandoned. An attendant hazard would be the
possible erosion of the profit through decline in the price of Sterling by the time the
exchange would be declared operative.

The risk potential in situations of the above type can only be "guesstimated,"
not calculated. The possible loss can be estimated as the difference between the
value of Hilton-Davis shares at the time of purchase (approximately $17) and the
level to which the shares might settle on their own investment worth as securities of
an independent operating chemical concern.

The next step is to obtain the market-price history of the shares. This information will disclose the influence of anticipatory transactions. Broad movement
during an anticipatory period could disqualify a situation from further interest, as
substantial increase in the price prior to the announcement of the plan could create
too great a risk in the securities under consideration.

A check of the past record of the market prices of Hilton-Davis disclosed the
following pertinent facts: The price range for the latter part of the year was $16 low
and $18 high. The shares had sold around $21 in June. The previous year's range
was $14.50 low and $21 high. The price of $17 was therefore midway between the
low and high. This was favorable and indicated there had been no price inflation due
to the proposed acquisition.

On the basis of historical price record one could assume a value around $15 to
$17 per share on their own merit. Thus a loss of possibly two points per share
might be incurred in the event the acquisition failed to consummate.

Analysis of the financial condition of Hilton-Davis corporation was made to ascertain what level the shares might be worth in relation to the earnings and finances of the corporation.

This disclosed earnings were on the incline. $1.68 per share was reported for the previous year as compared with $1.58 for the previous year. Furthermore, sales had advanced from under $2 million to more than $6 million in a few years-- a clear sign of product growth.

Current assets were in a strong position and accounted for a major portion of the book value, which amounted to approximately $10 per share. This status of low book value was common in chemical shares and deemed adequate to support a price of $15 to $17 in the market in association with other factors.

The price/earnings multiple is the relationship of the market price per share to the earnings per share. It is obtained by dividing the price of the shares by the earnings per share: $17 ÷ $1.68 = 10. The price of the shares at $17 was equal to 10 times earnings. This was reasonable and indicated no overvaluation.

Dividend payments of $0.80 per share, amounting to a 50% pay out of earnings, gave a return of 4.1%. The shares were not considered cheap nor overpriced at $17 on the dividend basis.

Further analysis of the corporation disclosed that only 147,771 shares of common stock were outstanding. There were 1,000 stockholders. The family of the late founder held the controlling interest, indicating that no serious objections to the proposed plan would be forthcoming. Furthermore, the shares would not be subject to severe pressure in the stock market should the plan not consummate.

The complete study of Hilton-Davis gave support to the probability that no serious loss would be sustained by holding Hilton-Davis shares until the acquisition had been completed. The dividend of $0.80 per share would suffice to pay for the money to be used.

Summing up the analytical steps we found the shares to be reasonably priced based on: (1) historical market-price levels, (2) earnings and dividends, (3) financial worth, and (4) probability of consummation of the plan in so far as the Hilton-Davis shareholders were concerned. The risk, calculable as a maximum loss of $2 per share, appeared small. The situation, then, contained the four elements of a special-situation investment, namely, "a corporate action was being processed," the security was undervalued in relation to the investment transaction, the situation permitted calculation, and the risk was minimal in relation to possible loss.*

---

*An evaluation of Sterling Drug's shares along similar lines would of course be desirable.

Another Choice - "Hedge"

The other choice for creation of an investment position would be to hedge. This procedure is sometimes misnomered "arbitrage." To hedge, or to take a hedge position, indicates the creation of two or more investment transactions that will tend to protect the investor against loss through compensatory price movements. (See page 7). Professional usage accepts the interchange of the terms hedge and arbitrage where applied to transactions of the type under discussion.

As our objective in a special-situation investment is to protect a potential profit, the hedge procedure would be the one to take, if permissible. The initial steps would be to purchase shares of Hilton-Davis at 17 and as soon as possible sell shares of Sterling Drug (short) at 64 1/4 in the ratio of 3 1/4 shares of Hilton Davis for each share of Sterling. Therefore, for every 325 shares of Hilton Davis purchased, 100 shares of Sterling would be sold (short). This would establish a potential gross profit of approximately 16% on the money invested, computed on a per annum basis.

How to Sell Short

"Short" as a securities market term means possessing at the time of the sale the securities one has sold. A "short sale" of stocks or bonds can be compared to the sale of clothing by a manufacturer for delivery six months hence, though he has not purchased the cloth at the time he accepted the order. Through the mechanics of the securities market and the facilities of a brokerage house, one may sell shares which one does not own. Then he may borrow the shares and deliver them to the party who purchased the "short-sale stock." At a future date the "short seller" may either purchase in the market or obtain through exchange in a merger or acquisition the number of shares he owes. He then delivers said shares to the lender and thus terminates the transaction.

Hedge Procedure

In taking a hedge position it is important to ascertain the availability of the stock for borrowing. The lender of shares does not bind himself beyond a call loan. This means that the borrowed shares are returnable on demand. The shares might become so scarce that the borrower might have to pay a premium for their use. The premium could amount to as much as $1 per hundred shares of stock per day, or whatever price the traffic could pay.

It is also possible for the loan to be called so that shares are not available at any price. The investor would then be forced to purchase stock in the market and so close the short side of the transaction. This, of course, would cancel the hedge position as the investor would be long without the balance he had planned.

A condition where securities would become unavailable for lending would arise where a fight occurred for control of a corporation. With shares in demand for voting purposes they would not be available for lending. Thus investors in short positions would be squeezed since they would be required to return borrowed shares and deliver shares they had sold short. As shares would not be available to borrowers, the short-position investor would have to go to the market to "buy in" shares to balance his short position. Because of the already strong demand by the parties battling for control, this would force him to buy at rising prices.

This occurred during a battle for control of the New York, New Haven & Hartford R.R., with the company's shares steadily rising up to the record day for voting. A large short-interest existed, reflecting hedge positions in the New Haven R.R. "Certificates of Beneficial Interest."* The latter securities would, at a future date, be exchangeable for common stock. The strong demand for New Haven shares removed them from the loaning market, forcing short positions to cover in order to deliver the stock owed. The stock was recalled from loans by the owners, who wanted to register the shares for voting.

Shares not being available for loan, the short investor, forced to purchase the shares in the open market, took a loss on his short position while the "Certificates of Beneficial Interest" in which he was long) had not moved upward in equal ratio. Thus the "hedged" investor could not offset the loss by sale of the "Certificates."

Expenses

The costs attendant on establishing a hedge position consist of charges to be paid the broker for executing the orders, and taxes in the form of documentary stamps issued by the Federal and state governments for transfer of property.

Another cost may be incurred where the shares which were sold "short" represent a corporation paying dividends. The dividends distributed by that corporation (in our example, Sterling Drug), during the time the seller remains short, would have to be paid by the short seller. This is a direct cost, as the seller is not entitled to the dividends from the stock he has borrowed.

Consequently, the length of time the situation would remain open is important. The dividend status of both companies must be considered to see whether a loss could occur from that source. Sterling Drug's dividends were $0.75 quarterly or $3 per annum. Hilton-Davis' dividends amounted to $0.20 quarterly or $0.80 per year. This indicated that, on a quarterly basis for each 100 shares of Sterling one was short, he would have to pay out $75, while for each 325 shares of Hilton-Davis held long he would receive a total of $65. In this case there would be a loss of $10 per each 100 shares of Sterling sold short, for each quarterly period. Loss of $10 per 100 shares would not be a significant item since it could be compensated for in the capital-gains profit resulting from the completed transaction.

---

*Hedge positions had been established wherein the investor was long of the "Certificates" and short of the common stock.

Findings of the Analysis. The Decision

A thorough study of Sterling in accordance with the procedure used for Hilton-Davis revealed the following: (1) Based on the relative values of the shares the plan was equitable. (2) The majority voting control of Hilton-Davis by the family eliminated doubt as to the outcome of the official voting. (3) The nature of the companies' products indicated no conflict with anti-trust laws, nor did they pose any commercial problems. The indeterminate period of time pending consummation of the acquisition was the only unfavorable factor.

The financial and stock market analysis disclosed that Sterling shares were fully priced. Hilton-Davis shares, however, would not suffer materially if the acquisition did not materialize. From this the investor can see the importance of an analysis of the acquiring company (Sterling). Here the investor had to decide whether or not to establish a hedge position, which required short selling of Sterling shares. If Sterling shares were undervalued, this would not be desirable. Conversely, if the shares appeared high, as they did in this case, it still would not be the determining factor.

The fact that Sterling shares were fully priced influenced a leaning towards a "hedge" position. Findings of the comprehensive investigation indicated the probability of the acquisition being consummated. However, the vital point of the duration was not conclusive.

The risk attendant upon failure to consummate the acquisition seemed average for either the long position in Hilton-Davis or the hedge position. The uncertainty of the duration period tipped the scale in favor of purchase of Hilton-Davis shares and awaiting the fulfillment of the "corporate action."

The acquisition processing took a year for final consummation. This was longer than desired but not unexpected. Sterling shares at the termination period were priced around 66. Thus, a profit of 20% was established over a period of little more than a year.

Origin of Mergers/Acquisitions

These marriages occur in response to various influences. Our interest in the latter is limited to their effect on the completion of the merger/acquisition. On learning to recognize factors which lead to merger/acquisitions, you then should be able to anticipate situations where this condition is inherent. "To be forewarned is to be forearmed."

Merger Based on Soundness

Where the reason for creation of the merger/acquisition plan is sound, the probability of completion is reflected in the price of the securities. The merger of

Merck and Sharp & Dohme was sound in respect to the complementary nature of their commercial activities. This special situation presents another interesting hedging operation.

The merger plan proposed an exchange of 2 1/4 shares of Merck for each share of Sharp & Dohme. Merck shares were priced around $23, and Sharp & Dohme around $45. The 225 shares of Merck to be received for 100 shares of Sharp & Dohme would be worth $51.75 per share, as compared with the market price of Sharp & Dohme of $45, or a spread of $6.75 per share. This was equivalent to a return of approximately 15% on an annual basis.

Stockholders' meetings for both corporations were scheduled three months hence. If the merger were completed at that time, then the return would be at the rate of 60%. Investigation via our standard procedure disclosed no important objectors, while the combining of the two companies seemed commercially desirable.

Because Merck shares had moved up from a considerably lower level immediately prior to the announcement of the plan, hedging appeared more attractive than direct purchase of the undervalued Sharp & Dohme shares. This was so because the risk attendant with a short position in Merck seemed minor, since the shares would probably recede substantially should the merger fall through. On the other hand, the purchase of Sharp & Dohme shares at 45 held little risk.

As expected, Sharp & Dohme shares advanced to 50 while Merck shares remained at 23. At these prices the profit potential was reduced to around 3%. Later market action, at the time of consummation in early May, saw Sharp & Dohme around the 45 level while Merck shares had declined to the 20 level. At the latter prices the spread was eliminated (20 x 225 = 45).

During the waiting period the probability of the merger consummating became more evident. When the profit potential had dwindled to 1 1/2 points, equal to approximately 3 1/2% return on an annual basis, or 14% return over a three months' period, professional hedging activities began. This influence generally indicates that the merger would be completed.

Professional hedging generally refers to investment dealers who are in a position to create hedge positions at lower costs than to the public. Frequently these costs differences represent the major portion of the profit in a hedge situation.

Another sound merger which offered profits through hedging was the following.

General Dynamics Corp. - Liquid Carbonic Corp. Merger

The official public announcement of the proposed merger was made toward the end of July, 1957. At that time General Dynamics was priced at 57 1/4 while Liquid Carbonic sold at 54 3/4, a spread of 2 1/2 points. The plan proposed a share-for-share exchange of common stock. The meeting of stockholders of both companies was scheduled for the latter part of September. During the interim the shares of both companies fluctuated within a 4-point range. Around mid-August the spread stood at 4 3/8 points with General Dynamics at 54 5/8 and Liquid Carbonic at 50 1/4. Thus opportunities for profit were present during most of the intervening period.

Since the spread was wide the merger possibility would have to be viewed with caution. Therefore this case required the examination of the financial position of each company in relation to the market prices. This disclosed, among other things, that while both companies paid equal dividends, General Dynamics' earnings for the previous year was 25% better than Liquid Carbonic's.

Marketwise, General Dynamics' shares were hovering around the low for the year, while Liquid Carbonic's shares were close to the high. Furthermore, Liquid's shares had moved up from a low of 38 for the year. This may have reflected anticipatory purchasing. This, too, was a sign for caution. In view of the foregoing, the investigation procedure described in this chapter would be used in full. This would include a check with the firm handling the proxies for the meeting. Other checking would include officials of both companies to locate the presence of significant opposition.

No pertinent obstacles appearing in the investigations, it seemed advisable to proceed with a hedge position. This required purchasing Liquid Carbonic and selling short an equal number of shares of General Dynamics. No technical problem of borrowing General Dynamics was present. The merger plan was approved by both companies, and the plan took effect as of Sept. 30, 1957. At that time the shares of both companies were priced at 50 1/2. Since the investment was held for about two months the rate of return ranged from 605 if purchased when the first announcement was made to 96% if purchased in August.

Acquisitions in Response to Economic Necessity

Chrysler Corporation's acquisition of the automotive facilities of Briggs Manufacturing Corp. exemplifies an acquisition due to economic necessity. The Briggs Company was confronted with the choice of loss of its major customer or sale of its automotive facilities to him. The decision to sell created an interesting special-situation investment. The facts of the case are presented on the following page. This analysis was used by the author at the time the situation became attractive for special-situation investment.

Rumors and denials as usual preceded the formal announcement of the proposed acquisition. Speculative trading had advanced the price of the Briggs shares to a level where the cream seemed to have been skimmed off. However, at the time the special-situation investor entered the transaction, the risk had been reduced to a minimum and the profit potential was satisfactory. In this situation it is important to note that while the cost of the shares was around $36 1/4, the actual risk money

SPECIAL SITUATION: BRIGGS MANUFACTURING COMPANY - Current Price: 36 1/4 NYSE

The cash purchase by Chrysler Corporation of substantially all the automotive and aviation facilities of Briggs Manufacturing Company is now effective. The transaction, which accounts for approximately three-quarters of Briggs Manufacturing assets, affords interesting profit opportunities to special-situation investors.

Briggs will effect a majority liquidation through distribution of the net proceeds of the sale via redemption and cancellation of a portion of the outstanding stock on a pro rata basis. This is equivalent to approximately $32.25 per share. There are outstanding 1,947,700 shares of common stock of the Briggs Manufacturing Company, which comprise the sole capitalization. The remaining assets, estimated at $9.50 per share, of which more than $3 is represented by cash, are applicable to the Briggs Manufacturing Company Beautyware plumbing business, which will continue in operation. It is understood that the company contemplates retention of its listing on the New York Stock Exchange.

Sales of Beautyware products in 1952 were in excess of $22,000,000. Net earnings, after taxes, of the Beautyware business are estimated at $1.50 per share. Such earnings should justify a market value of $8 to $9 per share. This division, which has been in operation since 1932, manufactures plumbing fixtures and porcelain enamelware for bathroom and kitchen appliances. The products are sold in every state of the United States and Canada through more than 600 distributors.

The indicated book value of Briggs stock is approximately $41.75 per share. However, the shares have an apparent work-out value of $40.25 to $41.25 per share based on the $32.25 per share to be received in liquidation plus $8 to $9 per share representing the plumbing business.

The current price of 36 1/4 reflects the strong cash position behind the shares. The discount from the estimated worth of $40.25 to $41.25 indicates a return of 10% to 12.9% on an outright purchase. If the Briggs shares are financed on 50% margin, with interest computed at 4% per annum, a return of 16% and 21%, respectively, would be attained. This is based on the expectation that the expressed intention of Briggs Manufacturing Management to distribute the equivalent of $32.25 per share to stockholders sometime during the latter part of 1954 will be fulfilled. It is our opinion that a liquidating dividend will be forthcoming nearer the mid-year rather than the latter part of 1954, in which event the <u>rate of return would be correspondingly increased.</u>

The examples below present graphically the computations per 100 shares for the two methods of participating in the Briggs liquidation:

Low Estimate				High Estimate			
Cash		50% Margin		Cash		50% Margin	
Liq. value	$4,025.00	Liq. value	$4,025.00	Liq. value	$4,125.00		$4,125.00
Cost	3,658.13	Cost	3,658.13	Cost	3,658.13		3,658.13
Est. profit	$ 366.87	Gross profit	$ 366.87	Est. profit	$ 466.87		$ 466.87
Return	10%	Interest	73.16	Return	12.9%	Interest	73.16
		Net profit	$ 293.71			Net pr.	$ 393.71
		Investment	1,829.07			Inv.	1,829.07
		Return	16%				21%

- 35 -

involved was approximately $4 per share, since the Briggs Corporation officials had indicated in the proxy statement that the sum of $32.25 per share would definitely be distributed within the year. The distribution was mandatory to obtain the benefits of a tax procedure.

While the indicated percentage yield (see preceding page) is based on an annual return, the actual percentage was substantially greater, the corporate action being consummated in nine months. During the waiting period Briggs Corporation paid dividends of $0.50 per share. The company stated that this dividend was based on the firm's anticipated operations from the plumbing division. This indicated that earnings from the plumbing division would probably be better than $1 per share. The Briggs shares subsequently moved to the 39 level, at which price the investor then might consider selling to establish a profit of approximately $2.50 per share, equal to 7% on the money invested. This would be equivalent to a return of 14% if the profit were established after six months. As the investment originally indicated a minimum profit of 10% to 12% per annum on a cash purchase, the investor should at this point evaluate the return in comparison with other investments to determine the desirability of remaining with the Briggs situation.

The Briggs shares continued to reflect the favorable aspects of the plumbing business along with the expected payment of $32.26 per share in liquidation. By the time the payment was made, the shares were priced around 43 1/4. Thus the situation showed a profit of 14% on an annual basis. However, as the situation matured in nine months, the return would be at the rate of 18%. This was considerably above the 10% indicated in the original presentation. The better-than-expected result occurs frequently with special-situation investments. This condition prevails because a special-situation is calculated to return a profit under the severest conditions.

Merger as a Result of "Family Sell-out" -
How an Indicated Small Profit Turned into a Substantial Gain

A frequent reason for the presence of merger/acquisition situations is management's desire to retire from active participation in the business. Often the management may be the family of the founder of the company and owner of a majority of the equity interest. Thus practical assurance of approval of the plan is present in such situations, as illustrated in the merger of Hickock Oil and Pure Oil Corp.

The discount or spread when the proposed merger was revealed amounted to approximately 6% on an annual basis. Investigation as per our standard procedure disclosed the following:

Hickock's capitalization consisted of 500,000 shares of Class A stock and 500,000 shares of Class B stock. The voting rights were equally vested in each class of stock. Pure Oil owned all the Class B shares and 28,731 shares of the Class A stock. The greater majority of the remaining Hickock Oil shares were owned by the family of the founders. The family had arranged for the merger.

This combination of holdings assured approval of the merger. The amount of outstanding shares was of minor importance and presented no risk of opposition or demand for an appraisal.

The only problem in this situation was the acquisition of shares of Hickock Oil. The creation of a hedge position through selling the equivalent number of shares of Pure Oil to be received in exchange for Hickock Oil shares could be accomplished without difficulty. No dividend payments intervened, and the duration period was expected to be exceedingly short. Accumulation of some Hickock Oil shares during July and August made possible a quick and substantial profit of approximately 40% on the capital invested. The merger was consummated in mid-August. Thus an apparent banking or small-profit deal actually contained a handsom gain, mainly because of the assurance of the completion of the merger plan.

Where Does Opposition Breed?

Opposition to mergers/acquisitions have their origins in discontent and the desire for self-benefit. You will see, in the American Woolen case which follows, that while opposition may create doubt it also presents opportunities for profit.

Opposition to a merger/acquisition often arises where liquidation of a seemingly "going concern" is proposed. This was the case in the battle over American Woolen Corp. Keeping abreast of the case was simple since the newspapers carried controversal material issued by both sides.

The American Woolen Company corporate-action epic started with the proposal to retire two issues of preferred stock and to consider disposing of eleven unnecessary and uneconomic mills. This partial-liquidation idea had been received favorably by many stockholders, besides three members of the Board of Directors.

Textron, Inc., desired control of this juicy plum and entered the picture by offering to exchange 1/5 of a share of Textron 4% preferred Series B and 1/2 share of Textron common for each share of American Woolen Common. At the then current market prices this offer amounted to $19 worth of securities as compared with American Woolen common's stock-market price at $17 per share. Textron stated in the offer that they would not retire the American Woolen preferred shares.

A stormy special meeting was adjourned by court injunction without taking any action. In the interim a New York syndicate put in a bid to acquire control of American Woolen at a price of $20 for 50% of the common stock. A stockholder's group stated that legal action would be instituted to prevent retiring the preferred stocks. Although voting at the reconvened meeting had favored the management's proposals, the new offers changed the conditions and a delay in carrying out the plan seemed advisable. Meanwhile the 7% preferred shares had moved to 91, up 18 points, while the $4 preferred rosed to 95, up 7 points. A court order restrained the company from redeeming the preferred stocks because the legality of the voting was being questioned.

The annual meeting had to be postponed because dissension made it impossible to obtain a quorum. Textron then improved their terms for the third time, offering 1/5 share of the $4 preferred and 1/2 share of Textron plus cash of $5 for each share of American Woolen. Textron had indicated, in a letter to stockholders, that this offer was equivalent to $24.10 per share based on a value of approximately $71 to $75 for the $4 preferred. However, the market prices suggested a worth of about $60 for Textron preferred, which would lower the estimated value of American Woolen to around $22. American Woolen at that time was priced around 18 1/4.

Textron, by then, had gained control of 200,000 shares of American Woolen, equal to one-fifth of the outstanding shares. 125,000 shares were acquired under the above offer. This voting strength was sufficient to block a proposed merger of American Woolen and Bachmann Uxbridge Co.

By May, Textron had acquired 300,000 shares of American Woolen and extended the public offer to purchase 100,000 shares at $23 per share. A few months later the proposal to merge the three companies, Robbins Mills, American Woolen, and Textron, was announced and subsequently approved.

For the terms of the finally approved merger and profit possibilities see pages 13 and 14.

Why External Opposition Should Be Evaluated

Recognition should be given to opposition arising from socio-economic sources, which can even force cancellation of a proposed plan. The following summary of the controversial Follansbee Steel Corporation sale demonstrates the significance of civic opposition.

Follansbee Steel Corporation directors had agreed to sell the company's assets for approximately $9 million. The sale of assets required approval by a majority of the stockholders.

The prospective buyer had arranged to sell part of the Follansbee, West Virginia, facilities to the Republic Steel Corporation, which intended to move the equipment to Alabama. Removal of these facilities would leave more than 700 of the company's employees jobless. The Town of Follansbee derives about 65% of its tax revenues from the steel plant.

Follansbee civic leaders declared that removal of the steel plant would leave the town in dire economic straits. A stockholders group then petitioned for an injunction to block the sale. The citizenry of the town was aroused and held meetings with the company's officials. The Senate anti-monopoly committee announced that they would investigate the proposed sale.

The stockholders subsequently approved the sale at the special meeting. However, a U. S. District Court Judge found evidence of a "breach of directorial obligation" on the company's part and moved to block the sale. He stated, "It is the conclusion and opinion of the court that inducements were present from the beginning of the negotiations to the employment of officers and executives. It is the further conclusion and opinion of the court that the failure to advise the stockholders by means of the proxy statement, and the omission of all reference to these inducements constitute a violation of the Security Exchange Act."

After much public wrangling the civic opposition was the victor to the extent that the steel plant would remain in operation in Follansbee, West Virginia, at least for three years. Thus the mainstay of the town was saved. This was achieved by sale of the property and ensuing merger with Union Chemical and Materials Corporation, which brought the dramatic battle to a close.

A few outstanding opposition instances follow:

American Cyanamid-Norwich Pharmacal proposal for merger had to be abandoned because of insurmountable legal difficulties, understood to have been brought about by the Department of Justice.

The Atlas Company is meeting opposition to its proposal of merger for its subsidiary companies. A committee representing minority stockholders of Rio de Oro Uranium Mines, Inc., filed a motion with SEC protesting its proposed merger with three other uranium companies into a subsidiary of Atlas Corp.

Cities Service Co.'s proposed plan to divide Arkansas Fuel Corp. into two companies is being opposed by a newly organized committee of Cities Service stockholders. Basis for opposition is desire for better terms than offered in the proposed plan.

Mt. Vernon Mills turned down an offer from a major textile company to buy its shares at $20 per share, and in August 1958, rejected an offer of $20 per share for control of the company.

Noma Lites, Inc., has actively opposed Textron's attempt to gain control of American Screw Co. Noma is reputed to own between a quarter to a third of American Screw Co.'s common stock. Since a two-thirds majority vote is required for approval of a merger, Noma could defeat the plan.

The Susquehanna Corporation's proposal to purchase the Vitro Minerals Corp. has been canceled because of stockholder dissension. The opposition threatened a proxy fight in an effort to prevent the proposed sale. The stockholders' protective committee and other large holders represented almost 50% of the 1,101,263 shares outstanding.

Where to Look for M/A

When searching the field for possible mergers/acquisitions, a good place to begin is with concerns which have taken the initial step by acquiring a stock interest in other corporations. This approach has additional possibilities in the area of spin-offs and appraisals, to be discussed later. However, since our interest at this point is in mergers/acquisitions, we will view the subject from that aspect alone. Profit possibilities may arise from the following actions:

1. An offer to acquire additional shares
2. An offer to merge or fully acquire the company
3. A rise in the market price of the shares in response to the "buying" influence

A recent merger proposal that appears to have profit possibilities is Porter Co.'s offer to Thermoid Co. stockholders. Porter Co. presently owns 40% of Thermoid common stock. The exchange ratio is 1/6 share of 5 1/2% cumulative Preference stock, $100 par value of Porter, for each share of Thermoid common. Since the Porter management also controls more than 80% of that company's shares there is little doubt of the consummation of the merger. Therefore a profit would be present if the Porter Pf. to be issued would be worth more than the current price of Thermoid common, which is priced around 13 1/2.

Based on comparative values of similar preferred shares and also giving consideration to Porter's financial rating, the new preferred could have a value between 96 and 110, equal to an indicated value of $16 to $18.33 per share of Thermoid common. The potential profit range is 18% to 36%, based on the above-mentioned price of Thermoid. However, the merger is scheduled to be consummated within a two months' period. If that is achieved, then the profit would be at the rate of 108% to 216%.*

An area of prospective mergers is the railroad field, with economic necessity as the major influence.

The following companies have been giving serious consideration to joining forces:

Norfolk & Western with Virginian Ry., Atlantic Coast Line with Seaboard Air Line, and Pennsylvania RR with New York Central.

The five-way merger possibility in: Bangor & Aroostook RR, Boston & Maine RR, Maine Central RR, New York N H & H. RR, and Rutland Ry.

---

*Merger was consummated in mid Dec. 1958. The Preference stock was priced around 90 at the date of issue and presently is priced around 95.

The table below presents, for illustrative purposes, a few of the outstanding corporations which have stock interest in other companies.

Company	Holdings in Other Companies, Approx. No. of Common Shares	Percent Ownership
American Can	172,320 Metal & Thermite Co.	21%
Basic Products*	46,236 Hevi-Duty Elec.	13
Bush Terminal Co.	162,000 General Cigar	34
Celotex	205,000 South Coast Corp.	48
Cities Service Corp.	1,257,977 Richfield Oil	31
Eastern Corp.	105,690 Rayonier, Inc.	2
DuPont De Nemours	4,508,622 Remington Arms	60
Olin Mathison Chem.	132,940 Marquardt Motors	24
	122,143 Reaction Motors	50
Oliver Corp.	74,800 Waukesha Motors	13
Radio Corp. of A.	1,158,563 Whirlpool Corp.	20
Revlon, Inc.	242,000 Schick, Inc.	20
Schenley, Inc.	34,400 Austin Nichols	17
Sinclair Oil	1,223,581 Richfield Oil	31
	1,091,692 Texas Pac. Coal & Oil	30
United Fruit Co.	241,100 Int. Ry. of Centl. Amer.	48

*Basic Products has recently offered to purchase an additional 75,000 shares of Hevi-Duty Electric. The offer price is $22 per share, while the stock sold at $19.75 on the day prior to the announcement.

CHAPTER 3

Liquidations

This chapter discusses profit possibilities in corporations which are in the process of liquidation. Investments of this type are concerned with basic asset values rather than the going-concern worth of a functioning enterprise.

A "liquidation" is the process of winding up the affairs of a business by realizing upon assets and discharging liabilities. The security holder receives his proportionate share directly from the liquidating corporation as one shares in the division of a pie. When the pie has been divided and served, the pie plate is empty. Similarly, when the final liquidating payment has been made the company ceases to exist. In a merger/acquisition, on the other hand, the business continues and the security holder generally is paid for his securities by the acquiring corporation in cash or other securities.

The life of a liquidation determines the percentage of profit. Since liquidations generally do not offer current income the main return is in the form of capital appreciation. Therefore the length of time money is invested exerts an influence on the profit. Should the distribution procedure take longer than estimated, the percentage return on the invested capital would be less, although the dollar amount of the profit would be as calculated. The most desirable liquidation investments are those where the major portion of the principal is returned to the investor within a short time. Then the residual investment, which may be small or at times nil, participates in distributions of the assets. In this type of liquidation the risk is at a minimum, as in the Southern Production liquidation described next.

Southern Production Co.

Sinclair Oil Corp. had agreed to purchase Southern Production's oil and gas properties while other assets were sold to Southern Natural Gas Co. The latter paid in stock for their purchases, while Sinclair paid in cash. Southern Production's directors had recommended complete liquidation, which, based on the above sales, would bring $44.40 per share. Southern Production stock was available on the New York Stock Exchange (NYSE) around the $40 level when the plan was announced. Thus an assured profit of 10% was indicated.

Note that the procedure for payments was divided into two main parts. The first distribution, which was made within six months, returned all the invested capital plus $1.61 per share. The balance of $2.74 per share followed during the second six-month period. This brought the aggregate payments to $44.40. However, bear in mind that no money was invested during the second six-month period. The latter condition is responsible for the substantial rate of return on the investment. Your activity in this type of situation merely required verifying with the company officials the particulars of the liquidating procedure.

Something for Nothing

Because corporate action is in progress during the life of a liquidation situation, uncalculated profit opportunities may arise. Windfalls and "romance," which are not uncommon in liquidations, should be viewed as an added incentive. This uncalculated expectation should be the "to-boot" item at no cost to the investor.

An illustration of the profits in "to-boot," the Continental Foundry and Machine Co., follows:

The point of first contact was at the time the sale of the assets was publicly announced. The liquidation plan provided for distributions in cash of $40 as the first payment and $5 as the second payment to take place within sixty days. The balance would be forthcoming as soon as feasible, though it was believed such payments would take no longer than twelve months, to complete the major portion of the liquidation. The stock was priced around 49 1/2 (NYSE) at that time.

The indicated liquidating value, according to company releases, amounted to $52 per share. Since $45 of the principal invested would be returned within two months, the situation offered an indicated profit of $2.50 on an investment of $4.50, an attractive return in a riskless investment.

The company's releases disclosed that substantial funds had been reserved for contingencies and that the company had a tax claim filed against the Federal government.

Since the assets had been sold to Blaw-Knox & Co. there was no risk to the invested principal.

The liquidation was substantially completed within the twelve month period. Stockholders received $58.55 per share in the following distributions:

First distribution within 2 months	$40.00
Second distribution within 3 months	5.00
Third distribution within 6 months	8.00
Fourth distribution within 12 months	5.05
Fifth distribution	0.50
Total	$58.55

The investor's money was in use during the following periods:

$49.50 for 2 months
9.50 for 3 months
4.50 for 7 months

After the third payment had been made the investor had a profit of $3.50 per share on his investment.

Analysis: We charged ourselves interest, at 5% for the money invested for three months, at which time $45 had been returned. This amounted to $0.41 for two months on the $49.50; on the $9.50 interest for three months amounted to $0.12. In this way the aggregate interest for the short-term period totaled $0.53 per share. This amount was to be added to the cost of the shares. Thus interest plus cost amounted to $50.03 per share.

After the second payment the investor would have but $5.03 per share invested in the situation. Six months later the sum of $8 per share was distributed. This resulted in a profit of $3 per share, equal to a 60% return on an annual basis or at the rate of 120%. However, the real romance in this situation began to unfold in the twelfth month when a payment of $5.05 per share was made. This was followed by a $0.50 per share payment one year later, and $1.79 per share distributed in November, 1958. This brought the total to $60.34 per share. While the latest payments were not calculated as assured assets in the approach to the situation, the possibility of such "to-boot" distributions had been indicated by the reserve fund and the tax claim.

The substantial profit of $10.31 per share which developed came out of a riskless investment that at first inspection indicated a mere $2.50 profit as a final distribution.

Types of Liquidations

Liquidations may be divided into two main classifications, voluntary and involuntary. These in turn may be divided into types.

Voluntary liquidations fall into any one of the following three types: complete liquidation, partial liquidation, and optional liquidation.

Involuntary liquidation can only be complete, since "involuntary" refers to the absence of choice, the security holders in this type of liquidation having no elective preference.

Involuntary Liquidations. Involuntary liquidations generally arise from two sources, namely, economic demise (bankruptcy) and/or statutory direction. Both conditions can occur simultaneously and did so, in the public utility field. Statutory liquidations were widely prevalent in the 1940's, reflecting the effects of the Public Utility Holding Company Act of 1935. Chapter 9 discusses this type of liquidation.

Voluntary Liquidations. The stockholders' reason for supporting a plan to liquidate is their belief that the corporation has greater worth dead than alive. As the legal owners they determine whether a corporation may voluntarily liquidate. The liquidation of a corporation, sale of resources, and change in the basic character of operations, in most instances, must be voted upon by shareholders.

However, to initiate a liquidation, sponsorship is needed to start the corporate action. The quality of the sponsorship often is a clue to the ultimate objective. Therefore the financial history of the sponsorship should be studied with the same care you analyze the company's balance sheet.

The Investor's Profit Margins in Liquidations

The major portion of the profit can often be mathematically figured because the essential statistical facts are available. Competition among investors often is keen since they can readily calculate the profit percentage on their invested capital. Thus profit margins sometimes just about meet the investor's requirements. In view of this close profit-margin condition, the investor's margin of error in a liquidation is small. However, the risk often is compensatingly small. The following case history illustrates the value of exactness in calculations associated with a liquidation and also how to apply pertinent data.

American Republics Corporation

The shares of this company were traded on the American Stock Exchange and priced around 68 1/2 on the day of the formal announcement of the terms of liquidation. Previous announcements had confirmed the intent to liquidate but had not stated the method. Investigation disclosed that a majority of the shares were owned by the management. This virtually assured consummation of the proposed plan, which required a favorable vote of 67% of the outstanding shares.

In this case checking with the company was the principal step in our procedure (full investigation steps are described in Chapter 2).

It was learned that the first liquidating payment would be substantial, in the neighborhood of $60 or more per share, to be distributed no later than May. The balance would be paid before the end of the year. A dividend of $0.43 would also be paid in January. The tax status had been cleared, and the only delay might arise from transfer of title of some of the oil properties. Appraisal of this liquidation situation follows.

Calculations: A purchase at 68 1/4 would yield a potential profit of $3.75 plus the dividend of $0.43, equal to a total of $4.18. The return on the investment of $68.25 would be 6%, based on a full year's duration. However, we must accept the indication of a $60 payment within a short time after transfer of the property. As this action would be expected to occur by March, we could then expect the payment of $60 or more to be made no later than May. Such payment would mean that the investor would have $68.25 invested for five months and $8.25 invested for slightly less than a year. Thus the return on the capital would be at the rate of 14% if carried on a cash basis.

American Republic liquidation qualified as a special-situation because the four basis elements were present:

1. The stock was undervalued in relation to the liquidating price.
2. A corporate action was in progress, i.e., liquidation.
3. The profit could be calculated and the duration was specific, within one year.
4. The risk was at a minimum, as inferred from the proxy statement.

Partial Liquidations

The partial-liquidation special-situation occurs frequently. It often turns up in a merger/acquisition and in the construction of a holding company (see chapter 9). It should not be confused with the sale of plant facilities or unneeded assets. Partial liquidation may be recognized when you see that a major disposal of operating assets is involved, with a mere fraction of the original corporation remaining. The value of this remainder generally holds the profit, or the major portion of the profit. The Briggs Manufacturing Co. special-situation investment (see chapter 2, part 3) is an illustration.

A current partial liquidation which offers profit possibilities along with an opportunity to apply analytical techniques of special-situations is Electric Auto Lite Co. For further discussion of this company and other partial liquidation situations (see chapter 13).

Optional Liquidation

An innovation in the liquidation field is the "alternative choice." In this type of action the investor has an opportunity to decide upon a course of action after the plan has become effective. In this flexibility arises the possibility of a special-situation inventment. An assured profit is feasible, contingent only upon specific corporate actions primarily involving time. The profit possibilities and procedures are described in the accompanying Willys Overland "liquidation" case history.

Willys-Overland Corp.   (Now Overland Corp.)

Rumors of a proposed sale preceded the formal announcement by Willys-Overland, on Mar. 3, 1953, of the plan to sell the assets, excluding cash, securities, customers receivables, and other current assets.

The market prices for Willys-Overland shares in mid-February, 1953, were: common stock, 12; preferred stock 80. In April, after release of the terms of the plan and other vital information, the shares advanced from early March levels of 13 1/2 and 88 to 15 and 98, respectively.

The proxy statement contained the notice of the meeting along with full details of the proposed "liquidation." The plan provided for the following:

1. Disposal of the assets for $60 million
2. Establishment of a fund of $3,250,000 for contingencies
3. Redemption of the preferred stock at the price of 104 per share
4. Eventual distribution to the shareholders electing to withdraw, an estimated $17 per share, depending upon the outcome of the contingencies
5. Disclosure that the corporation contemplates remaining in business as an investment company

The unique feature of the plan was an offer to common stockholders to withdraw from Willys-Overland by receiving their pro rata share value. However, neither the proxy statement nor the officials of Willys-Overland disclosed the exact amount of money or the date distribution would be made to shareholders.

The plan did state that on or about October 15, 1953 Willys-Overland would report its then financial condition and its plans for retiring the interest of stockholders who wished to withdraw from the business. In the meantime, Willys-Overland could use part of the proceeds of the sale to purchase shares of its common stock. It is important to note that the absence of such pertinent data as price and date of distribution detracted materially from the desirability of investing in this liquidating situation.

Significance of Voting Control

The proxy statement revealed that management controlled 36% of the voting shares. This favored the probability of consummation of the proposed plan since only 50% of the outstanding shares were needed to confirm the plan. Management generally can swing control of a company if they have 20% of the outstanding shares. This is so because a large percentage of stockholders as well as the shares held for banks and brokerage accounts generally go along with management. The foregoing combination is usually sufficient to retain control. In this situation management's 36%, plus the votes indicated above, would assure an excess of the required 50%. However, not until the closing days did the company announce the details of the optional liquidation plan, which were as follows:

Common stockholders were given until January 15, 1954, to decide whether to retain their investment in the company or accept an initial payment of $14 per share plus a receipt (stub) entitling them to receive 1/2,775,967 of a special reserve at the time of final distribution. Holders of 1,600,696 shares elected to accept payment, leaving 1,170,780 shares held by 2,154 stockholders. The special reserve fund amounted to $8,440,718. It was created to meet the following liabilities: expenses in liquidation and debt settlement existing on January 15, 1954, which had not been provided for.

The market value of the receipt at the beginning of 1954 was $2.75. Withdrawing stockholders received $14 in cash and held a certificate which had a value of $2.75. The combination totaled $16.75. The shares of those who retained their investment were then priced around $16.62.

Why the Plan Was Unattractive

When the plan was announced the stock was around $15. This price showed an indicated profit of 2 points equal to a return of 13% on an annual basis. Nevertheless the situation was not attractive. Uncertainties existed as to:

1. When the first cash distribution would be made
2. The amount of the principal distribution
3. The duration period required for complete distribution to become effective
4. The real asset value or liquidating value of the company

On Oct. 1, 1956, holders of the receipts received $2.50 as a partial distribution from the special reserve, which then amounted to $8,959,000.

Values in Residual Corporate Shells

A liquidation special-situation investment opportunity could be present after a corporation had disposed of its principal assets and retained one or more of the following potentials: an unresolved claim for taxes, favorable litigation, an undeterminable asset in a contingency. This latter item could be a carry-forward tax loss resulting from past operations. Lately the residual shell channel has become increasingly active since corporations with "tax losses" endeavor to capitalize on the last remaining asset. See chapter 13 for a discussion of this phase of investing and list of corporations currently in a tax-loss position.

Servel Corporation is presented here as a live example of a residual shell. The company disposed of substantially all its physical assets. The proceeds from the sale plus cash and accounts receivable totaled $15 million. Liabilities included possible refunds to the government on defense contracts and warranty obligations.

Complete liquidation would have resulted in the common stock receiving nothing for the equity interest. It was stated in the notice of meeting to stockholders that, in liquidation, there would be no capital applicable to the common stock. However, the stockholders have a powerful asset in the $17 million carry-forward tax loss. This accounts for the stock having a market value around $10 per share instead of being practically valueless.

In view of this "tax" asset the management has been studying possible acquisitions of available companies with demonstrated earning power. If this large loss carry-forward can be applied against earnings, then Servel's common stock will benefit. There are many companies whose shares have enjoyed substantial rises in response to the improved earnings resulting from effective use of the "carry-forward" tax loss. Allied Paper (formerly Thor Corp.) and Philadelphia Reading Co. are two classic examples.

Procedure for Investing in "Liquidations"

Each liquidation-investment situation has its own opportunities and procedures for attaining the inherent profit. However, in all liquidations there is this similarity to "spring housecleaning": hidden treasures may be discovered. The unknown factor adds romance to seemingly passive liquidation situations. Nevertheless, an investment in a liquidation must be founded on the estimated value of the known assets.

The analytical approach to a liquidation investment differs substantially from other special-situation analyses. A liquidation requires the marshaling of a corporation's affairs into a free-flowing current of dissolution. In most liquidations tangible assets have a calculable worth. The liquidating corporation must reduce those assets to distributable form such as cash or securities. Debts, taxes, and claims must be satisfied prior to complete liquidation.

Since the profit in a liquidation is based on estimated values, the more detailed the information you have about the assets, the more likely it will be that you will attain the maximum profit.

The accompanying illustrations discuss important procedural and analytical steps used in liquidation-investment situations.

What to Look for in a Liquidation

An investment situation does not qualify as a liquidation until the intention to liquidate, i.e., the "corporate action," has been clearly defined. Then the following factors become the key clues in appraising the liquidation's capital-appreciation possibilities:

1. The tangible assets
2. The tax status
3. The legal contingencies
4. The corporation's schedule of liquidating steps
5. The method of distributing the assets
6. The time expected for completion
7. The romance windfalls

The approximate value of assets other than cash or securities may be obtained from a recent balance sheet. The indicated preliminary price discussed for the sale may provide a tentative valuation. An appraised value of the property may be available which also may be used as a guide.

The approximate asset value would, in most instances, exceed the market price of the securities sharing in the liquidation. However, where contingencies have an assured minimum value, they can be treated as an asset and excess asset value need not exist.

Where to Find the Tax Status

The tax status of liquidating corporations must be considered in relation to possibilities of refunds and claims for additional taxes. In the latter case the amount estimated to meet such contingency should be deducted from the assets. The corporation's position in regard to previous years' taxes will usually be defined in the annaul report, the latest balance-sheet release, and the proxy statement.

The significance of the corporation's tax status in relation to the proposed liquidation tax may appear in the aforementioned publications. Direct questioning of the corporate officers and tax counsel will help clarify the tax picture. The importance of the tax status must be fully weighed, as this factor can be costly, since, in a liquidation, time is money.

Tax cases are complex, and the antitipated results cannot easily be appraised or even conjectured. Consequently, refund claims should be viewed merely as possibilities, not as tangible resources. The case of Boston Elevated Railway Co. illustrates a tax-liquidation situation that developed many surprises, including additional large profits.

The Boston Elevated Railway Co. sold its entire assets to the Metropolitan Transit Authority, an agency of the Commonwealth of Massachusetts, for the sum of $20,297,490. This was equivalent to a net of $85 per common share.

The question of who was to pay the capital-gains tax arose upon completion of the sale. The court held the company liable for the tax, and the Collector of Internal Revenue was paid $6,177,796, the amount of the capital-gains tax shown in the return filed by the company. Attorneys for the company filed a claim for refund, while the Tax Bureau commenced an audit to determine the final amount of the tax.

Point of First Interest

Interest in this situation began after stockholders received one payment of $40 per share. Deducting this distribution and the tax payment, a balance of approximately $19 per share remained for the common stock. However, the tax-refund claim indicated a prospective $1 million repayment from the U.S. Treasury, which would add $4 per share, increasing its total expectancy to approximately $23.

The situation appeared attractive since a decision from the Tax Bureau was understood to be forthcoming within a reasonable time. This was learned on checking the company's tax status with the company's attorney. The shares at $15.50 offered a minimum return of 20%. The assets, which consisted of bank deposits or the equivalent, would be considered riskless.

Subsequently, in late August of the same year, the shares declined to $12 on news that the U.S. Internal Revenue agent at Boston, on examination of the company's income-tax return for 1947, proposed an additional capital-gains tax of $3,229,096.

The company protested the report and carried the matter further. Subsequent investigation disclosed that the counterclaim of the tax agent had been instituted more as a protective maneuver than on its merit.

Progress Procedure

The situation remained dormant for more than a year, when the company distributed $10 per common share as a liquidating dividend. This of course reduced the amount of capital invested in the situation and also enhanced its desirability, as it left a residue of only $5.50, with the expectation of receiving $9 or more per share.

During this period the company's officials were contacted for continuous checking on the progress of the situation. The information thus secured led to the purchase of additional shares.

Two years later, shareholders were advised that a proposed settlement of the "Federal tax claim" was to return an amount equal to $6 per share to the company. This was $2 more than had been expected at the time the situation first appeared attractive. Instead of having to pay an uncalculated (unexpected) tax payment, the company garnered a windfall of 50% more than their hoped-for claim. Thus the combination of the earlier payment of $10 per share, the cash balance on the books and the $6 per-share tax refund brought the aggregate value to $26 per share.

Reflecting the favorable news, the shares moved to the $15 level. This was equal to a current value of $25 per share, giving effect to the $10 payment. The shares held that price for about a year, at which time the Court approved the amount of $16.86 to be distributed on each share as final payment. This brought the total distribution to $26.86 per share. Thus a profit in excess of $10 per share was established, as compared with the original expectation of only $3 per share profit plus a hope of $4 additional.

The situation showed a net profit of 45% after allowing for the $15 invested for 1 1/2 years, and the remainder including interest for 3 years.

The technical requirements in this situation were:

1. Examination of the balance sheet.
2. Maintenance of contact with the president of the company for progress on the tax claim.
3. Studying the information released by the attorneys through the companys' progress reports. This contained most valuable data.

Legal Aspects   (in Liquidations)

The more usual legal contingencies fall into categories such as damage suits, patent suits, contracts, trade claims, and stockholder suits. When the liquidating company is the defendant, note whether adequate reserves have been established to meet the contingency. Some claims may appear to be minor and of the nuisance type, but to a corporation winding up its affairs, legal actions can be a serious drain on the remaining assets, which probably are not producing any important income.

However, the dollar value of the legal matters can be measured in relation to the total assets to be distributed and thus be calculated into the appraisal of the investment situation.

Where the liquidating corporation is the claimant, the decision whether to purchase a lawsuit or not would be influenced by the cost. The decision would be positive if the cost were considered negligible in relation to possible gain.

Such a situation would be present where the assured assets to be liquidated equaled the cost of the security, and the loss of interest on the investors' funds would be slight.

Timing Schedule of Liquidations

The procedure used by the corporation in liquidation should be investigated to obtain the following information:

1. Method for disposal of the assets.
2. Collection of accounts receivable. Here the investor should note the quality of the debtors. A government debt, where renegotiation is not a factor, is of course valued at its full worth; also a triple-A corporate debt. However, a wide distribution of accounts receivable in certain fields would not warrant full value. Consequently, the estimated asset value must be adjusted accordingly.

3. Termination of production activities. Check work in progress, which may have a costly loss potential.

4. Settlement of legal claims, trade claims, warranties, bank loans, and capitalization prerequisites. Be alert to penalties or premiums which may be required to satisfy such claims. Information about the method of procedure and amount of liabilities can be obtained from the company.

5. Settlement of contracts with employees. This information generally can be obtained from the management and in proxy statements.

The importance of investigating liquidation "steps" is to uncover contingencies that would detract from the investment desirability of the liquidation situation and provide clues to the duration period.

Methods of Distribution of Assets

Liquidation can be completed via two methods, disposal of all the physical assets as a unit, and piecemeal or gradual, sale. In the former case the approximate sum to be distributed to the outstanding securities can be computed from the balance sheet. When the plant, property, and inventory are sold, simply add the sale price to the cash and negotiable securities. Then deduct the liabilities, including estimated liquidating expenses, funded debt, and preferred stock. The remainder is then divided by the number of common-stock shares outstanding, which dividend is the net, per share, to be distributed.

Distribution in Kind

The liquidation of a company by distribution of the assets in kind (for practical purposes this would be securities) could come within the unit-distribution method. Since the aggregate assets could be evaluated as a single unit, the distribution procedure would be as follows:

After satisfying liabilities and senior securities, the stockholders are entitled to a pro rata share of the portfolio holdings. The dollar value of the portfolio can be calculated where the securities are marketable. This total amount, when divided by the number of common shares outstanding, will reveal the dollar equivalent for each share. The actual sale of the portfolio securities to be received rests with the stockholder. He has two choices for disposal. One is to await actual receipt of the shares and sell at that time. The risk here is in the fluctuations of the market prices of the stock over the duration period. The other choice is to protect his indicated asset value by hedging,* through selling short/ the estimated shares to be received in liquidation.

---

*Hedging is discussed in Chapter 2.
/Short selling is discussed in Chapter 2.

An example of substantial profit potentials which resulted from a distribution-in-kind liquidation follows:

Associated General Utilities Co.   This situation came to light as a potential special situation in the fall of 1955. The shares were then priced (over-the-counter) around 62, but moved within the 80 level on news of the proposed liquidation. Nevertheless, opportunities for substantial capital gains were present at the higher levels as the liquidating work-out value was slightly under $100 per share, plus dividends. While special-situation investors did establish positions at prices well below the $80 level, we will use this higher price for our examples to show that opportunities for substantial capital gains are present after the information has become general knowledge.

On November 4, stockholders approved a plan of dissolution of the company. The principal assets were shares of General Public Utilities Corp. (GPU). The latter stock was selling around 36 1/2 on the NYSE. Associated's portfolio holdings of G.P.U. equaled a minimum of 2 1/2 shares for each Associated share after deducting liabilities and estimated liquidating expenses. The evaluation at that time appeared as follows:

Associated General Public Utilities Corp.

Capitalization, common stock, 53,674 shares

Assets:		Liabilities:	
Cash	$18,000	Misc. notes	$30,870
162,330 shares of G.P.U. @36 1/2	$5,882,000	Note	650,000
Less	681,000		$680,000
	$5,401,000	Estimated liq. expenses	$80,000
Less	80,000		
	$5,320,000		

This statement shows a per-share value of $98.72 before deducting full expenses. The indicated percentage gain on an annual basis, calculated on the estimated asset value of $98.72 per share, equaled 23.4%. This did not include dividends which would accrue on Associated. The plan indicated that a minimum of 2 1/2 shares of G.P.U. would be distributed in two payments in six months or earlier. The first distribution would be one share of G.P.U. The balance would be distributed within six months with a target date set for March 31. Based on the principal being invested for a six-month period, the rate of return would average 46.8%.

A distribution of one share of G.P.U. having a market value of 36 1/2 was made three months after the purchase of Associated at $80 per share. Thus the investor had but $43.50 (80 less 36 1/2 = 43.50) invested for the entire duration period, which was three months. With the second payment of 1.6 shares of G.P.U., the investor had received the cash equivalent of $94.90 per share. If we charge interest for the use of the invested money for the first three months, this amounts to $1 per share. After deducting this charge the profit amounted to $13.90 per share, equal to a rate of return of 62% on the investment of $43.50 for the full six-month period.

Hedging Transaction. The hedge operation in this situation revolved around the G.P.U. shares to be distributed. Since the Associated stockholder was assured of a minimum of 2 1/2 shares of G.P.U., he could sell short all or part of the 2 1/2 shares in anticipation of the distribution. As dividends would accrue on both securities, that factor would be a stand-off. Thus one could have purchased 100 shares of Associated around 80 and at the same time sold short 250 shares of G.P.U. around 36 1/2. This would have established an interim gross profit of $112.50 per each 100 shares. The balance could be sold when the liquidation had been completed.

The investigating procedure consisted of communicating with officers of the company. The main point that required checking was to find out whether sufficient votes to meet the two-thirds requirement of assets for liquidation would be forthcoming. This presented no obstacle. Thus the risk element was limited to the market fluctuations of G.P.U. Analysis of this public utility company indicated that the 36 1/2 price level was reasonably safe. The stock was readily available for borrowing.

The company paid a final liquidating dividend of $1.50 per share in October, 1956. This distribution brought the aggregate payments to $96.40 and the profit to $16.40 per share.

Piecemeal Liquidation

When this method is used, extra caution is needed in evaluations of stated assets, since the company continues in partial function. The semi-operative state makes it vulnerable to the hazards of mounting business expenses. A longer period of time than originally contemplated to dispose of the assets could erode values. Furthermore, the liquidator may not be overanxious to terminate a lucrative relationship, or the liquidating management may be overzealous and lose markets for the plants and properties.

On-the-site Valuations

Personal contact with the company can uncover much valuable information. A knowledge of the location of the plant and the nature of its facilities can help you assess the marketability of the assets.

An interesting piecemeal disposal of assets can be seen in the following case history.

Kalamazoo Stove & Furnace Co. The liquidators decided on a piecemeal disposal of assets because they believed it would yield a better return than sale of the company's assets as a unit. A mild demand for the particular physical assets of Kalamazoo Stove existed at that time, and there were expectations of a good price when the right buyer appeared. The investor's thinking in this situation was as follows:

The book value was $20.28 per share. Based on the Kalamazoo Stove market price of $16 per share, each dollar per share obtained above $16 would show a profit of 6% on an annual basis. Therefore, if the company was sold in its entirety at $18 per share, 12% would have been made on the invested capital, assuming the situation required one year to consummate. On the other hand, by the piecemeal method of sale, it might be possible to obtain the book value of $20.28 or more. A price of $22 per share could be envisioned under favorable conditions for the sale of certain properties.

Should $20.28 be the ultimate amount obtained over a two-year period, the profit would be the equivalent to a sale at $18 consummated in one year. In both cases the return on the principal would be at the rate of 12.5% per annum. However, the piecemeal method indicated a sale of the major asset and a distribution of $10 or so per share. This procedure opened another view on the situation. After the assumed $10 distribution, the investor would have only $6 invested per share. On the above estimated values of $20 to $22 the investor could expect to receive from $4 to $6 per share profit.

If the situation covered two years, the investor would have had $16 invested for one year and $6 for two years. He would receive a minimum of $20 per share at the end of the second year. The net profit would be approximately $3 per share after charging interest at the rate of 6% for the $16 used for one year. The return on the money invested would amount to 50%, which over a two-year period would be at the rate of 25% on the invested capital. This compared favorably with the 12% indicated on the total-sale basis. You can readily see that, on a percentage basis, it appeared wiser to work with the piecemeal liquidation plan rather than accept a one-price bid for the assets. The possibility of a larger profit is an influential factor in view of the minor risk based on the price of $16 for the stock. The Kalamazoo Stove special-situation, step-by-step procedure illustrates this.

Rumors of liquidation were common knowledge in the early part of 1952.

The first step for the prospective investor was to determine the then-current price, which was under 16 per share on the NYSE. Then the price range for the year and the daily range for the past two or three months were obtained. This would disclose any exceptionally active trading which, in turn, would reveal anticipation of the "liquidation" by others.

Step 2 was a study of the records of the corporation, to fill out a picture of the prior year's price range, earnings, dividend record, and, most important, the latest balance sheet. The price range was 15 5/8 low and a high of 18 5/8, indicating no excessive activity. The balance sheet showed a book value in excess of $20 per share, of which $15.40 was in net, quick assets. This latter factor indicated the absence of a large monetary risk, since the shares were priced around $16. From these data could be calculated:

1. How much can be realized.
2. The time needed to complete the liquidation.
3. How long will it take to recover the original investment or a major part of it. After the original investment has been recovered the final liquidation duration period diminishes in importance.

Inferences drawn from the rumors, combined with the factual data outlined in the foregoing, suggested that the situation would be attractive, since a minimum value of $18 per share appeared assured. Further investigation, therefore, was in order.

From this point on, the basic investigatory sources and procedures outlined in this and Chapter 2 become operative. Only the facts relevant to the liquidation are valued. The principal items in the situation being the assets, the balance sheet will disclose the amount of net quick assets. However, the physical condition of the inventories would have to be established in regard to quality and worth. This could be accomplished through direct communication with officers of the corporation, prospective purchases, or even a competitor. A competitor often knows more than you do about your own business.

The information thus obtained included the fact that a new group other than the officers and principal stockholders had acquired a block of stock sufficient to influence the policies of the corporation. Another significant fact was that sale of the stove business to Nash Kelvinator had been arranged.

Communication with the management and the "new group" revealed the existence of opposition to the liquidation procedure. This conflict became public knowledge through a proxy battle involving forces opposing a proposed merger with Maremount Automotive Products Co. Management favored the plan while the new group opposed it. The plan was decisively defeated at a special meeting. The majority of the stockholders said in effect that the approximate price of $18 per share which had been indicated as the value for Kalamazoo shares was inadequate.

Time was consumed in negotiations for the sale of the remaining assets. Meanwhile, the possibility of merger of the corporate shell was held in abeyance. The thinking here was directed toward obtaining some value for the listing on the NYSE. Subsequent sales disposed of the stove business and most of the other physical properties. A meeting of stockholders was called on Dec. 10, 1952, at which time stockholders voted to liquidate and terminate the corporate existence.

During the above proceedings the shares had advanced to the $18 level.

Investors' Choice. This rise in price posed the question of whether to take a 2-point profit over a seven-month period, which would be equivalent to 20% on the money, or stay with the situation. The answer revolves around the investor's ability to make use of his funds. For those who had more profitable ways it would be desirable to take the profit and terminate the transaction.

Those who remained, participated in a liquidating distribution of $11 per share in December, 1952. This was $1 better than our original assumption.

This payment was followed by three distributions totaling $5 per share in 1953, and $1 in 1954, making a total of $17 paid. The cost price then had been returned with a $1 cash profit. The market price of the shares at 2 1/4 reflected the $17 paid. Thus the value of the situation as of that date was $17 plus $2.25, equal to a total of $19.25 per share.

The corporation's balance sheet showed approximately $2.40 in physical assets, plus a reserve of $500,000 set aside for contingencies. Therefore the amount of the potential liquidation value was not precisely calculable. Nevertheless, it appeared that a sum slightly under the $20 originally estimated would be the minimum. On the other hand, the company might realize more for its remaining assets than indicated in the balance sheet. Furthermore, the corporate shell might have a value. The assets other than cash included land and buildings with 300,000 square feet of factory space. Should this be disposed of at favorable prices, it was estimated that $1 per share additionally would accrue to the common stock. In view of the various possibilities, the $22 maximum estimate might be achieved.

The remainder of the tangible assets were disposed of by 1957. Subsequently, in February, 1958, a distribution was made equal to $1.70 per share. This brought the total to $18.70. The Board of Directors stated that a further liquidating dividend would be forthcoming, although, because of contingent liabilities, it is not possible to anticipate the amount.

Why Are Liquidations Available?

The question is often posed as to why the shares of a company in liquidation are available at a discount from the estimated liquidating value. One explanation could be the absence of unanimity of opinion as to the liquidating worth. Another may be the desire of some security holders to assure the advanced price where the market level has risen in expectation of the liquidation. Sometimes the tax position of a stockholder warrants disposal of the shares rather than acceptance of the liquidation distribution. Then again, many securities holders cannot evaluate the situation and unwittingly sell too soon. Others may be just too lazy to figure the percentages. Whatever the reasons, a liquidation situation has attraction for the special-situation investor if the liquidation offers a profit of at least 10% on an annual basis and the risk has been reduced to a minimum.

A liquidation is additionally attractive because of the liquidity possible through daily marketability of the securities. A terminal-investment situation involving properties other than securities would generally arouse apprehensions of being "locked in." That condition does not exist where the liquidation occurs in a corporation whose securities are traded in the market. The securities markets offer a means for getting out of liquidation investments despite the fact that the corporation is not actively engaged in business. Broadly viewed, the ideal liquidation involves the purchase of cash or negotiable assets at a discount, combined with a romance element that could have important plus values.

The following companies are presently concerned with actual or prospective liquidation:

<u>American-Hawaiian S.S. Co.</u> SEC went to court in an attempt to have this company register as an investment company, or liquidate. However, dissident stockholders have asked the company to invite tenders for up to 40% of its stock or to liquidate. The company has stated that it hopes to continue in the shipping business.

<u>General Realty & Utilities Corp.</u> This company is in the process of liquidating. It is expected that liquidation may require three years.

<u>International Railways of Central America.</u> This company announced that it would consider an offer from the Guatemalan government to purchase its properties in that country. The government now has the matter under study. The road is 40.18% owned by the United Fruit Co.

CHAPTER 4

Spin-Offs

A "spin-off" is a hybrid corporate action having characteristics common to dividends, liquidations, and reorganizations. The corporate action which creates the profit potential is the distribution of an asset as distinguished from earned income. For practical purposes, distributions are in the form of securities.

Where the spin-off has characteristics of a reorganization, profit possibilities could exist in securities of either the parent or the spun-off company, since a significant change in the corporation would be taking place. This can be seen in Transamerica Corporation's recent mandatory separation of its banking interests from its insurance business.

Transamerica Corporation Spin-off

On Aug. 21, 1957, the Federal Reserve Board required Transamerica Corp. to get rid of its stock ownership of Occidental Life Insurance Co. of California. This was the first divestment order issued by the Board under the 1956 Bank Holding Co. Act. Transamerica's principal assets were bank stock holdings and insurance companies. The plan of reorganization provided for the separation of Transamerica's majority-owned banking interests from its other interests by transferring to Firstamerica Corp. (a new corporation) all Transamerica's directly held shares in its bank subsidiaries, and $20 million in cash. Firstamerica shares were distributed to Transamerica stockholders on a share-for-share basis. The plan became effective on July 1, 1958.

Our analytical approach to the Transamerica situation is similar to the methods used in liquidations and public utility divestments (discussed in a separate chapter).

The Transamerica spin-off was in the making for a few years. It was no secret that the company would be required to spin-off its bank holdings. Profit potentials existed in varying degrees from the anticipatory stage through the final days when the spin-off became a fact. The investment qualified as a special situation in the closing period. A discount from the calculated evaluation was present, the corporate action was being completed, and the risk was at a minimum. Special-situation investors had an advantage in their knowledge of the methods used to evaluate such an opportunity. Through this knowledge they could participate in the situation when the potential profits appeared greatest.

To clarify the significance of the separation of Transamerica's bankholdings from its insurance assets and to locate the profit potentials, it is advisable to set up the proposed two companies on a pro forma basis.

FIRSTAMERICA	TRANSAMERICA
Assets	Assets
Majority stock in 23 banks	Occidental Life Ins. Co.
	6 Fire and Casualty Ins. Cos.
Cash: $20 million	2 industrial Cos.
	2 real estate development companies.
	Minor subsidiaries

Capitalization

No. of shares outstanding: 11,372,022 for each company
Subsidiary debt: $20 million

Pro forma earnings including equity in undistributed net income on subsidiaries:

1957	$1.19		$1.79 plus 43¢ profit on securities
1956	1.12		$1.77 plus 38¢ profit on securities
1955	0.85		$2.13 plus 18¢ profit on securities

Equity Value As Carried On Books

$14.82 per share $16.38 per share

The key to this type of situation is to evaluate the assets in proper perspective. This means that, beside calculating the companies' worth on an asset and earnings base, consideration be given to growth potential as an independent operating company. This latter factor had greater importance, here, to the insurance holdings than the bank subsidiaries.

Therefore, in evaluating the insurance company, some value should be assigned to the effects of release from parental restraints. In this light, Transamerica as the holder of the insurance subsidiaries had an estimated value based on earnings, assets, and vision of around $25 per share. Firstamerica shares were appraised on prospective earnings, around $17 per share. The combined estimated values aggregated $42 per share. Other estimates of potential values of the two companies ranged from $40 to $50 per share.

Transamerica's $1.40, plus 20¢ extra annual dividend, helped defray the cost of capital for the duration. Its shares were priced around 37 as late as March, 1958, when the situation had but three months to go to consummation. At that time the indicated profit based on the aforementioned estimates showed a capital gain of 13%, plus a 35¢ per share dividend.

As frequently occurs when the consummation date approaches, spin-off situations become more desirable marketwise. Uncertainties disappear, displaced by wider awareness of the great expectations in the newer situation. Thus Transamerica shares reflected broader investor enthusiasm. At the completion of the spin-off, Transamerica stock was priced around $40 per share. The Firstamerica sold at 17, and Transamerica, Ex the distribution, sold at 23 1/2. At this point the situation showed a 9% gain. However, as the investment duration was for only three months, the return was at the rate of 36% on an annual basis.

No penetrating investigation was needed, since essential information had been furnished by the company. Even if, in this complex situation, the investor was not able to do the statistical work needed to assign fair values for each of the companies involved, comprehensive analyses were available, and the informed special-situation investor was in a position to judge the various analyses and so determine when and how to participate in this profitable spin-off.

The ACF Brill Motors, Inc., Spin-off

In the case of a spin-off which is part of a liquidation, the profit potentials would be discerned in the procedure. The ACF Brill Motors, Inc., spin-off is a case in point. This special-situation incorporated a partial liquidation, a distribution in kind, and a market valuation for the anticipated tax factor in a corporate shell. This example demonstrates the substantial profit potentials available to investors familiar with special-situation procedures in liquidations.

The reorganization of ACF Brill Motors proposed distribution of Hall Scott Motors, a subsidiary, on a share-for-share basis. Brill's assets at that time consisted of:

*Cash	$7 per share
Hall Scott Motors*	$3 to $4 per share
Total assets	Approximately $10 to $11 per share

*Hall Scott valuation was based on assets of $2.90 and indicated earnings of $0.50 per share. This valuation was in line with the standards of that year.

Brill shares remained around $7 per share for a protracted period. A profit of approximately 50% seemed a reasonable expectation in view of the indicated worth of $10 to $11 per share. This estimate indicated the presence of "undervalue." However, no official statement of liquidation had been issued; nor was a duration period for the Hall Scott distribution known. Nevertheless, the situation was attractive for the following reasons:

The distribution of Hall Scott having a $3 to $4 per share value would, after the stock was sold, leave the investment at only $3 to $4 per share in an asset having $7 in cash, equivalent to more than twice the remaining invested principal. Thus a minimum risk was indicated.

When announcement was made of the approval of the distribution of Hall Scott shares, the Brill stock had moved to the $9 level. At this point a short-term investor was in a position to establish a profit of 25% to 30% by selling out his stock purchased at $7 per share. Subsequently the Brill shares advanced to 12 5/8. During the latter period the shares fluctuated within a range which offered opportunities for investing at various profit potentials. After distribution of Hall Scott, Brill shares were priced around $11 per share and Hall Scott at $5 per share - an aggregate value of $16 per share. This amount, of course, was substantially above the $10 to $11 expected at first examination of the situation. In part, the better-than-calculated price rise in Brill could be traced to expectations that its tax-loss, carry-forward status would be used in the merger. This was accomplished subsequently.

Spin-off as a Dividend

Where the spin-off resembles a dividend, the profit potential may be negligible since no important corporate action would be in progress. Graham-Paige's recent spin-off of 20% of its wholly owned subsidiary Royal American Corp. ia an example. The value at the time of the spin-off was under 25¢ per share.

Undervalue in Spin-offs

In order to qualify as a special-situation investment, a spin-off profit potential should accrue at the time the corporate action (the spin-off) became effective. Where this is the case, it indicates undervalue. A discount from the estimated value could occur in the event the spun-off property were the controlling equity interest of an unseasoned company. The profit factor (the discount) would arise from two influences. One would be anticipation of economic benefits expected in the spun-off corporation, upon its release from parental restraints. The second would be in the marketwise seasoning of the securities to be spun off, during the period preceding the spin-off.

Essential to attaining the profit is to see the spin-off as though it has been accomplished. This will indicate the complexion of the new company, the quality of its securities, and the technical procedure for effecting the spin-off. There lie the sources of the profits. In the case of Transamerica, a typical spin-off, the profit potentials were in the insurance company holdings, since these were the assets controlled by the parent. Therefore the approach where controlled companies are being released is to evaluate the securities of the corporation which (in the case of Transamerica) would hold the insurance assets. As frequently occurs, comprehensive data pertaining to the situation were made public by the company in the notice of meeting. These included statements of assets and earnings. Besides, many investment services offered detailed analyses of the situation. Thus special-situation investors acquainted with spin-off procedure could readily recognize the profit potentials.

In the case of ACF Brill, the profit potential was in the procedure. The early return of a large portion of the investor's capital was the clue to the substantial profit available in this situation.

Background of Spin-offs

The recently increased use of the spin-off procedure may be traced, in part, to the many mergers and acquisitions of recent years. Not infrequently, after the marriage, a corporation may find itself with an asset of minor importance which does not fit within the scope of the company's activities. This may lead to the property being spun-off. In that type of spin-off, profit possibilities would arise mainly in the divested asset.

The Federal government, through its many agencies, is not infrequently the origin of a spin-off. The Public Utility Holding Co. Act, The Bank Holding Company Act, and anti-trust cases of the Justice Department have led to spin-offs. The recent directive by the Justice Department requiring du Pont de Nemours to divest itself of its General Motors stockholdings is a pending situation of wide interest; also Loew's, Inc., whose consent agreement to separate moving-picture production from theatre business may contain profit possibilities. The second spin-off resulting from the Bank Holding Co. Act was General Contract Co., now changed to General Bancshares, Inc.

In the foregoing pending instances the mandatory spin-offs could significantly change the character of each company. More profit possibilities in the case of du Pont might rise from the divestment procedure than from the spin-off. Loew's corporate action may disclose hidden values.

The analytical and investigating procedures for obtaining a profit in a spin-off situation follow the steps outlined in the chapter on Liquidations.

CHAPTER 5

Stubs

A stub represents a contingent, or a residual interest in a company. It comes into being as a result of a corporate action such as merger, acquisition, liquidation or reorganization. Among names for securities having characteristics of stubs are: Certificates of Beneficial Interest, Certificates of Participation, Certificates of Contingent Interest, Receipts, Scrip, and Liquidation Certificates.

Stubs have special-situation possibilities when:

1. They are corporate actions based upon an unliquidated asset such as a legal or tax contingency.

2. The assets are calculable.

3. The value of the assets exceeds the market price of the stub, which establishes "undervalue."

4. The foregoing make the capital risk minimal.

5. "Windfall" possibilities are present.

6. The market price level is low.

7. The return on the investment is capital gain. The profit potential is then calculated as a percentage of the cost. A stub priced at $2 per share, which has a $2.40 net asset value, has a 20% potential.

8. They are long-term investments since they rise out of basic corporate action.

How to Invest in a Stub

An investment position can be created by direct purchase or through purchase of the parent company's securities before consummation of the corporate action creating the stub. Examples of the latter are the Consolidated Retail Stores and Owens-Illinois Glass situations discussed in this chapter. The trading procedure is the same as for other stocks and bonds. The market place is either an Exchange or the unlisted market.

Since stubs may originate in various investment areas it would be helpful to classify them for easy recognition. Classification is additionally useful since a stub's category can point to its profit possibilities. The accompanying tabulation classifies stubs as to place of origin, issuing company, and type of corporate action which created them.

Place of Origin	Issuing Corporation	Type of Corporate Action
Merger/acquisition	Owens-Illinois Glass	Reserve for undesignated Claims
Reorganization	Consolidated Retail Stores, Inc.	Accrued-dividend claim
Recapitalization	Atlanta & West Point RR, Western Ry of Alabama	Reversionary claim Reversionary claim
Tax	Standard Gas & Elec.	Tax suit
Liquidation	Ridgeway Co.	Residual asset
Legal suit	Internat'l Paper Company	Contingent reserve claim
Dissolution	American Power & Light	Liquidation and tax ruling
Reorganization	New York N.H. & H. RR	Beneficial interest

Besides placing a stub in its proper corporate-action category, it can be subdivided into type of assets which support each claim. These are: fixed assets, participating assets, and fluctuating assets.

The fixed-asset stub is a discount situation against a cash claim. The Consolidated Retail Stores example discusses the stub in relation to a claim for a specified amount of money.

The participating-asset stub has value set within a minimum and maximum range. The Standard Gas & Electric case shows a stub which has a minimum value and possibility of a greater amount.

The fluctuating-asset stub generally is supported by a stated amount in property or securities that are subject to market movements. The New York, New Haven & Hartford CBI's (Certificates of Beneficial Interest) are an example of a stub's value tied to marketable-securities movements.

How to Approach a Stub

1. Place it in its proper classification.

2. Appraise the fixed assets and calculate the per-share worth. Since the fixed assets may be represented by marketable securities or property, do not lose sight of possible fluctuations in values. The value of the fixed assets, less liabilities, divided by the number of stubs, gives the per-share value.

3. Evaluate the contingencies, and note whether reserves have been established to meet them. These reserves should be prorated on a per-share basis to obtain an indication of potential values. These should be estimated at full value, partial, and at no value, to have a range of expectations.

4. Combine fixed values and contingency values to obtain a range of maximum and minimum potentials.

5. Calculate your cost price for the stub.

6. Figure the discount at which the stub is priced in relation to the estimated ultimate values.

7. Determine the cost for participation in "hope and expectations." This cost is the amount you pay over the assured assets.

8. Examine the situation for windfall possibilities. This may be present in litigation, tax disputes, recapture of unclaimed assets, and unaccounted physical properties.

Because a stub is, in itself, a corporate action, comprehensive information about it is usually available from the following sources: the issuing corporation, through notices of meetings and prospectuses; Federal agencies such as the ICC and SEC, and court files. It is also helpful to discuss the stub situation with associated legal firms, the accounting firm, a committee that may be in existence, and the company management.

Probably the best way to evaluate a stub is to know the reasons for its existence. This will show the potential worth and the probable duration period required for the stub's termination.

The following illustrations are, in most instances, living stubs. These investments disclose the technical procedure and the type of thinking used when studying their profit possibilities. Since a stub generally is created to meet a specific condition, no typical stub exists. Therefore each stub should be examined for a possible windfall, which often raises profits above the initial estimate.

Stubs Representing Undesignated Claims

Owens-Illinois Glass. Escrow certificates were issued in October, 1956, and were priced around 1 1/4 in the unlisted market. Currently the certificates are priced around 1 7/8, reflecting the approaching termination date and the absence of significant claims against the reserve fund. The certificates represent a potential participation in 92,587 shares of Owens' preferred stock, which was placed in escrow to protect Owens against any contingencies arising from the merger with National Container Corp. Each escrow certificate has $2.25 in par value of Owens 4% preferred stock held for eventual distribution to its holder. Normal termination of the escrow is December 31, 1960. This stub has an unusual feature in that the preferred stock is convertible into 1.05 shares of Owens-Corning Fiberglas Corp. until 1963, at which time the conversion becomes one share.

This stub offered at its inception an estimated profit of $1 for each $1.25 invested. Since the duration would be four years, the indicated rate of return is 20%. The present price of 1 7/8 reflects this rate of return. A purchase at 1 1/4 would now show a profit of 62 1/2¢, or a return of 25% for the two years during which the stubs would have been held. The quality of Owens' preferred stock gave the situation a minimum-risk rating, and the conversion feature, which could become valuable, offered romance.

Stubs Representing Accrued-dividend Claim

Consolidated Retail Stores scrip (stubs) came into being in October, 1957, at a price around 50¢ in the over-the-counter market. They subsequently rose to $1. This showed a 100% profit in one year. The stubs were issued to the former 4 1/4% cumulative preferred stock, series A, in settlement of accrued dividends. These certificates entitle holders to receive the accrued dividends in cash before any dividends are declared on the recapitalized preferred and common stock. The accrued and unpaid dividends amounted to $2.65 as of July, 1957. As the certificates were priced around 50¢, this was equivalent to purchasing a claim of $2.65 for 19% of its face value. Payments on these certificates depend upon the successful operation of the reorganized enterprise. There are 44,490 shares of old preferred outstanding, against which $142,000 of dividend scrip was issued. The reorganization of this company is discussed in Chapter 7.

Reversionary Certificates

A reversionary certificate gets its name from the turning action it represents. The action can be compared to the return of leased property at the expiration of the lease. The assets behind a Reversionary Certificate would become available after the contingency for which the certificates were created had been met.

The reorganization of the Georgia Railroad and Banking Company established two reversionary-certificate, special-situation investments. These reversionary certificates are presently available in the market at prices averaging a fraction of the value of the assets underlying the certificates. However, the assets which are represented by designated shares will not be available to the certificate holders until 1980. Nevertheless, intermediate profit potentials exist through market fluctuations. Then, too, the long-term characteristics of the certificates make them interesting as gifts to children and for speculative holdings by investment companies.

The two reversionary-certificate situations came into being in dividends declared by the Georgia Railroad & Banking Co. on July 7, 1954. The individual certificates represent the railroad company's reversionary interest in 12,180 shares of stock of the Western Railway of Alabama in one issue and in 7,000 shares of capital stock of the Atlanta & West Point Railroad Co. in the other issue. The shares are held by the lessees. Dividends and rents are paid to the railroad company.

The Western Railway of Alabama

Participating certificates, current market price $9 per share
Capital stock, current market price $95 per share

A Western Railway of Alabama certificate is entitled to one share of stock of the railroad company when the reversion becomes effective in 1980. The investor's problem is to establish a value for an asset that will not be available till two decades hence.

The Analytical Approach

The Western Railway of Alabama is affiliated with the Georgia Railroad and Banking Co. and the Atlantic Coast Line Railroad. The road extends from West Point, Ga., to Selma, Ala. The 133 miles of track operate mainly in Alabama. The line forms a connecting link of a through route from Washington, D.C., to Jackson, Miss. There are 30,000 shares of capital stock. Gross assets amount to $11.7 million. Funded debt totals $1.8 million. Net current assets are $1.2 million.

The earnings record has been good since the company's inception in the early 1900's. The dividend record parallels the good earnings record. Some dividends have been paid in every year since 1902, except for four depression years in the 1930's.

The recent year's price range of the shares was between a high of 108 and a low of 90.

Thus the railroad has (1) valuable trackage, (2) good earnings, (3) substantial continuing dividends, and (4) large asset value. The investor's thinking might see the present price for the certificates as the knockdown value of the property. On this basis, the loss would be the absence of a return on the investment, while the profit could be substantial in the light of the present value of the actual stock. The investment thinking depends on your conjecture of the future. Should you think that the railroad will not be functioning by 1980, and the property will not have a value even as junk, the certificates would hold no interest.

A point to bear in mind is that the certificates reflect, through the market prices of the shares and the certificates, the company's "going-concern" outlook. Three years ago the certificates were available around the $5 level; the present price is $9, and the price has touched the $12.50 level.

The case of the Atlanta and West Point Railroad Co. is similar. The statistical summary is presented, since the situation is alive.

Participating certificates, current market price	$5 per share
Capital stock outstanding in the amount of 24,644 shares, current price	$40 per share

Each Atlanta & West Point participating certificate is entitled to one share of the company's stock when the reversion becomes effective in 1980. The railroad is affiliated with the Atlantic Coast Line Railroad Co. The trackage covers 93.31 miles in Georgia and is a connecting link in a through route from Washington, D.C., to Jackson, Miss.

Gross assets approximate $9 million, while the fixed debt totals $1.2 million. The earnings record has been good. Dividends were paid in every year since 1916 except 1932 through 1939. The most recent dividend amounted to $3 for 1957. The shares have ranged in price from a low of 25 to a high 75 during the past decade.

Standard Gas & Electric Co.: A Tax-suit Stub

The stubs presently are priced around $3 per share on the NYSE. This is a liquidation. The stubs represent an interest in fixed assets and a tax-reserve fund. The fixed assets comprise marketable securities and cash amounting to approximately $6.20 per share as of Dec. 31, 1957. From this sum a reserve fund equal to $1.85 per share has been established to meet Federal tax liabilities for prior years, leaving the stubs an estimated minimum worth of around $4.35 per share. Additional value is contingent upon the outcome of the tax case, which is in the Appellate Division of the Internal Revenue Service. Comprehensive information about the tax case is contained in the company's annual report.

Since the probable profit may be estimated at $1.35 gross the situation shows a potential return of 45% on the investment. The tax matters pertain to the years 1942 to 1950, inclusive. While the nature of the tax status is complex, determination must be made. Therefore you could approach this situation looking toward a maximum duration period of four years. This would show a return of 11%. However, you should not lose sight of the tax contingency, which will have the final influence in this case.

Ridgeway Corporation: A Residual Asset

This stub, priced around $10 per share on the American Stock Exchange, offers participation in a residual asset resulting from a liquidation. The principal asset comprises a tract of 800 undeveloped acres in the vicinity of the International Airport at Miami, Fla. Besides this, there are small holdings in the Palm Beach area. Estimated land values indicate a liquidation value around $13 per share.

This situation illustrates the significance of sponsorship of a corporate action. Here we have a liquidation procedure controlled by management which has disposed of their stock interest. Since the company is in liquidation, the corporate books are closed and stockholders' meetings are not held. Because of this it is difficult to change management. Nevertheless, from the investor's point of view, it would be worth checking developments since a sale of the major properties would have profit possibilities.

The financial analysis is simple since no contingencies exist. The value of the land, less Federal taxes and the small amount of liabilities, will establish the amount to be divided among the outstanding shares. The acreage can be appraised through Miami real estate firms. The company is the most likely source of background information on finances, tax, and legal matters. The duration period is the point to watch, and this can be checked with the company.

International Paper Co.: Certificates of Contingent Interest

This situation developed a windfall of substantial profits shortly after issuance. The certificates were priced around 20 when first issued and now are selling around 69.

These certificates were issued in connection with the merger of International Paper and Long Bell Co. Each certificate represents a $\frac{1}{50,000}$ interest in a reserve fund presently aggregating 38,000 shares of International Paper common stock. The fund was established to protect International Paper against expenses and loss on account of Federal taxes of Long Bell Co., and a lawsuit brought against that company. The lawsuit has been settled. The tax matter is at the lower level of court procedure. However, a windfall possibility has come to light in the company's tax-refund claim against the government, which could make the company the recipient rather than the dispenser of funds. This possibility was reflectd in the certificate's sharp rise in price.

At this point the 38,000 shares of International Paper held in the fund have a market value of $4.2 million equal to $84 per certificate. This is 33% greater than the market price. Since the situation has had a dramatic change from a participation in a residual asset to a dynamic legal tax matter, some risk element is now present.

The most likely sources for information in this situation is the company and legal affiliates. The annual report carried complete discussion of the background of the certificates. Investigation and checking rather than financial analysis is the procedure.

Reclaimed Assets and Tax Windfall

The American Power & Light stubs are presented to show an unusual windfall resulting from a tax ruling. This kind of profit possibility should be borne in mind when analyzing each clas of stub.

The stubs came into existence as a result of the dissolution of the company in July, 1953. The undistributed assets on a per-share basis were as follows:

1. Cash, $0.95.
2. 1/43 share of Portland Gas & Coke.
3. A participation in the contingent assets described as follows: The Company has the right to receive the balance of cash and securities deposited for holders of its old stock issues if holders do not claim the deposits, together with miscellaneous unclaimed payments, amounted to $875,000 on Dec. 31, 1953.

The above assets had an estimated value of $2.50 to $3 per share. The stubs could have been purchased around the 2 1/4 level in January, 1953, with an expectancy of a minimum of 10% profit and a maximum of 30%. It was further expected that the cash and stock of Portland Gas & Coke would be distributed within the year. In that event the investor would have invested less than $1 per share with the potential of $1.50 to $2 as an objective. The final profits, as frequently occurs in special situations, were greater than expected. This additional benefit resulted from an unexpected tax ruling. The following steps trace the "stubs" course.

A purchase of 100 shares of American Power & Light stubs was made at (2 1/4) $225. The stockholders participated nine months later in the following distribution:

	Per 100 Shares
Cash	$95.00
Two shares of Portland Gas & Coke (sold at $18 per share)	36.00
Cash for fractional shares of Portland Gas & Coke	6.06
	$137.06

The residual amount invested after deducting the proceeds from the costs amounted to $88. The anticipated new element injected into this situation was the advice from the company that, for tax purposes, the cost price of the Portland Gas & Coke stock should be computed at 69 7/8 per share. This meant that at the sale price of $18 per share, a tax loss of 51 7/8 ($51.87) was created. This amount could be deducted from profits or charged against income tax where permissible.

This $51.87 per 100 shares of tax loss is a potent item to an investor in the high-tax bracket. Such investor could have established a loss of $518.70 on a 1,000-share investment, while a 10,000-share investment, costing only $22,500, originally could have established $5,187 worth of tax losses to be used against an equal amount of profits. Thus the stub situation would have been worth investment participation on a tax basis alone.

The final date for recapture of the unclaimed shares passed, and the company distributed $1.44 per share on Oct. 31, 1955. However, a small amount has been withheld for final expenses.*

Summing up, we see that an investment of $225 brought in $281.50 for a profit of $56.50. While the money was tied up for a period ranging from nine months to a year and a half, the substantial tax benefit combined with the profit made this a desirable situation.

The New York, New Haven & Hartford RR Co.: (CBI's)

The CBI's are traded in the unlisted market. The approximate price is 6, which is equal to $60 per stub. This stub is a leftover from the reorganization of the New Haven. The corporate action will be the exchange of the CBI's for common stock of New Haven. The indicated basis of exchange is 9.7 shares of New Haven common stock for each CBI. New Haven common is presently priced around 11 1/2 on the NYSE. Based on the above prices, the CBI's are selling at a discount of 50% from their estimated value. However, the exchange cannot occur until a settlement has been reached in the dispute over the sale price of the Boston & Providence RR (B&P) properties to the New Haven. The B&P stockholders have been fighting for better treatment than was proposed. It is understood that the case now will be returned to the ICC for a new separation study.

The CBI's were issued against a reserve fund of 1,073,852 shares of common-stock of the New Haven. The shares are held for issuance to security holders of the B&P, and unsecured creditors of the New Haven upon final court determination of the total unsecured claims. Settlement of the B&P controversy is the last hurdle to release of the shares.

The New Haven reorganization plan provided for acquisition of the B&P by the New Haven in exchange for cash and securities. As the case stands now, if the B&P is not awarded common stock from the reserve fund, then the CBI's rate of exchange will be the estimated 9.7 shares for each CBI. However, any withdrawal of shares in settlement of the suit will be at the expense of the CBI's.

The profit potential rests in the discount of the CBI's from the value of the New Haven commonstock. The important factor is the duration period. The CBI's

---

*The final distribution amounted to 95 cents, paid Oct. 23, 1958.

have had a volatile history, fluctuating between a high $30 a few years ago and a $4 low recently. The present 50% discount reflects the indeterminate outlook. Nevertheless, it is possible to participate in this situation either through direct purchase or by way of a hedge position. The direct purchase has two risks: the tying up of money without a return for a possible long time and the market value of the New Haven common stock. However, the hedge position could be of interest since New Haven common does not pay a dividend, and the discount spread has ranged in the past from 10% to the present 50%.

The procedure for the hedge position would be to sell short approximately as many shares of New Haven common as the number of CBI's owned would be entitled to receive. For example, sell 100 shares of New Haven commonstock short against 10 CBI's held as a long position. Profits accrue through the narrowing of the spread. This would occur with CBI's rising without a corresponding move of New Haven common. This, of course, is not a completely riskless situation. However, settlement of the legal complications would create an investment position. Awareness of the possibilities inherent in CBI's, combined with the public announcement of settlement of the case, could mean profits for those familiar with this type of situation.

Stubs have an additional attractiveness in that the knowledge gained from experience with them can be profitably applied to usual investment securities. It is not uncommon for a type of stub to have its counterpart in the conventional stock or bond. In this way stubs open new avenues for investment and profits. The characteristics of some securities are identical with stubs.

For example there is the <u>reversionary</u> feature in the Gold & Stock Corp. lease to Western Union. The agreement calls for the return in 1981 to Gold & Stock Corp. of a sum equal, on a per-share basis, to $241 per share. This is substantially more than the current price of the shares. Full details follow.

<u>Guaranteed Stock with Assured Appreciation</u>

Gold and Stock Telegraph Co. (listed on the NYSE) is under lease to Western Union Telegraph Company until Jan. 1, 1981, at a guaranteed rental of 6% on the stock of $100 par value. The part of the lease which is unlike other guaranteed leaseholds is the inclusion of a "reversionary clause" under which: plant and equipment stated at $432,203 plus the proceeds from the sale of securities which Western Union took over and subsequently sold amounting to $12,085,262 must be returned to the stockholders of Gold and Stock Telegraph Co. at the termination of the lease in 1981. The above item is carried on Western Union's books as a deferred non-interest-bearing liability and is included on the balance sheet in "Long Term Debt." The fund from the sale of the securities has a value equal to $241 per share of Gold and Stock Telegraph Co.

Thus the shares of Gold & Stock offer an assured income of approximately 3.4% based on the current price of 172 plus potential capital appreciation.

The capitalization structure of Gold & Stock consists of 50,000 shares, of which Western Union Telegraph Company owns 29,476 shares. Regular rentals have been paid and dividends disbursed quarterly without interruption. A court decision settled the question of tax liability, and Western Union is required to pay income taxes of Gold & Stock Telegraph Co.

The <u>dividend-arrears</u> medium has been employed in the issuance of other securities than stock, as in the case of R. Hoe & Co. In this instance the company issued "B" stock to settle accrued-dividend claims (see page 142.)

The American Power & Light tax windfall has opened a new channel in the tax area. When studying a liquidation or a divestment it would be advisable, where the situation calls for distributions in kind, to look for the tax cost price of the security, as it may give you a tax-loss base.

Stubs resulting from bankruptcy and reorganization proceedings can bring to light the possibility of participation in hidden assets. An example was in the Denver, Rio Grande RR 5/78 residual certificates, which participated in a claim of the stock of Utah Fuel Co., which was held as collateral by the trustee for certain DRG Bonds. When finally settled, this proved a rich windfall to the residual bondholders.

CHAPTER 6

Tenders

The corporate act of offering something for acceptance is called a tender. This chapter deals with the profit possibilities which are inherent in most tenders. However, the profit results from the application of your special-situation investment "know-how."

How Are Tenders Used?

A prospective purchaser offers to buy specified securities subject to the terms of the "tender invitation." By this procedure a security holder may offer stock and/or bonds to the prospective purchaser at a stated time and price.

Where Can I Find Tenders?

The following activities use tenders to:

1. Reacquire shares by a corporation.

2. Facilitate mergers and acquisitions.

3. Accumulate securities by corporations and/or individuals.

4. Facilitate redemption of shares during a partial liquidation of a corporation.

5. Facilitate sinking fund operations.

Why Are Tenders Used?

Tenders are used because they offer protective features.

1. The risks attendant upon open-market purchases are eliminated. A purchaser could find himself in an unwholesome position when a large accumulation of securities proves insufficient for his purpose. For example, a prospective purchaser seeks 80,000 shares of stock to gain representation on the Board of Directors or to get control of the company. In open-market activity, he might be able to purchase only 60,000 to 70,000 shares before the market moved beyond his maximum price. His stock holdings would then be in a vulnerable position; he would be a large stockholder without direct representation. However, through the use of a tender offer to purchase, he might have achieved his objective of 80,000 shares. In the event the required amount had not been offered, the purchaser could use the protective feature which would permit withdrawal of the bid if the minimum requirement were not met.*

2. The seller can obtain a better price for his securities than prevails in the market. Not infrequently after a tender offer has terminated, the investor may purchase the same securities in the open market at prices below the sale price through the tender. Also, the seller can use the tender when the invitation is offered, for disposal of substantial amounts of securities.

3. The tender offers immunity to market fluctuations. The tender by-passes the influence of a substantial buying order which creates upward pressure while it is being processed. Conversely, the tender removes the downward pressure when large blocks of securities overhang the market.

How Are Tenders Processed?

The execution is simple since all important information is given in the official "invitation for tenders" and also in the letter of transmittal. The latter is the form which, when filled out by the seller, is forwarded to the bank acting for the buyer. The forms can be obtained from the purchaser; an investment dealer, or the processing bank. The following page shows excerpts of a tender invitation and a letter of transmittal. The main features of a tender are:

1. The name of the company or principal making the offer.

2. The price to be paid for the securities. This stipulates whether the purchase price is fixed, a maximum price, or the lowest offerings under a maximum ceiling.

---

*Textron, Inc., ended, on Dec. 2, 1958, a month-long fight to acquire control of American Screw Co. Unable to obtain the desired 60,000 shares of American Screw, at its tender offer of $55 per share, Textron decided not to exercise its privilege of purchasing less than the desired amount.

FORM OF TENDER

Covering Tender of Shares of Common Stock of
Parmelee Transportation Company

(See Terms and Conditions of Tender on reverse side)

SCHRODER TRUST COMPANY, *Agent*
Trust Department
57 Broadway
New York 15, N. Y.

Certificates for shares of Common Stock of Parmelee Transportation Company are enclosed as follows:

Certificate Nos.	Number of Shares Called For By Certificate	Number of Shares Tendered*	Registered In The Name Of

* If this column is not filled in, all shares are tendered. If less than all shares are tendered, you are to return to undersigned a new stock certificate registered in the above name for the number of shares not tendered.

which are hereby tendered to the extent noted above, for purchase under and subject to all the terms and conditions of the Invitation to Tender Stock of Parmelee Transportation Company set forth in the letter of the Company dated September 30, 1958 (receipt of which letter is hereby acknowledged by the undersigned).

By execution of this Form of Tender the undersigned hereby sells, assigns and transfers to Parmelee Transportation Company the number of shares of Common Stock of Parmelee Transportation Company tendered as above stated.

Dated: October _____, 1958

SIGN HERE_____

PARMELEE TRANSPORTATION COMPANY

Invitation to Tender Stock

September 30, 1958

To the Stockholders of
PARMELEE TRANSPORTATION COMPANY:

As you know, your Company for some time past has been following the policy of acquiring shares of its own stock for retirement. Of the 506,445 shares of its issued Common Stock, the Company now holds 45,500 shares in its treasury, all of which were purchased in the open market.

The Board of Directors has resolved that it is in the best interests of the Company to purchase up to an additional 125,000 shares of its stock, to the extent they can be acquired at a price of $36 per share, or a total purchase price not in excess of $4,500,000, by inviting tenders of such stock.

Accordingly, the Company hereby invites tenders of stock from its stockholders at a price of $36 per share on or before 3 P. M. (Eastern Daylight Saving Time) October 15, 1958, and hereby offers to purchase at such price 125,000 shares (or such lesser number as shall be tendered) of the Company's stock so tendered, subject, however, to the right of the Company at any time prior to such date to revoke such offer by written notice to the Agent hereinafter referred to except as to shares already tendered to and received by such Agent. Tenders will be accepted on a pro rata basis if more than 125,000 shares are tendered.

Checker Motors Corporation, which holds 320,787 shares of the stock of the Company, has informed the Company that it will not tender any of its shares pursuant to this invitation but it has agreed with the Company that, promptly following expiration of the Company's offer contained in this letter, it will sell to the Company at $36 per share such number of shares owned by it, up to 100,000, as may be necessary in order for the Company to acquire a total of 125,000 shares (or as large a portion thereof as possible) as contemplated above.

Tenders must be received by the Agent for the Company, Schroder Trust Company, 57 Broadway, New York 15, New York, on or before 3:00 o'clock P. M. (Eastern Daylight Saving Time) October 15, 1958. Tenders must be made in accordance with and subject to the Terms and Conditions of Tender contained herein and on the reverse side of the Form of Tender, and the enclosed Form of Tender must be used. Tenders will be irrevocable. Stock certificates for shares tendered must accompany the Form of Tender. Promptly after the expiration of the tender period and upon acceptance of stock tendered, the Agent will remit to the tendering stockholder the purchase price for his shares.

3. The amount of money to be used.

4. The minimum and maximum number of shares or other securities to be accepted.

5. The period of time the offer will remain open.

6. The eligibility of securities holders. This defines whether there are limitations upon securities holders of a specified date.*

7. The procedure for acceptance of offers. It is important to know whether securities will be accepted on first-come, first-served basis or prorated.

8. The flexibility of the provisions. This permits latitude in determining whether the tender offer is effective or not. Some tender invitations are rigid to conform to charter provisions.

What Additional Profit Possibilities Are Behind Tender Invitations?

Besides being a medium for profitable transactions, tender invitations can act as a clue to corporate moves that hold special-situation investment opportunities. This would come to light:

1. Where a partial liquidation is under way. A clue may indicate the following:

    a. Full liquidation
    b. A merger or acquisition to make full use of a tax-loss carry-forward
    c. A subsequent tender at a higher price

2. Where a company or individual has been acquiring shares of another corporation. This could be followed by future purchases via tender to acquire complete control.

Besides the foregoing, the following romance condition is often present.

Windfall Profits from Tenders

Profit possibilities in tenders are not limited to the tender price and terms of the invitation. Applying special-situation know-how to information about a tender can bring profit opportunities without resorting to the tender. A case in point is Parmelee Transportation.

---

*Standard Oil Co. of N.J. extended an offer to purchase shares of Creole Petroleum at $90 per share. This was 10 to 15 points above the market price. However, the offer was restricted to registered owners of a date which preceded the date of the offer. This limitation prevented Creole's shares from reflecting the $90 price.

The company invited offers of common stock at a price of $36 per share. The number of shares to be accepted was 125,000. The company previously had purchased 45,000 of the 506,445 shares issued. Checker Motors Co., which owned 320,787 shares of the Parmelee stock, agreed to sell up to 100,000 shares if necessary. Since there were only about 200,000 shares of free Parmelee stock in the market, the tender invitation would take up more than half. Therefore it would be reasonably safe to say that any stock tendered would be taken up.

The thinking at this point is: What is the possibility of the shares selling at higher levels than the tender price prior to the expiration? What is the loss potential if the shares are purchased close to the tender price and the tender offer is accepted?

Since the shares were priced around 35 3/4 and the tender price was 36, the loss would be the commission and the taxes less $25 per each 100 shares. The record shows that quite frequently the shares involved in a tender offer do move above the tender price prior to the expiration date. Therefore it would be a reasonable risk to purchase shares around the 35 3/4 price and then either present the tender or sell in the open market, whichever would be higher.

In this instance the shares moved to the $40 level within a short period of time. Thus a substantial profit was established without tendering the stock. It is interesting to note that of the publicly held shares, only 10,837 were presented for tender.

The step-by-step procedure for participating in tender invitations is shown in the operation by which Warner Bros. Pictures reacquired a substantial block of its shares.

The Warner Bros. Pictures, Inc., tender was designed to reacquire $20 million of its stock at prices not exceeding $28.50 per share. Rumors and newspaper items about a pending corporate action preceded the formal tender invitation. From around $23.50 the stock advanced to $26. The maximum profit figured on the above prices was equal to a return of 20% and 9.4%, respectively, on an annual basis. The company's notice stated that offerings would be accepted at the lowest prices and that the transaction would be consummated about two months hence. The tender invitation appeared attractive in light of the profit possibilities. Limitations as to price and the amount of money to be used suggested the following question-and-answer approach:

1. What percentage of the total outstanding shares could $20 million purchase? This indicates the likelihood of stock offerings being accepted. If the percentage that could be purchased is large, then the possibility for selling to the company is good. Based on a price of $28 per share, the $20 million could purchase 710,000 shares equal to 25% of the outstanding stock. This is a large percentage of its shares for a company to purchase.

2. What position in regard to the tender would be taken by large stockholders? In this case, members of the Warner family stated they would tender an aggregate of

100,000 shares at $27.50. This would leave them with 160,000 shares. Another large holder, representing almost 40% of the outstanding stock, indicated no intention of tendering shares. This information discloses the actions of the principal stockholders.

3. <u>What possibility did the company have to exhaust the entire $20 million?</u> 25% is a large percentage of any stock issue. In this case almost 50% of the outstanding issue was certain not to be offered. This meant that the $20 million could buy approximately 50% of the free stock. Such a large percentage would, of course, be difficult to obtain unless the tender price were substantially beyond estimated values. As this condition did not exist here, the possibility of having all stock accepted seemed good.

4. <u>What risk is involved if the tender is not accepted?</u> Generally the stock will decline to a level around the pre-tender time. However, in this case, the possibility of a substantial reduction in the amount of outstanding shares could exert a stabilizing market influence. This premise proved true in the Warner case as the stock sold around 29 1/2 subsequent to the expiration of the tender.

5. <u>Is the stock worth owning as an investment?</u> Because the situation appeared attractive in light of the foregoing, it was desirable to examine the stock from the financial view. This procedure follows our basic financial analysis. The answer to this question combined with the answer to question 4 gives the key to the degree of risk in the situation.

Since the financial analysis warranted purchasing the stock and dividends sufficient to pay for the use of the money were indicated, the situation was satisfactory from that approach. The corporate-action analysis indicated a strong probability that all shares offered would be accepted. In view of these conclusions the tender invitation was worth pursuing.

Warner Bros. Pictures purchased nearly $18 million of stock at prices up to $28.50 per share. Our illustrative purchases were offered at prices ranging from $28.25 to $28.49 per share, in recognition of the tender terms, which indicated acceptance of lowest offerings first. Since the investments were not held for more than three months the rate of return ranged from 36% to 80%.

Sinking-fund Tenders

The most widely known and oldest use of the tender is for corporate sinking funds. In such funds money is specifically earmarked to meet expenditures or debt. Sinking funds have provisions which apply to a specific security. The objective of the sinking fund is to reduce the amount outstanding or eliminate the particular security from the capital structure. Money is made available for the sinking fund (SF) from earnings. However, when the provisions so state, sale of assets may require part or all of the proceeds to be applied to the SF.

Sinking-fund tenders are classified as fringe special situations in view of the dependence upon chance for the success of the SF operation. This speculative status arises from the use of the lottery method for obtaining the securities to be purchased.

A successful investment practice is to acquire, at a price below the SF price, securities of a corporation where SF provisions are in force. Investor thinking can be summarized as follows: Where the security is attractive on its merits, it then has the additional interest of possible sale to the corporation at an SF price which would yield a profit. On the other hand, should the security not be sold to the SF within the first year, a similar opportunity would arise in following years. This would continue until the entire outstanding securities subject to the SF operation had been purchased. Thus, at some time or other, the SF price would be attained.

While SF provisions make the use of the tender mandatory, a voluntary corporate use which offers profit possibilities is present where the tender is used to assist in furthering a corporate change. Through the use of tenders, a corporation may purchase its nonredeemable securities. In this way a corporation could reduce the amount outstanding and possibly eliminate entirely an undesirable security such as a high-dividend or high-interest-rate preferred stock or bond.

Thus the American Bank Note Co. made recurrent use of the tender to reduce the outstanding number high-dividend-rate preferred shares. The preferred stock carries a dividend rate of 6% and is noncallable. There are 46,575 shares outstanding. The company has offered, at various times, to buy up as much as 25% on one occasion. However, the number of shares presented for sale have always been substantially below the desired amount. In view of the record this situation offers profit opportunities at the company's next tender offer.

Procedure: Seven steps should be taken in preparation for such a tender, or in a similar situation:

1. Establish the quality of the preferred stock. This can be done via our basic financial analysis.

2. Establish a price at which you would care to own the preferred stock as an investment. This price should have some relationship to the previous maximum tender prices.

3. Compare the 6% dividend rate with the money market. This is to confirm your belief that, from the company's viewpoint, the preferred is a high-cost security which should be eliminated, since the company could obtain funds for less than 6%.

4. Inquire at the company about the possibility of a tender invitation within the year. A negative or noncommittal reply would not terminate your investigation as long as the desirability of eliminating the preferred stock remains.

5. Verify the number of preferred shares outstanding.

6. Prepare a statistical review of the price range of the preferred stock for the past few years. This should be done on a monthly basis, except for the most recent period of eight weeks, when a weekly range would be preferable. This will show the range within which the stock may be purchased.

7. Find out what success previous tenders had. These data are available at statistical services and may be obtained from the company. The previous record should be correlated to the amount of money that is expected to be used at the next tender. If no figure is available, use an average of the past tenders. This would serve as a clue as to the probabilities of your stock being accepted. If previous tenders were not met in full, the next might also fall short of company expectations. This would indicate that your chances of having stock accepted would be good.

Anticipating the Use of a Tender

This interesting approach offers substantial rewards. The first requirement is that most of the characteristics of a special situation should be present. The financial analysis and investigation procedure used in locating special situations should reveal the presence of tender possibilities.

Your anticipation of the use of a tender would most likely be fulfilled in the following conditions:

1. The company is in the process of partial liquidation.

2. The company's business activities are undergoing a significant change (See Eastern Steamship Corp. which follows).

3. There is increased activity in the securities of the company.

4. The company's shares are being accumulated by outside interests.

5. The company has been reacquiring its own shares through tenders (See American Bank Note).

The status of partial liquidation, where tenders might be used, can be recognized by the presence of the following conditions:

1. The company has discontinued its principal commercial activities.

2. Cash or equivalent on hand is above normal.

3. Plant facilities have been or are in the process of being sold.

4. Despite the foregoing the company continues its corporate structure. This would be for the following reasons:
   a. The tax status of large stockholders.
   b. The tax position of the corporation.
   c. The benefits which might accrue to the liquidating management.

The accompanying illustration of Eastern Steamship Lines, Inc., provides a comprehensive analysis of a special situation that offered substantial profits as a result of anticipating the use of a tender. The following excerpts are from the actual study used at the time the situation was developing:

EASTERN STEAMSHIP LINES, INC.

A Special Situation: Approximate Price, 18 3/4

The equity shares of Eastern Steamship Lines, presently priced close to the net current asset value of $18 offers the additional attraction of having approximately $5 per share in property and equipment, plus a claim against the United States Government that could have a value of $5.45 to $10.90 per share, equivalent to a discount of 33% to 43% from the possible asset value. An inference drawn from the wording of the Court of Claims' decision suggests the claim could be settled at any time for $2,000,000, which would be equivalent to $5.45 per share. If we assume a compromise at $3,000,000, which would be the equivalent to $8.18 per share, then the total asset value would amount to approximately $31, or 66% greater than the current market price.

The disappearance of coastwise shipping from the Atlantic seaboard has converted Eastern Steamship Corporation into an Investment Fund, for the present, rather than an operating shipping company. Current activities are limited to the profitable operation during the summer season of the SS Yarmouth from Boston to Yarmouth, Nova Scotia. The company's only other vessel in operating condition, the SS Evangaline, is idle, while efforts to utilize or dispose of the vessel and other fixed properties are being carried on. The asking price for the SS Evangaline is understood to be around the $850,000 figure. The SS Yarmouth, a sister ship, is also in the market for sale.

Other assets to be disposed of include Pier No. 18 in New York, and a parcel of waterfront property in Norfolk, Virginia, valued at $125,000. Two small claims against the Government and unspecified miscellaneous assets of apparently minor importance, have not been included in this appraisal.

The estimated value of the above mentioned property and equipment amounts to approximately $1,800,000, equivalent to approximately $5 per share, while the portfolio of marketable securities and other assets have a current value of $6,727,000, equivalent to $18 a share. After deducting liabilities, the net balance amounts to approximately $8,447,000, which is equivalent to $23 per share.

A special feature in this situation is the claim against the United States Government, which arises from an action brought by the company against the Government with respect to the SS Arcadia (now tied up in Norfolk, Virginia) to recover the amount which the company claims it is entitled for reconditioning the vessel sufficiently to place it in its condition when taken by the Government, before its war service, and for the Government's other redelivery obligations. The company's claim in this suit is for $4,000,000.

Analysis of the Situation

The investment would carry itself since the $1 dividend was secure in light of the substantial portfolio holdings. The investment was undervalued; it was calculable; it was at a minimum-risk level; and the corporate action was developing. Thus the four special-situation elements were present. Purchase of the shares and patience were all that were required of the investor.

Progress Report

The situation was inactive until the claim against the United States was settled and paid. The company received $3,400,000 in full settlement of the S.S. Arcadia claim. This was followed by the sale of the S.S. Evangeline and other properties. The asset value then was estimated to be around $32 per share. The company was out of the steamship transportation business. The shares were priced around 21-22, equal to a discount of 31% from the asset value. The time for anticipating the use of a tender had arrived.

The investigating procedure was limited to keeping in touch with company's officials and attorneys. From this checking point two pertinent facts were available, namely: (1) The probability of settlement of the claims, which took place as indicated. (2) The intention of the company to present management's views as to future operations of the company. The fact that management had future plans combined with the high liquid assets and investment characteristics of Eastern suggested the possible use of a tender to reacquire shares. This information was subsequently imparted to all the stockholders. However, bear in mind that it had been available before to all who took the trouble to inquire.

How to Calculate the Probable Tender Price

Marketwise, where a tender is under consideration, shares generally sell at a discount of 10% to 15% from asset value. On this basis, Eastern's shares would have a "tender value" of around $27 to $29 per share. This means that up to $24 could be paid per share since, at that level, the situation would still show a minimum profit of 12% on an annual basis, plus the $1 per share dividend.

The notice of the special stockholders meeting contained a plan to reacquire shares through a tender invitation at $27 per share. Also disclosed was the accumulation of a large block of shares by a privately controlled corporation. As so often occurs with special situations, this one also had greater profit possibilities than originally calculated. After the tender invitation expired, the shares moved to the $40 level.

A trait worth noting in special situations is that frequently the opportunity to invest in the situation is offered at more than one price level. As the situation unfolds, profit opportunities continue. Eastern was no exception, as can be seen by the presence of opportunities between the 18 3/4 and the 24 level.

Tender-Invitation Used to Acquire All the Shares of a Company

The Commodore Hotel, Inc. An offer was made to the stockholders of the Commodore to buy, at $18 per share, all the outstanding stock. The stock was priced around 16 3/8 on the American Stock Exchange. The profit potential was 10%. Since the duration period would be no more than four months, the situation would be worth investigating. Consummation of the tender was contingent upon acceptance of 322,089 shares of the 483,132 shares outstanding.

The key to this type of tender situation is, of course, in the contingency. However, by checking with the company, it was ascertained that owners of 258,568 shares had agreed to exercise the tender. Thus only 13% of the remaining stock would be needed. This would not pose a problem. Therefore consummation seemed assured. Nevertheless, a financial analysis should always be made, just in case of error, as well as to estimate the possible loss.

The use of the tender to acquire all the outstanding shares was successfully closed within four months. Final payment totaled $18.07 per share, which netted a return at the rate of 30%.

There follows a summary of the principal steps in tender situations:

1. Calculate the expected profit. This is the difference between your cost price and the prices at which you offer your securities.

2. Make certain of the following facts:
   a. Procedure for exercising the tender, whether it is a fixed or lowest-offer tender.
   b. Contingencies as to minimum amount of securities required.
   c. Amount of time prior to effective date. Since markets and conditions change, always present your tenders at the latest possible date. This does not apply to the first-come, first-served type.

3. Analyze the financial status of the security, so you will know what you own if your tender is not accepted.

4. Analyze the market-price movements of the issue. This will help as a guide in pricing the securities and give you a level to which the issue might decline after the tender.

5. Weigh the competition to see if they may have an advantage.

6. Be sure you know the percentage of the outstanding shares that could be purchased through the use of the entire amount of money allotted for the tender use.

CHAPTER 7

Reorganizations

A reorganization is a corporate action designed to bring about relief from financial stress to a company confronted with economic demise. A reorganization takes place when a company's credit has collapsed and creditors have taken over the operation of the business. The creditors, who may comprise commercial interests, bondholders, and preferred stockholders, hope to regain more through continuation of the business than through its liquidation. In the reorganization a major portion of burdensome debts are eliminated and something new is added. The corporate action which implements the reorganization takes place within the capital structure.

The Profit Play

The profit possibilities arise from the investment opportunities opened up by the differences in value of the securities of the old company and the estimated values of the securities of the new company to be received in exchange. The profit is in the prices obtainable for the new securities in the open market. The market's evaluation of the significance of the settlement of claims is seen in the prices of the new securities in relation to their face value.

Let us illustrate with a situation in which we deal with bonds of a company in the process of reorganization. We assume an arbitrary price of $780 as the cost of a $1,000 bond which has an accrued interest claim of $50. The bond has a claim of $1,000 principal and $50 of interest, or an aggregate claim of $1050. Let us assume that, under the reorganization plan, the above bond was allocated a new mortgage bond having a face value of $1,000 and an income bond with a face value of $50. This was in settlement of the $1050 claim. Let us further assume that "when-issued" prices (or estimated values) for the mortgage bond was $870 and the income bond $30, a total of $900. This indicates a profit of $120 since $900 less $780 (the cost) equals $120.

An oft-repeated reason for higher prices for the "new securities" is: As the date for consummation of the reorganization draws near, the "new" securities often give recognition to the favorable potentials of the reorganization plan by reflecting a value as a "going concern." It would be helpful, at this point, to bear in mind that, as the plan approaches consummation, the probability of the reorganized company paying interest and dividends becomes more realistic. Such expectation contributes to the value of securities and counteracts the depressing effect of earlier uncertainty. Furthermore, the old securities are subject to pressure of selling orders by security holders who do not care to continue in the reorganized company or who act out of tax considerations. Then, too, the old security may be available at a discount from the estimated value of the new security. This prevails because of uncertainties about the duration period and doubt regarding completion of the reorganization plan. The causes for doubt are similar to the obstacles met in mergers/acquisitions discussed earlier.

Where Can I Find Reorganizations?

A reorganization is possible wherever trouble is present. The sources of information about reorganizations are the newspapers, financial publications, and investment services. Wherever you hear of a corporation operating at continuing losses, having extreme losses, or with accumulated interest and dividend claims, the possibility of a reorganization exists.

It's No Secret

The intent to reorganize is usually known well in advance of the actual presentation of a reorganization plan. There is no need of haste when studying the facts of the case.

One should be mindful that a protracted period preceding consummation may permit the "plan" to be revised to meet changed economic conditions, as in the Missouri Pacific Railroad reorganization, to be discussed later.

How to Recognize a Special-situation Reorganization

Be alert to:

1. Financial embarrassment or insolvency of a corporation.
2. Efforts to continue the existence of the enterprise.
3. Presentation of plans to reestablish the corporation on a sound basis.

4. Compromise or agreement on a plan by authorized persons or groups.

5. Approval of the plan by the regulatory or official bodies. (A reorganization may need the approval of a Federal regulatory body such as SEC, ICC, FCC, (the Federal Communications Commission), the Federal Court, and state agencies, as well as the various creditors and securities holders.)

6. Formal approval by creditors and stockholders.

7. Certification by the court having jurisdiction. Plan declared operative.

8. Exchange of old securities for securities of the new corporation.

How to Get the Profit

The approach to establishing a special-situation investment in a security in reorganization is as follows: (1) Apply our basic securities analysis, to establish a value for the new securities based on a pro forma financial projection. Should the analysis indicate an adequate value above the market level of the "old" securities, carry the investigation further. (2) As the corporate action in a reorganization is the consummation of the "plan," our investigation would be concerned mainly with the activities leading to that end. Therefore careful consideration should be given matters pertaining to the opposition, such as:

1. The quality of opposition. Is it sincere, well founded, and financially strong?

2. The quantity. What percentage of the creditors does the opposition represent?

3. Status of the opposition in relation to the various securities. Do they oppose the entire plan, or are they seeking to improve the lot of a specific issue?

The Significance of the Opposition

Because a reorganization is a legal procedure, the opposition's activities could be followed through published court proceedings, communications of protective committees, announcements of the company, and records of Federal or state agencies. It would be helpful to discuss the case with informed persons at these sources. The information thus obtained could give clues to the progress being made, facilitating the calculation of the duration, and enabling you to decide whether or not to invest in the reorganization.

Protective Committees

A reorganization generally leads to the formation of protective committees, groups of creditors and/or other interested parties. Generally, they represent each class of creditor and security holder and receive their power and authority from the creditors and the voting strength of the shares they represent. An example

- 89 -

is the communication of a committee formed by preferred stockholders of the Missouri Pacific Railroad given below.

Protective Committee for Holders of Preferred Stock of the Missouri Pacific Railroad Company

CHAIRMAN
HARRY W. HARRISON
123 SO. BROAD STREET
PHILADELPHIA, PA.

116 NASSAU STREET NEW YORK 38, N. Y.
Phone WOrth 4-4613

SECRETARY
ROBERT E. SMITH
116 NASSAU STREET
NEW YORK N. Y.

September 9, 1954

Fellow Missouri Pacific Preferred Stockholder:

Herewith summary of the plan of reorganization for your railroad, as proposed by the Interstate Commerce Commission. If no further hearing is ordered by the I.C.C., and if both the Court and the securityholders approve the plan, the reorganization may be completed within a year or even less.

However, if the Commission holds a further hearing, before it submits the plan to the Court, or if the Court, after approving the plan, holds a further hearing before confirmation, conclusion of the proceeding will be considerably delayed. Also, if the Court, after hearing, rejects the plan, or if an appeal is taken from the Court's approval, extended delays will result. Consequently, much work and effort must be expended on behalf of the present preferred stockholders in support of the plan.

An authorization blank is enclosed. If you have not previously sent in your authorization and pro rata advance, we urge that you do so promptly, so that we may know what funds are available for the preparation and presentation of the preferred stockholders' case. The issues at stake, and the inherent value of your preferred stock, are so great that no preferred stockholder should risk a "free ride" on the shoulders of his fellow preferred stockholders.

Sincerely yours,

Harry W. Harrison, Chairman

It is not unusual to find a separate reorganization plan presented by each committee. The purpose of each is to obtain the best terms for the respective securities, or at least to protect the interest and rights of the specific security. The difference in treatment of securities when more than one plan exists will give a clue to the amount of compromise that will have to be effected to complete a reorganization.

The investigation outlined on pages 88 and 89 would uncover the legal requirements and/or obstacles, the extent of governmental interests, the significance of the creditor's attitude, the objectives of the committees, and their voting strength. The number of votes, amount of securities, and percentage of total claim will affect the reorganization plan.

How to Establish an Investment Position

Outright Purchase. There are two methods for creating an investment position in a reorganization. One is to purchase the "old" securities to hold for consummation of the reorganization. This will be discussed later in this chapter in a step-by-step analysis of the Consolidated Retail Stores reorganization. Outright purchase is particularly recommended if the securities accrue interest payable at consummation. When interest does not accrue, then the gross profit should include a reasonable charge for use of the money for the estimated duration period. This type of investment is vulnerable to a delay in reorganization which could be costly in that time could consume the profit.

Hedge Position: The second approach is to purchase the "old" securities and sell, on a when-, as-, and if-issued basis, the new securities to be received in exchange. This procedure is described in the Consolidated Retail stores analysis.* The profit, of course, is established via the higher prices at which the when-issued securities are sold.

Since when-issued transactions in reorganizations of commercial and industrial companies do not generally come into existence until the reorganization plan is approaching its final stages, duration should not be a serious factor. Nevertheless consideration must be given the estimated duration period, since a protracted delay could be costly. On the other hand, a delay may offer an opportunity to enter the situation at a later date. This would be desirable where a company's securities are accruing interest during the waiting period.

The Banking Stage. It is possible to create an investment position at the final stage. This is the "banking," or "money," stage, since the profit that remains is based on the use of money to facilitate the exchange of securities. This profit may amount to only 2%. However, 2% earned in a moneh, is equivalent to a per annum return of 24%. This is the period when the date has been established for the exchange of securities, and consummation of the reorganization is a matter of the technical deposit of the old securities in exchange for the new.

---

*See Chapter 2 on Arbitrage and also the Missouri Pacific reorganization in the following chapter on Railroads.

Summary of Step-by-step Procedure

The following outline presents a simplified procedure for investing in reorganization situations, summarizing the steps to be followed:

1. Determine the possibility of a reorganization, from data on unpaid corporate indebtedness, obtained from newspapers and financial publications and services.

2. Set up the reorganization plan on a pro forma basis.

3. Mathematically calculate the profit that is, the difference in value between the "old" and "new" securities.

4. Decide which class of security appears most attractive.

5. Investigate probabilities of consummation of the reorganization. This includes ascertaining the strength of the opposition and significance of legal contingencies.

6. Examine windfall possibilities in hidden assets and tax refunds.

7. Set up an investment position through purchase of "old" securities and, where a hedge position is to be taken, sale of "new" securities.

8. Check the progress of the situation. Be alert to possibility of new influences which may affect plan.

9. Observe the market action of the securities for an opportunity to establish a profit prior to consummation.

10. Complete the transaction. In light of tax influences you may consider the following: (a) extending your investment into the following year; and (b) establishing a long-term profit as opposed to a short-term profit.

The foregoing outlines general reorganization procedure. Variations exist in each type, as will be shown in the ensuing discussion of reorganizations in commercial enterprises, railroads, and public utilities. Because the public utility and railroad reorganizations of the 1940's presented unique and numerous special-situation money-making opportunities, separate chapters are devoted to them. Similar situations have arisen in present-day markets through the separation of bank stock from insurance holdings required by law. Transamerica Corp. and General Contract Corp. are recent examples; and the pending divestment of General Motors shares by du Pont de Nemours is an indication that other areas may open to this type of reorganization.

The Consolidated Retail Stores reorganization presents an ideal illustration of an opportunity for substantial profits most readily recognized by those investors whose sights have been oriented toward special situations. The company's difficulties had been aired in the newspapers a long time before the formal announcement of a reorganization.

Official notification of the proposed plan of recapitalization and debt arrangement was presented in the notice of a special meeting to stockholders. The company had been operating since September, 1956, under Chapter XI of the Bankruptcy Act. The special meeting was called for Sept. 10, 1957. The plan was released to the public on Aug. 2, 1957. The market prices of the securities at that date were: preferred stock approximately 10 1/2; common stock approximately 2 7/8.

The gist of the plan was an offer by Mr. A. M. Sonnabend, who proposed to settle the debts of the defunct company in return for control of the corporation. Depending on various optional factors in the recapitalization, Mr. Sonnabend's stock interest in it would range from 45% to 56.8%. The details of the plan follow.

Creditors of the company with claims under $100 and those with priority claims would be paid off in cash totaling $141,397. Other unsecured claims would be settled by issuance of non-interest-bearing ten-year promissory notes for 85% of the claim, totaling $4,656,993. The 15% balance of each claim would be satisfied with two-year, 5% convertible notes, of which $821,821 would be issued.

The plan proposed reclassification of each outstanding share of common stock into one-half share of recapitalized common and each preferred (4 1/4%) stock into one share of 5% preferred and four of the new common shares. The new preferred would be convertible into five new common shares.

The new preferreds would also receive warrants for accrued dividends amounting to $2.65 as of July 1, 1957. The estimated values of the new securities and the package to be received as related to the preferred and common stock follows:

For each share of 4 1/4% preferred the holder would receive:	Estimated Value
☐ One share new preferred ($20 par) convertible into five common shares	$10
Four shares new common stock	8
One warrant for accrued dividends, nominal value*	
Estimated value of securities to be received	$18
For each old common share the holder would receive:	
☐ One-half share of new common	$ 2

The foregoing projections were based on estimates made around mid-August. As the old preferred was priced around the $13–$14 level, a substantial profit potential existed through purchase of the shares. Contrariwise, as the old common was

---

*The warrants were not given any indicated value. However, after consummation of the plan they did command a price of around $0.50 per warrant.

priced around 2 and the holder would receive only half a share of the new stock, the common was too high. Consequently profit possibilities via a hedging procedure were contingent upon selling the old common stock short.

Approach to Analysis of the Plan

Two elements in this situation stood out sharply. Complete liquidation would give the creditors about $0.50 on the dollar, while the equity interests would be wiped out; and potential values in the reorganized company would come mainly from the use of the $3.8 million tax-loss carry-forward. This, and the sale of unprofitable stores, could inject hope for the reorganized company.

The financial statements and reorganization-plan material contained all the needed information. The determining factor was the obvious benefit to be derived from going along with the plan. Opposition did exist, but its position was weak, since no other workable plan had been submitted, nor was one in view.

The Consolidated Retail Stores Corp. reorganization is an illustration of procedures valuable in trading opportunities which often arise in reorganizations. Here it was possible for the informed investor to participate via two kinds of trading positions, namely (1) a straight long position of the old preferred, (2) a hedge position created by selling part or all the common while retaining a long position in the old preferred. The investor's thinking proceeds as follows:

How to Talk It Over with Yourself

If the old common had a nominal value of $1 per share based on the recapitalization and debt adjustment plan (keep in mind that the tax loss gives value to the new equity position), then the new common would be worth $2 per share, since it would be issued at the rate of one-half share for each old common.

The preferred, in effect, would receive nine shares of new common, four shares directly and five shares available upon conversion of the new preferred. Thus, at $2 per share, the nine shares of new common would be worth $18 plus the value of the warrant. As the preferred was available around the $13-$14 level in August-September, a purchase then of a straight long position would have worked out as follows:

Buy, 100 shares of old preferred at 14, cost	$1,400

At the time the plan was confirmed in October the following transaction was possible:

Sell, 100 old preferred at 18 1/2, proceeds	$1,850
☐ Gross profit (duration 2 months)	$ 450

- 94 -

Second Example - Hedge Position

Investors could have hedged this situation as follows:

Buy, 100 preferred at $14, cost	$1,400
Sell 1,800 shares of old common short at $2 per share ☐ (each 100 old pf. is equal to 1,800 old common)	$3,600
$1,400 from $3,600 leaves gross profit of	$2,200

The profit is subject to commision charges and taxes.

Partial-hedge Position

In the following instance we have sold but half of our full common potential. The objective here is to cover the old common when it declines to its $1 estimated value (which it did). After covering the 900 shares of common stock, the next move would be to sell the preferred around the time the plan has been consummated. The following tabulation shows how this approach would work out and how it is processed:

Buy, 100 old preferred at 14, cost — $1,400
At the same time:

Sell, 900 old common short at 2, proceeds — $1,800
Subsequently,

Buy, 900 old common at 1, cost — $900

☐ Gross profit — $900

Sell, 100 old preferred at 18 1/2, proceeds — $1,850

☐ Gross profit on preferred transaction — $450

Combined profit of short sale and long preferred — $1,350

A thought to bear in mind is that the foregoing trading procedures have similar application where an exchange of securities is in operation.

Equitable Office Building

This reorganization history has interest because of unusual legal developments. Here we see the anomalous situation of a court-approved reorganization plan that never became effective, though the new securities to be issued under the plan had been admitted to the NYSE.

The Equitable Office Building filed a petition in the U.S. District Court of New York for reorganization under Chapter 10 of the Chandler Act. At the time of the filing, the company's capitalization consisted of $4,754,000 of 5% debentures due in 1952, and common stock. From the time of the first reorganization plan through the maze of legal maneuvers, the company's debentures offered speculative opportunities and headaches. The price of the debentures ranged from a low of 18 3/8 in 1944 to a high around 200 in 1946. Thereafter the debentures remained around the 130 level until completion of the reorganization.

The debentures appeared attractive in light of safety of assets supported by improving earnings. The latter were estimated to be around $0.60 per common share. This suggested eventual payment of principal and accrued interest.

The price range discloses the many opportunities for profit that existed in this situation over a long period.

Bonds	Low	Approximate High
February, 1944	18 3/8	29
May, 1944	31	32
December, 1944	44 1/2	45 3/4
May, 1945	81	83
December, 1945	133	137
January, 1946	147	200
February, 1947	129	136
October, 1947	127	130
December, 1947	130	130

The final plan gave the debentures cash equal to the principal ($1,000 per debenture) with interest thereon at 5% per annum from Nov. 1, 1944, to date of payment. The common shares received one new share for five old and a warrant which subsequently expired.

Surprise Ruling

The chronological steps in the case follow: A plan of reorganization was filed Feb. 24, 1944, and court hearings commenced on May 11, 1944. The Trustees subsequently filed a plan, dated May 5, 1945, which, as amended, was approved by the court on Dec. 4, 1945, and then submitted to creditors and stockholders on Jan. 1, 1946. Each debenture was to receive 100 shares of new common stock and $600 in new debentures. The plan was approved by the stockholders and confirmed by the Federal District Court on May 1, 1946. The NYSE authorized the listing of the new common shares to be issued. However, consummation was postponed to abide by a higher court ruling, that of the U.S. District Court of Appeals, that amendments could still be offered in a reorganization for the company.

This ruling was a surprising deviation from precedent, as it transcended the all-around approval of the reorganization described above. Other reorganizations which had been approved by creditors and security holders and confirmed by the Court had been considered inviolate, with consummation a foregone conclusion. However, the U.S. District Court ruled that any responsible individual still might offer a plan to pay off the debentures. The City Investing Company then made an offer which provided for payment in full of all creditors. This offer was not accepted and expired on Oct. 17, 1946. In the above ruling the Circuit Court had reversed an order of the Federal judge which had denied stockholders the right of amendment because the plan had been confirmed in his court. The Circuit Court ruling was that the confirmation order was not a final decree.

On Oct. 24, 1947, Federal Court confirmed the plan representing revision of the plan submitted by the Manufacturers Trust Company and others, which was duly consummated on Dec. 1, 1947.

Discussion

In a situation where a plan has not yet been formulated, it would be desirable to obtain preliminary estimates of assets and earning power. This information can be secured from officers of the company, protective committees, investment brokers, research services, and individuals having association with the company. This introductory investigation may reveal such pertinent data as (1) potentialities that have been dormant; (2) the strength and objectives of the interested groups; (3) greater values in fixed assets such as real estate. The latter might have more significance in a bankruptcy or reorganization than in a going company, since an evaluation of real estate could be made at appraised market worth. In recent years this has proved substantially above book value. The value of real estate is more important to the first-mortgage bondholder of a company when in reorganization than when it is in a solvent though retrogressive condition.

An illustration of the foregoing is the Hudson & Manhattan Railroad Co. (see chapter 8) now in bankruptcy and pending reorganization. Here we have a combination railroad-real estate company whose net railway-operating income has been declining sharply while its real-estate assets rose in indicated value above the present market prices for the first-mortgage bonds.

It may be advisable to acquire senior securities at the inception of a reorganization development, where the specific securities have been under market pressure in anticipation of the distress climax. These securities may well rebound on re-examination of the company under a reorganization status which would (1) free some valuable assets; (2) relieve operating pressure; and (3) open up opportunities which were locked in during the declining-earning period.

While the court reversal was most unusual, a special-situation investor would not have found himself in a vulnerable position since he would have entered the situation when the risk was of minor significance. That condition would have been at a price around its analyzed worth.

CHAPTER 8

Railroad Reorganizations

The railroad-reorganizations which gave rise to so many special situations began around the time of the Second World War. Numbers of major rail lines were operating under Section 77 of the Bankruptcy Act. While that period has come to a close, the investing know-how gained then can be used to advantage today in liquidations, spin-offs, recapitalizations, and reorganizations under the Chandler Act.

Among the technical procedures developed to effectuate investment opportunities among the "old" and "new" capitalizations of railroads was a method for creating tax benefits through establishing long-term profits and short-term losses. These were valuable during the existence of a previous capital-gains tax law. Another procedure was trading in when-issued contracts discussed in the following pages.

The Three-step Approach

Special-situation profit opportunities in railroad securities existed in three principal categories:

1. Arbitrage positions when the reorganization development had reached an advanced stage
2. Long position in the bonds of the railroad company being reorganized
3. Long position in the when-issued securities of the new corporation resulting from the pending reorganization

The foregoing investment mediums were interrelated, having originated from the same source and being part of the same reorganization plan. Therefore analysis of the reorganization routine would reveal the opportunities inherent in all three mediums. Since these are present in the arbitrage procedure it would be helpful to study the Denver & Rio Grande situation, which demonstrates the technical procedure for setting up an arbitrage position. (See below.)

DENVER & RIO GRANDE, WESTERN RAILWAY
Arbitrage

The Federal District Court approved the ICC plan for reorganization and final consummation is generally expected in about a year.

BUY:	$10,000 Denver Rio Grand 4's/1936 @ 53	$5,300.00
	Approximate commission and taxes on completed arbitrage transaction	65.00
	Total cost	$5,365.00

ITEM SELL: "When-issued" new securities issuable under Plan of Reorganization:

A	$3,189.20 Denver Rio Grande 1st Mtge 3-4s, 1933 @ 87-3/4	$2,798.52
B	$2,170.80 Denver Rio Grande Income 4-1/2s, 2018 @ 56-1/2	1,226.50
C	32.160 shares Denver Rio Grande Pfd @ 41-1/4	1,326.60
D	48.240 shares Denver Rio Grande Common @ 18-3/4	904.50
	Accrued interest on above 1st Mtge bonds (estimated)	191.35
	Proceeds	$6,447.47
	Purchase cost	5,365.00
	Net spread	$1,082.47

BUY:	$10,000 Denver Rio Grande 5's/1978 @ 48	$4,800.00
	Approximate commission and taxes on completed arbitrage transaction	65.00
	Total cost	$4,865.00

SELL: "When-issued" new securities issuable under Plan of Reorganization:

$2,500.10 Denver Rio Grande 1st Mtge 3-4's, 1933 @ 87-3/4	$2,187.58
$1,596.10 Denver Rio Grande Income 4-1/2's, 2,018 @ 56-1/2	901.79
31.075 shares Denver Rio Grande Pfd. @ 41/1/4	1,281.84
69.213 shares Denver Rio Grande Common @ 18-3/4	1,297.74
Accrued interest on above 1st Mtge bonds (estimated)	150.00
Proceeds	$5,818.95
Purchase Cost	4,865.00
Net spread	$ 953.95

If the arbitrage is completed in a year, the capital return would be approximately 20%. However, if the transaction is carried on a conservative margin basis, the return would be over 40%. Even if the arbitrage takes an additional year, the cash return would be 10% per annum and the marginal return over 20% per annum.

Arbitrage Position

The goal of an arbitrage investment is the immediate establishment of a profit collectible in the future. As you will note in the Denver & Rio Grande arbitrage, the bonds cost $5,365, while the sale of the securities to be received in exchange brought $6,447.47. These transactions created a paper profit of $1,082.47. The item of "accrued interest" should be borne in mind as it pertains to the Denver and Rio Grande first-mortgage 3 - 4's of 1993 to be issued under the reorganization plan. It is Wall Street procedure to allocate the interest payable on the when-issued first-mortgage bonds to the seller. The interest would reduce the cost for the use of the money when the situation required a longer period for consummation than had been calculated. The interest in this instance was estimated to cover a 2 1/2-year period.

The net profit would be collectible at consummation of the reorganization plan. At that time the "old" bonds could be deposited with the bank or agency clearing the reorganization plan and the new securities would be received in exchange. These securities would then be delivered against the previous sales as indicated by the when-issued contracts.

Long Positions

The second approach would be to purchase "old" bonds such as the Denver Rio Grande 4's of 1936 and await consummation of the reorganization. The interest to which the bond is entitled would accrue to the bondholder during such holding period and be paid via the reorganization plan. Of course, purchase of the "old" bonds would be made only where the expected future price appeared, after analysis, to be reasonably assured. The financial appraisal should include the basic analysis described in Chapter II. Net earnings are figured in estimates of the value of railroad shares; using traffic movement, i.e., car loadings, as guide to the earnings trend. Valuable financial data and railroad-operation statistics were available at the ICC. A good portion of the potential profit was based on a projection of earnings. The risk remained at a minimum since cost price was in line with the current evaluation. Then, too, the package value of the when-issued securities acted as a guide for the not-too-distant future price that was expected. Based on the foregoing, a long position would be considered.

The outright-purchase approach offers additional investment opportunities which can be applied in reorganizations. This procedure is so designed that a selected security can be acquired at a price substantially below the prevailing market. To accomplish this a part or parts of the "new package" is sold on a when-issued basis. A package is an assortment of securities issued as a single group. For an example, see page 99, under the column "Item Sell." Here items A, B, C, and D make up the package of "new securities" to be received in exchange for the "old" Denver Rio Grande 4's/1936 noted in column "Buy."

How to Own the Preferred Stock at Low Cost

Let us assume you chose to accumulate the preferred shares. You could purchase them on a when-issued basis around the 41 1/4 price. However, by purchasing the old bond (Denver & Rio Grande 4's/1936) and, in turn, selling the first-mortgage, income bonds and common stock, items A, B, and D for a total of $5,120.85, which included the interest to be received, your net investment would amount to only $245 ($5,120.85 deducted from $5,365), which is equal to $7.61 per share of new preferred stock.

How to Establish a Low-cost Income Bond

The cost to the investor who desired to retain the new income bonds works out as follows:

Cost of Denver & Rio Grande 4/36	$5,365.00
Proceeds of sale of items (in exhibit A-C-D plus interest	5,220.97
Net Cost	$ 124.03

Thus the $2,170.80 worth of income bonds (item B) would cost only $124.03 for the lot.

How to Establish a Low-cost First-mortgage Bond

To establish a low cost for the first-mortgage bonds, the investor would dispose of the income bonds, preferred and common stock (items B, C, and D). This would give him a cost of around 53 for the new bonds as against the when-issued market price of 87 3/4. It should be borne in mind that the investor has in effect diverted his potential profit into the cost of the security he retained.

Cost of Denver & Rio Grande 4/36	$5,365.00
Proceeds from sale of items B, C, and D (does not include first-mortgage bonds)	3,648.95
Net cost	$1,716.05

The cost divided by the amount of bonds bring down the net cost per $1,000 bond to $530.

The foregoing offered a practical and profitable procedure for special-situation investors.

Investment in When-issued Securities

A third much-used approach was through the medium of when-issued securities. This method offered three main advantages, as follows:

1. (a) The cost of carrying the securities could be low since margin requirements could have been arranged at minimum levels. (b) There is no interest charge on the debit balance since money is not required to be paid by the broker until the securities are issued. Thus the money deposited for margin is used to protect banks and/or brokers against possible loss. However, should the market price of the when-issued securities decline, then the holder would be required to maintain the agreed-upon margin requirement by putting up additional funds.

This "markup to the market" is the difference between the price at which a when-issued security has been sold and the market price at any given time. An investor who sold a when-issued security at a price of 79 could be called upon to deposit 10 points, or $10 per share, for each share he had sold, if the stock or bond was priced in the market at 89 subsequent to his original sale. A purchaser at 89 would be required to meet the markup to the market when the security declined to 79. The money deposited as margin often was sufficient to cover the markup to market demands, and thus expedited the technical procedures.

2. In an investment position through when-issued securities, failure of the reorganization plan to consummate incurs minimal risk. The only loss the investor can suffer is the commission charges.

3. When-issued contracts can be used as negotiable instruments. The when-issued contracts could be sold at a percentage of the existing profit or loss, prior to the reorganization becoming effective.

The Denver & Rio Grande arbitrage described earlier, illustrates this procedure. If an investor purchased the 32.16 shares of preferred stock at 41 1/4 (item C), he in fact had entered into an agreement or contract with the seller to purchase said shares "when, as, and if they are issued." Let us assume that more than six months hence (for tax purposes), the investor wishes to establish a profit as the shares have moved up to the 50 level. If he were to sell the shares, the only way he could do that would be the reverse of his purchase, i.e., to sell another contract to deliver 32.16 shares at a price of 50 on a when-, as-, and if-issued basis. This might incur cost of margin for an open contract, and he then would have two contracts outstanding. However, he still would not be in a position to close the transaction as the contracts would be contingent upon consummation of the reorganization plan. He then would hold one contract to purchase at 41 1/4 and another to sell at 50. However, the method simplified and benefited the investor because it simply required that he sell the specific contract or agreement which he had entered into at the price of 41 1/4. This contract had a potential value of the difference between 41 1/4 and the market price of 50, or 8 3/4 points on the 32.16 shares. This equaled $281.40.

However, it could not become actual until the reorganization plan had been consummated. But it did become possible to sell that contract with the $281.40 potential profit, at a discount, depending upon the state of the reorganization plan. The investor could terminate his investment with a net profit of $253.26 if the discount was 10%. The discount then would amount to $28.14, which, subtracted from $281.40, would leave $253.20 profit which was established whether or not the plan consummated.

While the above illustration relates to a railroad security, this approach can be used in other instances where when-issued contracts for securities are in existence.

Case History

The Denver & Rio Grande reorganization is typical of railroad reorganizations. It brings into sharp focus the periods when special-situation transactions appear appropriate. Its history of years of legal seesaws includes rejection of one plan, approval of a second, followed by court reversal and final confirmation.

Despite the delays, special-situation investment proved profitable and in certain respects even more successful than calculated. That the situation also contained a windfall is not unusual with special-situation investments.*

The Denver & Rio Grande reorganization-investment interest was based on (1.) announcement of the modified reorganization plan, (2.) the concurrent trading in the when-issued securities, (3.) the belief that consummation would take no more than two years. An added attraction of this situation was the fact that investors were entitled to interest on the new first-mortgage bonds upon completion of the plan. In addition, there were tax potentialities and a possible windfall in a hidden asset.

With minor deviations, most reorganizations of railroads in bankruptcy adhered to a standard design. This provided for exchange of the outstanding debt, and in some instances the equity interest, for new debt and equity shares.

On June 14, 1943, the ICC issued a modified reorganization plan superseding the rejected plan of 1939. The District Court of Colorado approved the ICC plan on Oct. 25, 1943, and submitted it to creditors for voting on Mar. 23, 1944. The plan was confirmed by the Court on Nov. 1, 1944, and ordered effective in December of that year. However, in early May, of 1945, the U.S. Tenth Circuit Court of Appeals reversed the Federal District Court's approval of the ICC plan. On Nov. 10, 1946, Supreme Court countermanded the stay order and ruled that the reorganization be carried out. The District Court thereupon signed the final decree of Apr. 10, 1947, and the property was transferred to the reorganized company on Apr. 11, 1947.

---

*The windfall came in the valuable properties of the Utah Fuel Corp., which benefits the Rio Grande 4's and the D.R.G. of '78.

While speculative activity in the outstanding securities prevailed during the earlier years of the bankruptcy, this was based on expectations of price appreciation in the market rather than calculated on values. However, when the ICC issued its modified plan, trading in the new securities presented arbitrage possibilities, and it became possible to deal in the "old" and "new" securities.

The arbitrage spread in the Denver & Rio Grande situation was approximately 20%. The purchaser of a $1,000 bond of the D.R.G. Consolidated mortgage 4% of 1936 at a cost of $530 would receive, upon consummation of the reorganization, the following securities:

	Allocation	Market Price	Amount
New first-mortgage bonds 3 - 4's, of 1993	$318.92	87 3/4	$279.85
New income, bonds 4 1/2's, 2018	$217.08	56 1/2	122.60
New preferred shares	3.216 shares	41 1/4	132.66
New common shares	4.824 shares	18 3/4	90.45
Accrued interest on above first-mortgage bonds, (estimated)			19.13
Total			$664.69

It was possible to simultaneously dispose of the when-issued securities at the indicated market prices. Based on a cost of $530 plus expenses, a potential profit of 20% was created. Since consummation was not expected to be protracted, the return, based on a two-year holding period, was satisfactory. This return was a minimum of 10% increased by the interest of 3% on the new first-mortgage bonds which accrued to the investor.

While consummation was not until April, 1947, the rising market plus the capital-gains tax law benefited the special-situation investors. It became profitable to reverse one's position by selling out the "old" securities at a substantial long-term profit. Bonds purchased at 46 in 1943 were then selling at 78 in 1946. The when-issued securities which had advanced in equal ratio were repurchased or "covered." The net result was that $1 of short-term losses, established by closing out the short position was offset by $2 of long-term profit.

The following describes the application of the foregoing "tax" maneuver. If the "old" bonds were sold at 78, a long-term profit of 32 points could be established, the cost being 46. The when-issued contracts were disposed of at equal losses amounting to a total of 32 points. Thus no profit or loss actually prevailed. However, the net position from a tax point of view would appear as follows:

    Net long-term taxable profit   16 points (50% of 32)
    Net short-term taxable loss   32 points

The net short-term loss of 16 points could then be charged off against other profits. Thus 16 points could be made tax-free. The tax law has subsequently been altered eliminating the above type of transaction.

Hudson & Manhattan Railroad Company Reorganization

This is at the stage where investigation for special-situation investment possibilities is advisable. Consummation could take place within a twelve-month period.

The Trustee has presented a plan for reorganization, and hearings have been completed. Because this situation is alive, this would be a good place to present the ten typical legal steps which confront a company in reorganization, from the time it has been place in trusteeship until release from court jurisdiction.

1. Trustee is required to propose a plan of reorganization.

2. The plan is filed with the Court, and hearings are held.

3. The plan is then referred to Federal and state agencies such as the ICC, SEC, and PSC.

4. The Court determines whether the plan is fair, equitable, and feasible.

5. The Court enters an order approving the plan.

6. The creditors and stockholders receive a copy of the plan and security holders file proof of claim.

7. This is followed by voting upon the plan.

8. The plan is accepted by creditors holding two-thirds in amount of claims filed of each class, and by stockholders holding a majority of stock.

9. The Court holds hearings to consider confirmation of the plan.

10. Confirmation by the Court is followed by the requisite regulatory approvals.

The following analysis of Hudson & Manhattan presents the case as it exists and indicates the profit possibilities.

HUDSON & MANHATTAN RAILROAD COMPANY

A Potential Capital Gain of between 18% and 33%

Refunding Mtg. 5%, due 1957   Approx. price 51 NYSE

Progress in connection with the reorganization plan indicates that consummation could become effective by spring 1960. Hearings conducted before the court regarding the Trustees' proposed plan have been concluded. The program is not now complicated by objections from any important group of claimants, and the development of serious opposition appears unlikely. However, a new party could enter the situation at any time.

On Dec. 5, 1958, SEC approved the basic provision of the plan. The Commission further concluded that the reorganization plan is fair in providing that present preferred- and common-stock holder shall not participate.

The present capitalization is as follows:

Funded Debt:	Amount(000)	Accum. Interest*(000)	Full Claim(000)	Per $1M
First Mtg. 4 1/2% bonds, due '57	$885		$1,045	
First Lien & Ref. Mtg. 5%, due '57	26,868	$5,846	32,914	$1,220
Adjustment Inc. Mtg. 5%, due '57	16,814	14,389	31,203	1,850

Preferred stock   52,500 shares

Common stock   399,999 shares

*To Aug. 31, 1952, since Aug. 1, 1954

Summary of the Reorganization Plan

The company presently is being operated by the Trustee under Chapter X of the Bankruptcy Act. The plan is based on the separation of the valuable real-estate holdings from the unprofitable railroad operations.

To accomplish this a new railroad company will be organized as a subsidiary of the real estate company. The railroad assets will consist substantially of the present railroad properties.

The real estate company will retain all other assets, including the railroad company common stock. Its principal assets are its twin 22-story office buildings in New York and cash. The new capitalization will be as follows:

Funded Debt	Amount	Interest Charges	
5% Prior Lien Oblig.	$ 2,500,000	$100,000	
6% New Bonds 20-year	$10,038,100	600,000	
Class A common stock			590,476 shares
Class B common stock			58,849 shares

- 106 -

The Class A and B stock will represent the same per-share equity in the assets and earnings of the real estate company. In the separation of the two operations the plan considers the possibility of sale of the railroad properties by allocating a contingent interest to the equity stock in the proceeds of the sale above $17 million.

The new bonds and Class A and B common will be distributed pro rata as follows:

	New Bonds	Class A	Class B
First Mtg. Bonds:			
Per $1,000 face amount	$340	20 shares	
Ref. Mtg. Bonds:			
Per $1,000 amount	340	20 shares	
Adjustment Inc. Mtg.:			
Per $1,000			3 1/2 shares
Equities, nil			

The accompanying table shows work-out values based on (1) indicated assets, (2) contingent interest in the railroad properties, and (3) estimated earnings. This shows comparative recent market price and also possible appreciation.

Issue	Current Price	New Bonds	Work-Out Values Class A Low	High	Indicated Package Val. Low	High	Apprec. Pot. Low	High
Ref. Mtg.	51	$340	13	17	60	68	18%	33%

Discussion. Since the Hudson Manhattan Company has been operating at a deficit due to railroad-operating losses, it is not expected that the new company will be faced with Federal income taxes for a period of five years after consummation of the reorganization. Real estate properties have produced profits over the years which, in 1957, amounted to $1,208,910. After allowing for interest on the new bonds, earnings would come to approximately $1.13 per share, before sinking-fund charges.

Railroad operations have improved this through (1) increased fares, (2) economies on service, (3) increase in commuters. The delivery of 50 modern passenger cars is also contributing to improved operations. Should the Hudson River ferries discontinue their routes, the Hudson Tubes would benefit further.

By itself, under present conditions, the real estate operating income would be sufficient to meet the interest requirements of the First 4 1/2's and Refunding 5% bonds. However, the properties are in need of repair and extensive modernization, for which the company will use the $2.5 million obtained from the insurance companies. It is hoped that the rehabilitation will draw additional important tenants to the buildings. Nevertheless, the possibility is present that revenues could be adversely influenced by vacancies.

An important element in this situation is property value. The real estate is assessed for about $16-$17 million. In the present real estate market, buildings usually bring considerably more than their assessed valuations. Estimates of the property values range from $17-$20 million. The latter figure is based on an accepted trade multiple of six times the gross rentals of $3.4 million, which amounts to $20 million. The present market price of the Refunding 5's places a values on the properties of around $14 million. The present market price, however, does not give consideration to the value of the railroad properties in the event of sale. Since the proposed plan treats with this possibility as being quite real, we can assume, as a working base, that if only $4 million net would be realized for the railroad, it would be worth about $6 per share to the combined A and B shares.

Sufficient funds have been allocated to the railroad for two years' operations. The plan expects that one of the following three possibilities will have materialized by that time:

1. The road will have been abandoned.

2. Revenues will have materially improved because of increased traffic resulting from abandonment of the ferries.

3. A Metropolitan Transit Authority will purchase the road.

In light of the combination of substantial asset coverage, estimated earnings of about $1.12 per new share and possible cash value for the railroad, it would be fair to estimate the value of the new Class A shares at between $13 and $17 per share. Based on these projections, the Refunding 5's would have a work-out value ranging from $600 to $680 per each $1,000 bond. This is equivalent to an appreciation of 18% to 33%.

An additional feature has been the 6% and 6 1/2% payments made, respectively, in the past two years against arrears. From a tax viewpoint, these payments are treated as a return of capital. It is possible, though not anticipated, that further distributions will be made at the rate of 6% per annum until consummation of the proposed plan.

Based on the foregoing values and estimated possibilities, the present price of around 51 for the Refunding 51s appears to have little risk.

An Epic Case History

The Missouri Pacific Railroad reorganization is particularly interesting because its historical background is replete with profit-making opportunities. Special situations were present in both investment and arbitrage position in the bonds.

Prolongation of the bankruptcy proceedings worked to the advantage of all the security issues. Throughout the entire reorganization proceedings plans were continually revamped to give consideration to changed economic conditions. The final plan follows:

Table 1 graphically shows the "old" securities and the amount of "new" securities, to be received in exchange. Table 2 shows the when-issued market prices of the new securities. Table 3 shows the market prices of the old securities and the value of the "package" or aggregate of new securities to be received and the spread of profit potential. When referring to the Table 3, keep in mind that the spreads in price between the old and new securities tend to diminish as the effective day of the reorganization approaches. The spreads presented here reflect prices based on a near-term consummation. Six months previously the spreads were considerably wider.

Table 1

Old Securities	Cash	First Mortgages (New Securities) 20-yr A4 1/4s	35-yr B4 1/4s	50-yr C4 1/4s	Income Bonds 65-yr A4 3/4s	75-yr B4 3/4s	90-yr Deb.5s	Common Stock (par) $100 "A"	"B"
All equipments (Assumed)									
MOP Ref.									
A5s'65	$296	$500	$ 500						
F5s'77	292	500	500						
G5's78	308	500	500						
H5's80	313	500	500						
I5's 81	296	500	500						
Gen. 4's 1975	None				$ 800	$1,073			
Conv.Deb. 5 1/2s	None				200	200	$1,819		
Serial 5 1/4s	None			588	1,354	217			
B.St.L.& So.	196	800	1,000						
C.Br.U.P.	123	640	640						
L.R.& H.S.W.	None	220	220	1,360					
$5 Pfd	None							2.645	1/20 shares
Common									

- 109 -

WHEN-ISSUED MARKET PRICES

Table 2

1st Mtge. Bonds Price	Income Bonds Price	Common "A" Price	Common "B" Price
20 yr. 94 1/2	65 yr. 72	25	9
35 yr. 94	75 yr. 65		
50 yr. 93	90 yr. 50		

Table 3

Old Issues	Market Price	"New Package" Value	Spread
MOP Ref. A5s '65)		$1227	3.9%
F5s 77)	118	$1227	3.9%
G5s 78)	(Various prices	$1227	3.9%
H5s 80)	around this level)	$1227	3.9%
I5s 81)		$1227	3.9%
Gen. 4s 1975	118	$1267	7.4%
Conv. deb. 5 1/2 1949	109	$1178.50	8.5%
$5 Preferred	59	66.12	12%
Common	9		

The "package" values in Table 3 are based on when-issued prices shown in Table 2.

Arbitraging of railroad securities was a profitable activity during the heyday of railroad reorganizations. The arbitrage procedure then and today is standard for all types of hedge positions. The following is a graphic presentation of the steps used in setting up an arbitrage position. The price of the Missouri Pacific, 5/77 at 91, reflects the clearance of interest arrears paid in 1954.

Typical Arbitrage Transaction

PURCHASE:

    $10,000 Missouri Pacific
        5s of 1977, at 91 $9,100

SELL—New securities expected to be received on a
        when-, as-, and if-issued basis:

$5,000 Missouri Pacific 1st. mtg. 35-year bonds, at 94 1/2	$4,725
$5,000 Missouri Pacific 1st mtg. 50-year bonds, at 93 1/2	$4,675
Credit accrued interest to Oct. 1, 1955*	318
Proceeds	$9,718
Less costs	50
Net proceeds	$9,668
Expected profit (subtract $9,100 from $9,668)	568
Rate of return	6%

*Interest accrues to the new first-mortgage bonds from the date of the plan to consummation and will be received by the maker of the arbitrage.

A return of 6.2% would be obtained if the arbitrage consummated in one year. However, should consummation be effective in six months, this would equal an annual return of more than 12.4%. By carrying the above position on a 50% margin and assuming interest charges at the rate of 3 1/2%, the profit would be at the rate of 20% if consummation took six months. If the arbitrage were open for twelve months, then a profit of 10% would be obtained.

Interest Payments Treated as a Return of Capital

During the past decade one issue was outstanding in this reorganization for special-situation interest. This was the first and refunding mortgage bonds, 5% due 1977 through 1981. Here the principal was not in jeopardy. Interest payments were treated, taxwise, as a return of capital and is nontaxable as income but is a reduction of cost. Interest accrued after the purchase date is fully taxable as income.

At frequent intervals during the many years the road was in reorganization, the market price of the first and refunding 5s offered satisfactory investment opportunity. This occurred in 1950 when the bonds were selling around 99 ($990 for a $1,000 bond) and unpaid interest of $235 per $1,000 bond had accrued.

Since the economic condition of the railroad permitted a fair-investment classification for this issue, the situation justified investment consideration. It is interesting to note that, for the special-situation approach, outright purchase of the bonds offered greater possibilities than the arbitrage route. This was so because the bonds offered the following potentialities:

1. Payment of the $235 of accrued interest was being made via $50 disbursements or more per year.

2. Yearly interest was accruing at the rate of $50 per bond.

3. The possible increase in market price was in line with securities of equal quality.

While other securities in the Missouri Pacific system offered interesting opportunities, the first and refunding bonds met the requirements for special-situation investment. Besides, the issue offered these advantages:

1. The principal was invested at minimum risk. The financial status of the road assured full treatment for these bonds.

2. A satisfactory return for the use of the money invested was assured. The 5% interest, which was amply secured, accrued when not paid.

3. A profit potential existed for many years. This varied in increasing amounts, reflecting the money and security market in general. Patience was all that was required to obtain it.

4. The situation offered long-term capital gains, which is a favorable factor taxwise.

5. The duration factor in this situation was not decisive. Delays and changes in the reorganization plan would not be harmful since senior position of the bonds assured satisfaction of the full claim. The use of the money was adequately compensated for by the yearly interest payments.

The analytical approach to this type of situation is direct, since all the pertinent material is readily available. The daily newspapers publish pertinent news. Analyses of the financial position and the pro forma status are also supplied by the company, the ICC, the SEC, and various investment services. The Missouri Pacific reorganization had additional interest because of the success in obtaining some recognition for the equity securities in the reorganization plan. This achievement is considered a major victory in the history of railroad reorganizations.

CHAPTER 9

Public Utility Holding Company Reorganizations

The Public Utility Holding Company Act of 1935, under "due process of law," brought about the dissolution of many public utility holding companies and created numerous profitable special situations. Large utility empires were required to divest themselves of holdings of operating utility companies. These corporate actions brought to the investing public the equity interest of many excellent electric, gas, and water companies, among them Union Electric Co., Southern Co., Middle South Co., and Ohio Edison Co.

One might question the practicability of studying the public utility holding company reorganizations since that period is over. But the investing procedures developed to meet the several types of situations created by the divestment process, are worth remembering since time has shown their usefulness in comparable situations.

One new area where divestment procedures are applicable is the "spin-off" (see Chapter 4), which has characteristics similar to the public utility holding company divestment procedures. It is also probable that future break-up of mammoth industrial empires will offer analogous investment opportunities.

Where to Look for the Investment Opportunities

The special-situation investments created under the divestment procedures were located first in the outstanding securities of the top holding companies. A holding company is exactly what the name implies. It holds the control, either in toto or of a sufficient percentage of the subsidiary corporation. The latter may or may not be the operating corporation. The accompanying chart shows the structure of a grandfather holding company. This name applies because the top holding company controlled another holding company, which in turn controlled a holding company which controlled the operating companies.

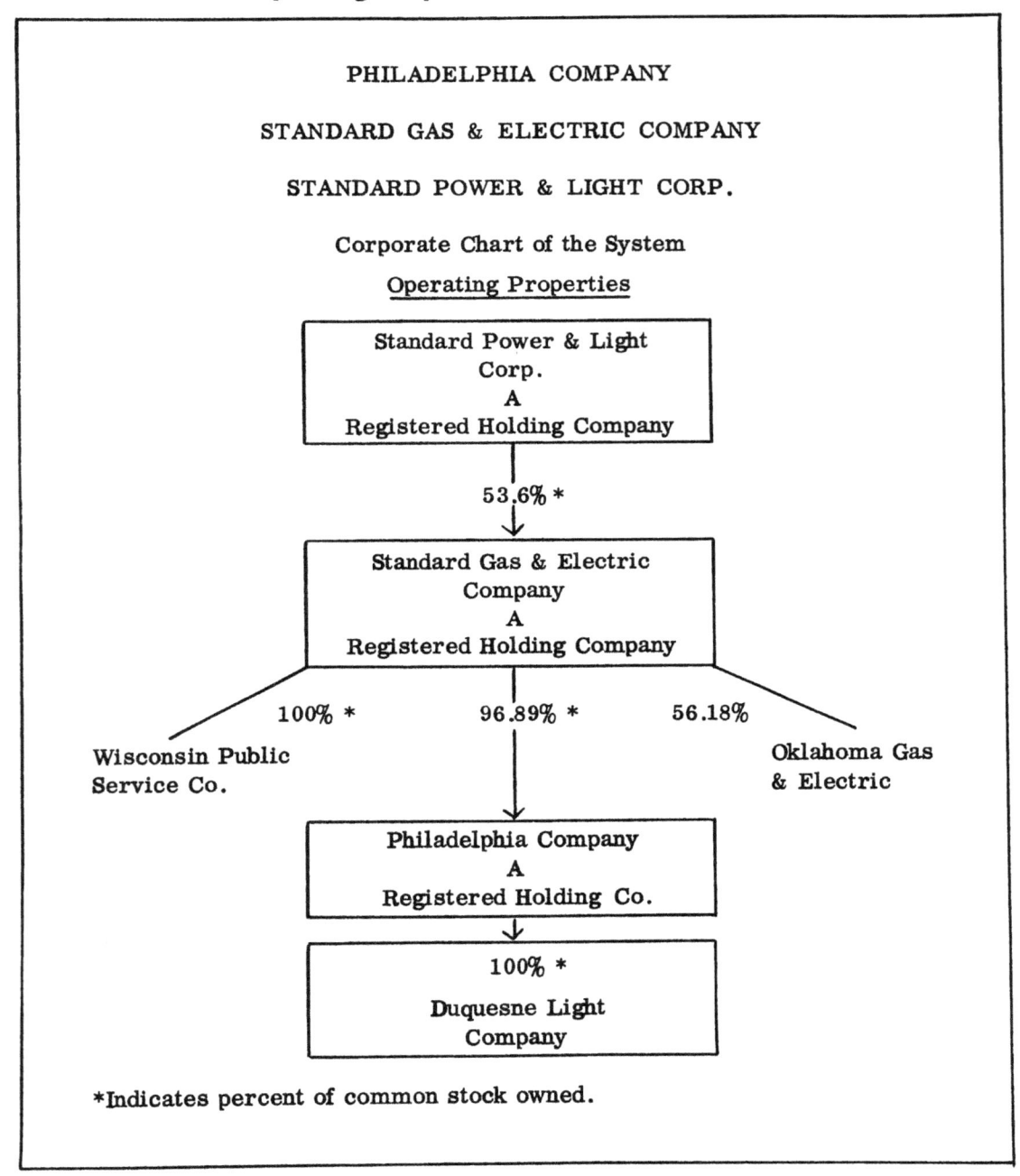

PHILADELPHIA COMPANY

STANDARD GAS & ELECTRIC COMPANY

STANDARD POWER & LIGHT CORP.

Corporate Chart of the System

Operating Properties

```
        ┌─────────────────────────────┐
        │   Standard Power & Light    │
        │           Corp.             │
        │             A               │
        │  Registered Holding Company │
        └─────────────────────────────┘
                      │ 53.6% *
                      ▼
        ┌─────────────────────────────┐
        │    Standard Gas & Electric  │
        │           Company           │
        │             A               │
        │  Registered Holding Company │
        └─────────────────────────────┘
           /          │           \
       100% *      96.89% *       56.18%
        /            │               \
Wisconsin Public     │          Oklahoma Gas
Service Co.          ▼          & Electric
           ┌─────────────────────┐
           │  Philadelphia Company│
           │          A           │
           │ Registered Holding Co.│
           └─────────────────────┘
                      ▼
           ┌─────────────────────┐
           │       100% *        │
           │   Duquesne Light    │
           │       Company       │
           └─────────────────────┘
```

*Indicates percent of common stock owned.

- 114 -

The Investor Approach to a Divestment

The first step was the valuation of the component companies, for which operating and financial statistics were needed. During the first stages of the divestment period such data were not available. Therefore calculations of the worth of a subsidiary operating company were based, in part, on dividends distributed to the parent company, plus the meager operating statistics. To this you would add the direct assets of the holding company, such as cash and facilities. The combined value of the subsidiaries' and the holding company's assets, after deducting liabilities, would then be divided by the number of outstanding shares to arrive at an estimated worth for the holding company shares. The dearth of information, of course, left room for subsequent upward adjustments. Because of this lack of adequate information, the holding company shares were generally at a discount from the estimated worth of the aggregate assets.

The corporate action of divesting subsidiary holdings was preceded by submission to the SEC of plans to accomplish this program. The release of the plans brought with it disclosure of the internal operations of the parent and subsidiary companies. This included valuable data on physical assets, operating practices, base costs, and intercompany relationships.

How to Locate the Profit

Participation at the first stage of a holding corporation divestment could be accomplished through purchase of the senior securities, those which have first claim to the company's assets. The next step would be to wait for the official presentation of the plan. This generally brought to light statistical information about the subsidiaries which were to be divested. It is important to bear in mind that the profit possibilities were in the valuations of the subsidiary companies which were being separated from the parent company.

A bit of historical background, at this point, will clarify the economic position of public utilities at that time. Many holding companies were in financial straits, the bonds of some being in default, with the corporations operating under the jurisdiction of the bankruptcy courts. In other cases vast dividend arrears had accumulated on the preferred shares of the holding company and/or its subsidiary companies.

Since the investor's first contact with the holding company under divestment was during unfavorable economic conditions and the financial statistics were sparse, his evaluations of the subsidiaries generally were low. However, two considerations affected the value of the underlying subsidiaries: (1) The release of subsidiary companies from parental control disclosed hidden assets plus latent earning power which gave the subsidiaries greater worth than at the first calculation. (2) The subsequent improvement in the national economy produced a continual flow of investment opportunities all the way from the senior securities of the top holding company down through the equity shares of the smallest subsidiary. Not infrequently, the expected special-situation profit matured in the original investment prior to the culmination of the contemplated corporate action. The divestment situation then offered opportunities for profits in other securities of the same corporation. This was broadly in evidence during the divestment procedure of the Standard Gas & Electric Co., analyzed toward the end of this chapter. The investor made his first investment in the bonds of Standard Gas; then, after obtaining satisfactory profits he moved on to the $6 or $7 preferred stock, and next to the $4 preferred, each investment returning profits. (See the case of International Hydro Electric Corp. on page 120).

The "Parts" and the "Whole"

Since the subsidiary companies to be released would become independent concerns, their earning power could be revalued excluding the holding company's influence, which had often restrained growth of their earning power. As a result their values had frequently been underestimated. It was important, in the utility divestment era, to recognize that the sum of the parts could come to more than the whole. Analysis of American Power and Light (see following page) shows this through the divestment-program evaluations and demonstrates the analytical approach to the profit opportunities. The aggregate value of the companies to be distributed exceeds the market price of the parent company.

Why the Public Utility Divestment Period Offered Many Profit Opportunities

1. A vast new field for exploration of special situations was opened by the many companies complying with the Act. This lasted for a number of years.

2. The many different types and sizes of corporate capitalizations gave opportunities in each classification of securities. From the special-situation approach senior securities were the most desirable since they offered the greatest protection and profit.

3. The numerous economic classifications of the corporations presented a diversity of opportunities.

4. The concept of divestment of holdings by utilities was a new idea. No precedent on which to base one's actions had been established. The presence of much uncertainty was reflected in the market prices of the securities. But this increased the profit possibilities because certain fundamental values existed on which the special-situation investor could rely.

SEC released comprehensive and reliable data which aided the investor in appraising the situation. The investor was also reasonably certain that the divestment would eventually be completed. While he could not be sure that a "plan" would be operative prior to court approval, he could be sure that the values he purchased would not now be wasted. Therefore a public utility divestment situation was attractive because the assets could be acquired at a discount sufficiently below the estimated values to indicate a profit.

AMERICAN POWER & LIGHT COMPANY
A probable capital gain of between 25% and 40%

$5.00 and $6.00 Preferred	Common Stock
Liberal current return with appreciation possibilities	Liquidating situation selling at attractive discount

Recent developments in connection with the Dissolution Plan for this company suggest that consummation may be expected before the end of this year. Hearings conducted before SEC regarding the proposed Divestment and Recapitalization for this holding company have been concluded and all parties of record to the Proceedings, including representatives of both classes of preferred stocks, the common stock, and Electric Bond & Share Company, are apparently in agreement on the objectives of the Plan. In order to expedite the program, the usual procedure requiring preparation of a report on the Proceedings by the Staff of the Commission, filing of briefs and oral arguments has been waived. The mutual consent to short-cut the proceedings should result in an early decision by the Commission, as the program is not now complicated by objections from any important group of claimants, and the possibility of opposition developing before the District Court appears unlikely.

Capitalization

The American Power & Light Company has no funded debt or notes outstanding, the sole capitalization consisting of preferred and common stocks as follows:

Series	Shares Outstanding	Dividend Arrears (Per Share)	Price Range 1948 - 1949
$6.00 Preferred	793,581*	$43.57	95 1/2- 83 3/8
$5.00 Preferred	978,444*	35.53	86 1/2- 69 1/4
Common	3,008,511	—	11 5/8- 6 5/8

* Regular quarterly dividends are now being paid.

Summary of Distribution Plan

A plan providing for the distribution of certain portfolio assets and the reclassification of this company's presently outstanding preferred and common stocks into a single class of new common stock is now before SEC. It proposes a distribution of 82% of the company's assets to holders of the two series of outstanding preferred stock, with the balance of 18% of the assets going to this company's common stockholders.

On the basis of the assets allocated to preferred and common stockholders under the proposed plan, indicated work-out values compared with recent market prices and possible appreciation appear to us as follows:

Issue	Recent Price	Work-out Value	Indicated Appreciation Per Share	Per Cent
$6.00 Preferred	91 1/2	118.04	$26.54	29%
$5.00 Preferred	79 3/4	99.38	19.65	24.6
Common	10	13.93	3.93	39.3

In the absence of an official opinion and order from SEC on the question of the Plan's fairness, we are unable to give the exact schedule or distribution dates for the portfolio securities. It seems reasonable, however, to expect, in the light of the satisfaction indicated by all interested parties to the proceedings, that liberal dividend-paying common stocks of important and well managed operating utility companies will be distributed in the not too distant future.

Why Profits Were Available

The opportunities for profit were present because the investing public lacked means of evaluating the companies to be released. Consequently, those who availed themselves of the SEC releases acquired knowledge which led to purchasing, through the indirect medium of the parent company, low-priced securities of the subsidiary companies. The estimates were frequently substantially exceeded by the prices attained in the actual results, because the majority of divestments were completed during the rising-price era of the 1940-1950's.

Outline of Procedure for Setting Up a Divestment Situation

1. Set up the situation in table form. This will enable you to compare the existing securities with those to be distributed. (See the following page). In this example the capitalization shows the existing securities, while the accompanying tables show the securities to be distributed to each class of security.

2. Evaluate each item to be received. This may be an estimate or a market price.

3. Deduct the cost of the parent company's security from the sum of the parts to be distributed. The remainder is the profit.

4. Deduct from the estimated profit, commissions, taxes, and interest charges.

5. Divide the cost into the profit to obtain the percentage of profit.

6. Give due consideration to the length of time it will take to obtain the profit. Note whether interest and/or dividends are being paid or accruing.

A discussion of the above steps in a hypothetical case follows: In compliance with the law Company "A" proposed to distribute its assets to its security holders. Financial data pertaining to subsidiary companies were made available so that earnings as well as assets could be used to determine a price for their shares. However, in instances where the subsidiary was not 100% owned, the shares generally were traded in the market, consequently, a price had been established. Where an estimated value was needed it could be calculated from a range of high and low estimated values for the specific subsidiary company. The value of all the shares to be distributed was then totaled in both the low and high estimates. This established an approximate range of values for the holding company's shares. The difference in values between the holding company's shares and the estimated values would, of course, be the anticipated profit. Trading procedures permitted establishing the profit prior to consummation of the divestment plan. This was accomplished by selling short the shares which were to be distributed.

COMMONWEALTH & SOUTHERN CORPORATION
Distribution and Liquidation Plan Receives Court Approval

CAPITALIZATION

Bank Loan 2 1/4%, due 9/15/51		$3,000,000
*$6.00 Dividend Series Preferred	(shs)	1,441,247
Common stock	(shs)	33,673,328
Option Warrants	(wts)	17,588,956

*Arrears as of July 1, 1949, were $17 per share, redemption price, $110.

Recent Developments

Justice Paul Leahy of the U.S. District Court at Wilmington, Delaware, yesterday handed down a decision, approving the distribution and liquidation Plan of this corporation. The amended Plan was filed with SEC in July, 1948, and received approval of that regulatory agency on November 23, 1948. Hearings on the question of the Plan's fairness were conducted on December 30th with all interested parties participating. Yesterday's decision was the outcome of the arguments made before the court last December.

Unless the findings of SEC and the opinion of the District Court are appealed to a higher court by counsel representing a group of common stockholders, it is expected that the distributions pursuant to the terms of the plan will be made on or about October 1, 1949.

Allocations and Estimated Work-out Values for Common and Preferred Stocks

Under the terms of the plan as approved, each share of Commonwealth & Southern Corporation $6 Dividend Series Preferred Stock is scheduled to receive 2.80 shares Consumers Power Company common; 0.55 shares of Central Illinois Light Company common; plus $1 cash per share. The common stockholders are to receive 0.35 shares Southern Company common and 0.6 shares Ohio Edison Company common.

The Table which follows indicates our estimate of Work-out values applicable to the participating security holders. No provisions are made in the Plan for continuing the Rights of the 17,588,956 outstanding Option Warrants.

For Each Share of $6.00 Preferred to Be Distributed:	No. of Shares	Estimated Price Per Share	Value
Consumers Power	2.80	(a) 33	$92.40
Central Illinois Light	0.55	(b) 32	17.60
Cash distribution			1.00
Total indicated value per share			$111.00

(a) Based on recent selling price on NYSE for minority interest.
(b) Estimated value based on earnings ratio of 10 3/4 times earning of $2.98 per share reported for the year ending May 31, 1949.

For Each Share of Common Stock to be Distributed:	No. of Shares	Estimated Price Per Share	Value
Southern Company	0.35	(c) 8 1/4	$2.89
Ohio Edison Company	0.06	(d) 28 1/2	1.71
Total indicated value per share			$4.60

(c) Estimated value based on earning ratio of approximately 8 times earnings of $1.07 reported for the year ending May 31, 1949.
(d) Based on recent selling price on NYSE for minority interest.

The Preferred and Common stocks of the Commonwealth & Southern Corporation offer a means for employing idle funds seeking capital gains, while at the same time presenting an opportunity to acquire stocks in operating electric utilities located in areas showing growth possibilities. The indicated market discounts below ultimate work-out values for the portfolio issues to be distributed may be carried forward as the cost base for the new securities received on a non-taxable exchange basis.

There follow case histories and step-by-step procedure of two holding company situations.

INTERNATIONAL HYDRO-ELECTRIC SYSTEM (HYDRO)

The Hydro system was directed by SEC to institute proceedings for its liquidation and dissolution pursuant to Sections 11(b) and 11(d) of the Public Utility Holding Act of 1935.

Since 1944, Hydro had been operated by the Trustee appointed by the District Court of Massachusetts. Capitalization of Hydro originally consisted of $30 million of 6% debentures due in April, 1944; followed by 142,799 shares of $3.50 cumulative preferred, $50 par, on which dividend payments had ceased subsequent to July, 1934, and 856,718 shares of Class A stock.

The debentures were in default, since the principal had not been paid when due in 1944. Interest, however, had been paid in full. Assets of Hydro consisted of Gatineau Power Corp. common stock, New England Electric common stock, all the common stock of Eastern N.Y. Power Corp., plus miscellaneous holdings. (See page 123).

Price range of the Hydro securities for the year 1944 were:

	High	Low
Debentures	77 1/2	56
Preferred	22 1/2	7 1/2
Class A	3 7/8	1 3/4

Investors were attracted to this situation by the corporate actions which developed during the spring of 1946.

One significant development was the approval by SEC of the reorganization of New England Power Association (name subsequently changed to New England Electric System). Consummation of this reorganization brought the Hydro liquidation a step nearer. However, of more direct influence was the acceptance of $10 million from International Paper Co. by Hydro in settlement of its suit against that company. This cash, combined with the portfolio holdings value at market prices, was equivalent to $2,000 of assets for each $1,000 debenture.

The Reasons for the Debenture Attractiveness

Hydro paid interest on the debentures at 4% per annum, though the debenture rate was set at 6%. Thus 2%, or $20 per debenture, accrued annually. Accumulations amounted to 5%, or $50 per debenture, by April, 1947. A 2% payment in April, 1946, would be treated taxwise by the recipient as a return of capital. Thus a purchaser of the debentures at 97 would reduce his cost price to 95, or $950 per $1,000 debenture. As the debentures would then have a claim of 105 ($1,050), a minimum of 10% profit could be expected, while at the same time the debentures should bring a return at the rate of 4.2% per annum. Safety, combined with the satisfactory return on the money invested made the situation attractive.

The accruing of unpaid but collectible interest, was additionally beneficial as such funds, when paid, would be taxable as capital gains and not as income. This factor made the debentures particularly attractive for investors in the higher income brackets.

Effect on the Preferred Shares

The Hydro situation contained further interest in view of the extensive asset protection offered to the preferred shares. After allowing for full payment of the debenture's claim, the value of the remaining assets amounted to $125 per share of preferred stock. The preferred shares had a claim of $50 per share, representing the liquidating price plus $45 per share for accrued dividends.

Reflecting the improved condition of Hydro's portfolio, the preferred shares had advanced in the market from a low of 39 in 1946 to 73 1/2; at the same time the debentures were priced at 97.

The Package Deal

In view of the safety afforded the debentures and the apparent 170% asset coverage behind the preferred, a "package deal" comprised of debentures and preferred in the ratio of $10,000 worth of principal amount of debentures and 100 shares of preferred stock seemed opportune. The total amount invested in the package would approximate $17,000. The preferred shares would not carry themselves, as dividends were not being paid. However, the estimated capital appreciation of 28% plus the accumulation of $3 yearly from cumulative dividends gave the package combination special-situation status.

The basic elements were present. The investment was priced at a discount; the corporate action was the pending liquidation. The situation was readily calculable, though the duration was not fixed; and, finally, the risk was at a minimum since the asset protection was high-grade and substantial.

Hydro's class A shares, reflecting the more favorable outlook for liquidation, advanced from $6 to $15 per share. However, the shares did not have the elements of a special situation at that time.

Numerous plans were filed in connection with Hydro's liquidation. Hearings started in October, 1947, before the SEC and continued through June, 1948. During this period the preferred and Class A shares fluctuated widely, along with the trend of the general securities market. The preferred dipped to 45 1/4 while the Class A receded to the $5 level. However, the debentures remained firm.

An important point in the Trustee's plan for the liquidation pertained to the method for raising funds to settle the claim of the debentures. By July, 1949, the principal payments on the debentures had reduced the unpaid balance to 60%. This factor enhanced the situation's attractiveness since less money would be invested to obtain the profit.

The Trustee's plan required the sale of enough Gatineau Power shares to raise $5 million and the borrowing of $10 million under a secured bank loan. This step was consummated, and the debentures were paid off in full on August, 1950. Prior to the payment, the debentures had registered a high price of 71, equal to 111, or $1,100 per original debentures.*

The elimination of the debentures gave increased desirability to the preferred stock. The latter had moved up to 81 1/2 by October, 1950, while the Class A had risen to 10 3/4. The claim of the preferred shares at that time had increased to $107.60.

A New Development

A group of Class A stockholders initiated efforts to have Hydro remain in existence as an investment company. This was motivated by the desire to take advantage of the substantial losses which Hydro could establish and which would entitle Class A stockholders to valuable tax savings. The proponents of the plan showed that the investment of Hydro in the New England Electric stock amounted to approximately $57 million, while its market price in December, 1949, was only $5 million. Thus nontaxable distributions could be made on the Class A stock for a considerable number of years. The investment-company idea awakened interest in the Class A shares.

Hydro's schedule of investments changed only to the extent that Gatineau Power shares were sold to meet the payment to the debentures. The total estimated value of Hydro's assets amounted to $35,622,000 which, after deducting the bank loan, resulted in a per-share equivalent of more than $170 on the preferred shares against its claim of $107.60. The improved status of the assets was further augmented by the increasing dividends received from Hydro's portfolio holdings.

Several plans were filed with SEC proposing methods for settling the preferred claim and/or liquidating Hydro. Early in 1951, reports indicated that negotiations were in progress looking toward sale of Hydro's subsidiary, Eastern New York Power, for a sum considerably in excess of the estimated value placed on it by appraisers and arbitragers. The Trustee also, at that time, filed with SEC an application seeking approval of resumption of dividends on the preferred. This was granted on Apr. 1, 1951. The arrears on the preferred than amounted to $61.25 per share.

---

*As $400 of principal had been paid, that sum, when added to the price of 71, or $710 per bond, brought the total to $1,100 per bond.

- 122 -

The preferred had moved up to the 100 level by July, 1951, while the Class A was priced around 19 3/4. The rising prices in the securities market was reflected in Hydro's assets. The equity behind the Class A shares rose to $23.87 after allowing for full payment of the claim of $111.25 on the preferred.

The tabulation shows the capitalization and portfolio as of July, 1952.

Capitalization

Bank Loan 2 1/4% Due July, 1953		$ 6,680,000
$3.50 Preferred stock ($50 par) 142,799 shares	$ 7,139,950	
Preferred dividend arrears $61.25 per share (*)	8,746,439	
Preferred stock at $50.00 per share Plus arrears $61.25	$15,886,389	$15,886,389

*Preferred stock dividend arrears to 1/15/52. 87 1/2¢ per share paid as of April and July 15th/52 as <u>liquidating distributions</u>, equivalent to regular quarterly dividends.

Portfolio assets and cash

No. of shares Owned		% of Outstad'g Issue	Market Price	Approximate Value
320,000	Eastern N. Y. Power Co. Common	100%	(∤)	$14,400,000
1,099,024	Gatineau Power Co. Common	66%	18	19,782,500
587,572	New England Electric Sys.	8%	13	7,638,500
	Cash (Approximate)			1,200,000

*Indicated value of the assets before reorganization expenses, $43,021,000.
∤Based on offers for the physical assets.

Based on the foregoing tabulation, total assets and cash of Hydro were $43,021,000. Therefore, after providing for payment of the bank loan of $6,680,000, the remaining assets applicable to Hydro's $3.50 Preferred and Class A Common stock would amount to $36,341,000. With the full claim of the Preferred stockholders provided for (at liquidating value of $50 per share, plus dividend arrears of $61.25 to Jan. 15, 1952) or total claims of $11.25 per share for a sum of $15,886,389, there remained $20,454,611, equivalent to $23.87 for each share of Class A Common.

The situation remained quiescent for almost two years. Then on Mar. 27, 1953, an amended plan, on which representatives of committees of preferred and Class A shares agreed, was filed with SEC. The plan consisted of two steps.

Step 1 called for the retirement of the preferred shares by giving holders 5 1/2 shares of Gatineau Power Common, plus a dividend adjustment. The dividend rate on Gatineau common being $1.20 annually while the rate on Hydro preferred was $3.50 annually, this created a difference of $3.10 annually based on the proposed distribution of 5 1/2 shares of Gatineau. The common stock of Gatineau was priced around 21 1/2. Therefore the work-out value of the preferred in settlement of their full claim would be in the neighborhood of $118.25, plus dividend accruals.

Step 2 of the plan provided for continuation of Hydro as an investment company. The division of Public Utilities of SEC had indicated that it would support a plan embodying the provisions of the above-mentioned agreement. To expedite the retirement of the preferres shares Hydro was required to dispose of its holdings of Eastern New York Power. Funds raised from the sale of these properties would pay off the bank loan and facilitate retirement of the preferred.

On June 16, 1953, the Federal Court sanctioned sale of certain of the Eastern New York Power properties to Dartmouth College. On July 6, 1953, the Niagara Mohawk Power Corporation announced purchase of a number of properties of Eastern New York Power Corporation.

On Oct. 1, 1953, SEC announced its approval of the above plan providing for the exchange of 5 1/2 shares of Gatineau Power for each share of Hydro preferred. Gatineau was then priced around 21 1/2 on the American Stock Exchange. Hearings before the U.S. District Court for the District of Massachusetts were scheduled for November, 1953. The Court approved the plan, and Dec. 2, 1953, was fixed as the effective date for the exchange of the preferred shares. Besides the 5 1/2 shares of Gatineau common, preferred holders of Hydro received $2.50 in cash as accrued dividends. The total was equivalent to $120.75 per share of preferred, a sum considerably more than the $111.25 representing the claim. The financial history of Hydro shows the complete routine of investor's participation in a special situation. The essential steps can be summed up as (1) calculating the asset value; (2) comparing the market prices of the securities in relation to the asset values; (3) keeping abreast of developments through official channels.

THE CASE OF STANDARD POWER & LIGHT -- STANDARD GAS AND ELECTRIC DIVESTMENT

The Standard Power & Light reorganization presents an investment approach which may be applied wherever major assets are subject to distribution. The following discussion shows the thinking associated with corporate actions pertinent to this case. The problems met here are typical of reorganizations.

Summary of Historical Background

Standard Power & Light was the parent holding company of Standard Gas & Electric Co. During the dissolution proceedings carried out in compliance with the

Holding Company Act. The final steps which resulted in Standard Power remaining as an investment company have been completed. Previously completed steps accomplished the retirement of all bonds and preferred shares of both Standard Power and Standard Gas & Electric. The wind-up moves in the corporate simplification process required the liquidation of Philadelphia Company. Standard Gas may continue as a shell to preserve valuable tax-loss benefits. However, a pending tax suit must be settled prior to further moves.

The following concept must be understood to have existed at the time of the dissolution proceedings. Changing values and conditions may require the altering of the entire concept of the above reorganizations. Nevertheless, the values used here are considered the move conservative and consequently less vulnerable to price erosion. As Standard Power and Light's largest asset is the investment in Standard Gas and Electric, the clarification of the latter's status and estimated worth would be essential. Pertinent details describing the computations used in appraising the share value of Standard Gas will be found in the latter part of this discussion.

Problems

The problem confronting Standard Power and Light is contained in its capital structure. While the company's apparent capitalization is comprised of 1,320,000 shares of common and 110,000 shares of common, Series B, that capitalization does not reflect a claim by H. M. Byllesby and Company, arising from an agreement dated June 28, 1940, therein H. M. Byllesby and Company surrendered for cancellation 330,000 shares of common stock, Series B, reserving the right to receive, upon any distribution of the assets of Standard Power & Light Corporation, proportionate share of the assets of the corporation in parity with holders of common stock and common stock, Series B, in an amount which would have been the distributive share of the 330,000 shares of the common stock, Series B.

Assumption

No public indication regarding a settlement of the above claim had been given. However, the investor's thinking would call for a discussion with officers of both companies, which might disclose the probabilities regarding a compromise. Such course gave substance to the belief that the Byllesby claim might be settled on a basis of 80% of the total dollar value. The 330,000 shares of Class B were valued at $4,455,000 in the market. Settlement on an 80% basis would amount to approximately $3,564,000. This capital loss would be reflected in Standard Power & Light's assets and revenues. If we assume an earning power of 5%, then the loss of income on the $3,564,000 would amount to $178,200. In order to pay the claim the company would have to dispose of some investments or borrow. This solution of the Byllesby claim would diminish the equity interest of Standard Power & Light. At the time of this writing the shares (at 14) appeared to have fully discounted the Byllesby claim.*

*Settlement of the claim was consummated on Jan. 31, 1955. This was accomplished through payment of $4,900,000 in cash and securities.

Elimination of the Byllesby claim in the foregoing manner would result in Standard Power and Light having an estimated asset value of $15.53 and an indicated income of 78¢ per share. The effect of the Byllesby claim can be seen from the tabulation and discussion which follows.

Standard Power & Light Corporation's portfolio, as of Dec. 31, 1953, contained the following investments, which have a market value of approximately $27,378,594, equivalent to $18.03 per share.

No. of Shares	Investments	Approx. Price	Amount	Approximate Div. Rate	Approximate Income
1,160,000	St. G & E Com.	12 1/2	$14,500,000	--	$ 790,855
281,500	Duq. Lt. Com.	29	8,163,500	$1.60	450,400
2,066	Louisville G & E Com.	41	84,706	1.80	3,718
3,801	Mt. States Power Com.	17	64,617	0.84	3,192
118,444	Okla. G & E Com.	27	3,197,988	1.50	177,666
6,519	So. Colo. Pwr. Com.	13	84,747	0.70	4,563
51,000	Wisc. Pub. Serv. Com.	19	985,036	1.10	56,100
			$27,080,594		$1,486,494
	Other Assets		298,000		
			$27,378,595		
	Less current liabilities and bank loan		1,590,000		
			$25,788,594		

    Asset value per share $18.03

Standard Power & Light's income (as indicated in the foregoing tabulation) could be in the neighborhood of $1,486,495. The $790,855 income ascribed to Standard Gas was obtained by taking 53% of Standard Gas' present income, which reflects the percentage of Standard Power & Light's interest in Standard Gas. Operating costs of Standard Power & Light as an investment company could be covered by approximately $150,000, which would leave a round figure of $1,300,000, equal to 80¢ per share on the 1,430,000 shares outstanding. However, as indicated in the foregoing and giving effect to the conjectured settlement of the Byllesby claim but with no consideration for the Pittsburgh Railway dividend,* The net income would be approximately $1,130,000, equal to 78¢ per share. As an investment company, Standard Power & Light could distribute 90% or more of its income. Thus dividend payments could be estimated at 70¢ per share. At the present price of 14, this would show a nontaxable return of 5.0%. To an investor in the 50% tax bracket this would be equivalent to a yield of 10%.

---

*These shares are held by Standard Gas & Electric.

Cushion

Pittsburgh Railway Company, an important holding of Standard Gas & Electric, recently declared a dividend of 40¢ per share, amounting to $164,305, the first since December, 1952, when 60¢ was paid. No consideration was given this dividend in the computation of Standard Gas income as disposal of this asset is mandatory. To assume the earning ability of such funds when invested would be too conjectural at this time. However, the possible income from such funds does provide a cushion for additional earnings to offset the estimated income loss from settlement of the Byllesby claim.

Standard Power and Light indicated its intention of continuing as an investment company. The 14% discount from estimated asset value of $15.53, after allowing for settlement of the Byllesby claim, is valuable from the point of view of safety, plus the potential profit resulting from the possibility of achieving parity of market price and asset value.

It is interesting to note that the Supreme Court recently gave the "go ahead" to United Corporation's steps to meet Government reorganization requirements to become an investment company. United Corporation shares listed on the NYSE are priced around the asset value and dividend disbursements are nontaxable. Standard Power & Light Company's distributions are and will continue to be nontaxable. This valuable asset, i.e., nontaxable distributions, arises from the losses which can be established through the sale of Duquesne Light Company shares (Standard Power & Light must reduce its holdings of the security to under 5%) in amounts to offset income each year. It is estimated that this favorable tax situation could prevail for more than 20 years, based on the indicated income of Standard Power & Light as shown in the foregoing tabulation. Standard Power & Light declared a distribution from capital surplus of 25¢ in 1953. As Standard Power & Light's major holding is Standard Gas & Electric, and that company is a holding company in the final stages of divestment under the Holding Company Act, it would be advisable to establish a value for the share of this subsidiary holding corporation in order to obtain a complete picture of the Standard Power & Light special situation.

STANDARD GAS AND ELECTRIC

Approximate price 12 1/2 NYSE

The Standard Gas-Philadelphia Company investment portfolio, approximate market values and income, are shown in the following tabulation:

No. of Shares	Investments	Approx. Price	Amount	Div. Rate	Approximate Income
836,775	Duq. Lt. Com.	29	$24,266,475	$1.60	$1,338,840
24,264	Duq. Lt. 4% Pfd.	47	1,140,408	4.00	97,056
3,178	Okla. G&E Com.	28	88,984	1.50	4,767
46,834	Wisc. Pub. Serv. Com.	19	889,846	1.10	51,517
547,678	Pittsburgh Rwy. Com.	7-1/2	4,107,585		
			$30,493,248		$1,492,180
	Other assets		4,912,749		
			$35,406,045		
	Less liabilities		8,196,000		
			$27,210,045		
	Per share		$12.58		

Standard Gas & Electric's capitalization is comprised of 2,162,000 common shares. Each $2,500,000 change in asset value is equivalent to Standard Gas. Therefore each $1.15 of value in Standard Gas is worth $1,334,000 to Standard Power and Light, which, brought down to the equity interest, is equivalent to 93¢ per share based on 1,430,000 shares of Standard Power and Light common and Class B.

Contingencies

As indicated in the tabulation, the net value of the Standard Gas holdings aggregates $12.58 per share. However, there are two financial items which could influence the value of Standard Gas shares materially. One is contained in a reserve fund for income taxes for years prior to 1950 in the amount of $3,935,267 and the sum of $1,260,672 held for accrued taxes and accounts payable. These amount to $5,185,939. Standard Gas & Electric's tax counsel states, in the 1952 annual report, "While the Treasury Department has only completed examination of the consolidated tax returns for the years 1942-45, inclusive, the reserves on the company's books appear to be adequate. In fact Philadelphia Company has claimed a large tax loss in 1950 resulting from the reorganization of Pittsburgh Railway's system, which, if allowed in full, would not only eliminate the holding companies' tax liabilities but would also result in further tax refunds in addition thereto."

The complex nature of the tax situation suggests a prolonged period of examination and negotiation before a settlement can be reached. Consequently, for the purpose of this analysis, we are assuming a compromise on a 50% basis. Such settlement would cancel out approximately $2,500,000 of contingent liabilities. This amount would increase the gross assets of Standard Gas by $1.15 per share and raise the asset value to $13.72 per share.

Claims for Fees and Expenses

The second item relates to the heavy claims for fees and expenses attendant upon the dissolution of Standard Gas. These totaled $5,500,000, of which $600,000 has been paid. No reserve has been created to meet these claims. However, Standard Gas is vigorously contesting the claims as exorbitant. While the exact amount of fees and expenses that will finally be approved by SEC for payment (and the respective courts having jurisdiction) cannot be predicted, it is believed that the amount will be substantially reduced. A reasonable conjecture would be a 50% compromise. This would create a liability of approximately $2,500,000, equivalent to $1.15 per share.

Based on the foregoing, the net result would give Standard Gas an estimated value of $13.25 per share, only 67¢ above the $12.58 indicated by the portfolio holdings. However, one should not lose sight of the varied combinations and possibilities inherent in such complex relationships:

1. It is conceivable that a substantially greater tax refund than assumed above could be attained, which would more than offset the entire claim for fees and expenses.

2. If we assume a 50% settlement for fees and claims, then each $2,500,000 released or obtained through the tax situation over the first $2,500,000 so obtained would add $1.15 per share to Standard Gas. If $7,500,000 were released and/or obtained through the tax channel, then $5,000,000 of it would redound to the common stock assets, or $2.30 per share, thus raising the total assets based on this assumption to $12.57 plus $2.30, or $14.87 per share.

3. If we assume settlement of the "fees and expenses" at $2,500,000, and no requirement to pay out funds for taxes, in which case the $5,000,000 held as reserve would be released, then Standard Gas' per-share worth would increase $1.15 to $13.72.

4. On the other hand, should there be no tax relief and the claims for fees and expenses allowed in full, Standard Gas would have a liability of $5,000,000. However, offsetting tax adjustments related to this specific conjectured liability would absorb about 50% of the cost. Thus Standard Gas' assets might be depleted by $2,500,000, equal to $1.15 per share, which sum, deducted from the $12.57 base asset value, would leave a remainder of $11.42 per share.

5. A more optimistic approach assumes a settlement of the claims and fees at 50%, or $2,500,000, and a tax refund considerably in excess of the $5,000,000 in reserve. Each $2,500,000 after settlement of the claims for fees and expenses is equivalent to $1.15 per share of Standard Gas. Therefore $10 million obtained through tax negotiations would increase Standard Gas' per share by $3.50 raising the worth to approximately $16.

However, for the purpose of this study, we are using the indicated worth based on the tax settlement offsetting the liability for fees and expenses. We are mindful of the extremes in portfolio values from the $11.42 level to the $14.87 and $16 or even higher level. This range of values suggests that any deviation from our appraised price of $12.57 would not exert a significant influence on the value of Standard Power and Light during the period of reorganization.

Note: The claims for fees were settled. This was followed by distribution of the major portion of the assets during 1957. The only remaining obstacle to complete liquidation is the undertermined status of the Federal liabilities for the nine-year period 1942-1950. The present status of Standard Gas, now reduced to a "stub," is described in the chapter on stubs.

CHAPTER 10

Recapitalizations

A recapitalization is a corporate action that takes place within the capital structure of a company. It is an intimate corporate relationship that must be resolved by the outstanding securities holders, who make up the membership of the corporate family. A recapitalization, then, is an action designed to bring about a change in the outstanding securities. Our interest in recapitalizations in previous chapters was limited to their use as a means to swing a merger/acquisition or reorganization. The profit possibilities were in the development of the terms of the corporate action rather than in the capitalization per se.

Capitalization represents the ownership of a corporation. Ergo, a recapitalization is an operation localized within the ownership, and the security holder should be alert to guard his rights in the corporation. The capitalization of a company resembles a set of sensitive balances in that the slightest change in one of the weights, in this case a security issue, may affect all the other securities. The intent of a recapitalization is to benefit the corporation which, in the final accounting, should be the equity stockholders. A recapitalization, then, is the reweighing of the relationships of the outstanding securities of the corporation.

Change signifies profit possibilities. This chapter deals with the various changes that can take place in the capital structure of a corporation, and recapitalizations that qualify for special-situation investment. Visible profit potentials may be regarded as evidence of a probable special situation.

Where to Look for Recapitalizations

Recapitalizations are found in maladjusted corporate structures, often the result of adverse economic conditions. The specific motive may be:

1. To reflect emergence from economic distress
2. To relieve economic pressure.
3. To facilitate an inner corporate maneuver
4. To take advantage of lower rates for borrowing money
5. To establish an improved corporate credit rating

Who Approves a Recapitalization

The approval of all who are, in any, concerned with the capitalization of a corporation is required to complete a recapitalization. This could include commercial creditors as well as bondholders and shareholders. Commercial creditors' approval would be required when their status in regard to the corporate assets would be jeopardized by the proposed recapitalization. Should the proposed recapitalization plan disturb the positions of the commercial creditors, that group would be a hurdle to be cleared.

Recapitalizations do not require the consent of creditors unless financial aid is being extended. However, since many corporations were, at times, indebted to the RFC,* it is well to know of existing restrictive provisions contained in RFC loans. This information can be found in the corporation's annual report, proxy statement, and prospectuses and statistical reports issued by financial publications. RFC loans have been the basis for that agency's injection into capital changes of many companies.

Establishing an Investment Position

The investigatory and analytical approach often may proceed while the approval of the aforementioned principals (parties) is being awaited. You will find it helpful to relate each class of security that is outstanding and involved in the recapitalization plan to the new set of securities to be issued. It is there that profits are to be found. The securities to be received must be worth more in the market than the existing issue in order to secure a profit.

The method used is to compare the old and new capitalizations as though they represent two separate corporations. It would be helpful, where possible, to construct a balance sheet and earnings statement covering a five-year period: (1) two years earlier, (2) the present year, and (3) two years hence. Then examine the financial statements to compare earning power, capital assets, and underlying values

---

*Reconstruction Finance Corp.

for each class of security. This would disclose whether there would have been or will be any improvement or loss from the recapitalization. The position of each security in regard to earnings and assets should be established on a pro forma basis, that is, as though the new basis had been in effect.

Objectives of the Financial Study or What to Look For

The purpose of the financial study is to determine whether a proposed plan is fair and equitable. This can be determined from the manner in which it proposes to achieve its objective. All securities concerned should benefit in some way. No class of security should relinquish a favored position unless it has been satisfactorily compensated. Neither should a junior security receive preferential treatment.

The allocation of the earnings, dividends, capital assets, and voting rights should be compared with the "old" status.

If the purpose of a recapitalization is to relieve a debt condition, then the possible dilution of the common earning power may be part of the plan. This, in itself, is not necessarily objectionable if, through achievement of the plan, the common would then earn dividends. However, a loss of preferential position of a bond or preferred stock might not be satisfactorily compensated by increased dividends. Such exchange offer would not be acceptable where safety would be more desirable than additional income. That type of recapitalization would not be considered fair and equitable. The American Car & Foundry Corp. plan of recapitalization (See page 136), illustrates a rejected plan and discloses the causes for rejection.

The study of Chicago Eastern Illinois Railroad which follows illustrates a recapitalization special-situation investment. It is interesting to note that this type of recapitalization, of which it was the first, has spread to other investment areas besides the railroads. Industrial and commercial enterprises have found the exchange of stock for debentures, useful. The procedure followed here is applicable to all recapitalizations of this type.

CASE HISTORY OF CHICAGO EASTERN ILLINOIS

This railroad's then unique recapitalization offered profit opportunities. Reversing the usual procedure, the investor was offered debentures for his Class A stock. The profit potential was in the stronger position of the new security. When the proposed plan was announced, the indicated minimum-profit potential ranged from 20% to 25% plus a dividend return at the rate of 8% per annum.

The situation met the four elements of a special situation, though on a fringe basis. The corporate action was the exchange plan. The investment was undervalued in relation to indicated worth on consummation of the corporate action. It could be calculated, though the duration was uncertain. The risk was not great, though not at a true minimum. An additionally favorable factor was the desirability of the creation of debt in exchange for the Class A stock. The recapitalization would benefit all concerned. Thus it could be expected that the plan would be consummated.

The plan, as proposed by the corporation, invited holders of the Class A stock to exchange their shares for the company's 5% debentures due Jan. 1, 2054, having the same face value as the par value of shares of stock exchanged. The par value of the Class A stock was $40, and holders were entitled to receive $40 principal amount of debentures in exchange for each share.

Analysis:

The change from equity interest to creditor status should benefit the latter in relation to the benefit to the corporation's financial standing. This would be reflected in a higher value for the debentures than prevailed for the stock. In investigating the potential advantages, begin by examining the financial position to see where the benefits fall. Compare the old and new capitalizations. The capitalization of the company as it existed, and pro forma, assuming all shares of Class A stock were exchanged, follows:

	Actual	Pro Forma
First Mortgage 3 3/4% bonds, Series B, due May 1, 1985	$ 7,844,000	$ 7,844,000
General Mortgage income 5% bonds, due Jan. 1, 1997	12,350,800	12,350,800
2%, 3 1/8% Equipment Trust obligations	11,354,000	11,354,000
5% Income Debentures, due Jan. 1, 2054	None	15,350,040
Conditional sale agreements equipment	6,039,914	6,039,914
Class A stock, $40 par, 383,751 shares	15,350,040	None
Common stock, no par	411,229 shares	411,229 shares

The elimination of the Class A stock and the inclusion of the 5% debenture are the only capital changes. The significance of the capitalization change is the interest to be paid on the $15,350,000 of debentures. Under the new setup this constitutes a charge before taxes, whereas dividends on the Class A are calculated as earned after taxes. Interest on the debentures amounts to approximately $770,000 annually, equal to the dividends paid on the Class A stock. However, as the debenture interest is charged before taxes and Federal income taxes estimated at 50% rate, one-half the cost of servicing the debentures would be saved, equal to about $400,000 annually. This savings would boost the indicated coverage on the new debenture to 3.6 times, which, as shown in the accompanying earnings table, would exceed the coverage for the Class A stock. The next step would be the examination of the corporation's earnings. The record shows that since reorganization, the company's earnings have been sufficient to cover the $2 per share dividend on the Class A stock in every year except 1946 and 1949. The following table shows net income and earnings on Class A stock for a ten-year period:

Ten months ended:	Net Income	Per Class A
Oct. 31, 1954	$1,351,373	$5.25 X
1953 (year)	2,712,559	6.07
1952	2,715,119	6.03
1951	2,196,960	4.68
1950	3,019,310	6.93
1949	364,422	1.09 D
1948	1,131,662	0.03
1947	1,274,461	2.20
1946	515,907 D	4.20 D
1945	1,364,436	2.74

X = Estimated for the year.
D = Deficit.

The savings from taxes would amount to almost $1 per share since there are 383,751 Class A shares outstanding. Over the five-year period, from 1949, fixed charges amounted to $890,000 annually. This was covered about 4.2 times. If we add the $770,000 interest payable on the new debentures, total charges would amount to $1,660,000, which would be covered by a satisfactory 2.25 times.

In view of the good financial condition, it would be reasonable to estimate a value for the new debentures in relation to the other outstanding securities. The General Mortgage income bonds were priced around a 5.5% yield. The Class A stock at 25 returned a yield of 8%. While the new debenture would not warrant an equal price with the General Mortgage income bonds immediately, they could be worth a price in between the bonds and the Class A stock. This would be a 6% yield, which would be equivalent to a price around 36 5/8 for the Class A shares. This level would appear to be a reasonable objective. Thus the situation offered substantial attraction. Therefore investigation as to the probability of the plan consummating was warranted. This required, first, a study of the benefits and objectives of the plan as released by the company. Excerpts from this report follow:

1. The Class A stock was originally issued in reorganization to the General Mortgage bonds. Because of this, it was believed that there would be no serious objection to the return to debt from equity interest.

2. The new income debentures would represent debt with a fixed maturity date.

3. The exchange ratio would retain the same investment proportion for the company.

4. The income would be the same.

5. The interest on the debenture would be paid at specific times when and to the extent earned, not exceeding $2 per $40 of debentures, whereas dividends are not paid unless declared.

6. Dividends are payable only after taxes, while interest on the debentures is a charge before taxes.

7. The debentures would have a sinking-fund provision.

The management's cooperativeness enabled the investor to obtain sufficient information upon which to make a decision. Thus the risk could be calculated along with the probability of consummation.

The special meeting for the plan was held in February, 1954, and was substantially favorable to the plan. The ICC would have to pass on the plan before it could become effective. At the annual meeting in May, the company stated that the plan was delayed while awaiting action by Congress relative to the tax legislation. The shares during this period fluctuated around the 25 level and continued to offer the same opportunity as indicated in the analysis. The ICC approved the plan in December, 1954. This action was followed by the offer to exchange the shares for debentures. By this time the shares had moved up to the 30 3/4 level. It is interesting to note that the General Mortgage bonds also advanced in price to 101 1/2, which offered a return of 4.93%. A satisfactory profit has been established by those who entered the situation inasmuch as the Class A shares had sold at 32 3/8 while the bonds had established an equivalent high of 80 1/4.

A Recapitalization to Eliminate a High-cost Nonredeemable Preferred Stock

The American Car and Foundry (A.C.F. Industries) first plan of recapitalization was defeated because it was not considered fair and equitable. However, the management stated, in a postmeeting release, that they had received intimations from a substantial number of stockholders and representatives of stockholders who opposed the plan, that their objections were based on details rather than on the basic objective, which was the elimination of the 7% noncumulative, nonredeemable preferred stock.

The company claimed that the high dividend rate, the noncumulative features, and the archaic method of computing dividends on the preferred were disadvantageous both to the company and the shareholders. Dividends had been paid on the preferred out of earnings on an unconsolidated basis, incorporating dividends received by the parent company from subsidiaries but not allowing for the equity in undistributed earnings.

Under the plan, holders of the 7% preferred were offered two shares of $50 par, 5% cumulative convertible preferred for each share held. The new preferred would be convertible into common at the rate of 1 1/8 shares for each preferred. There were 300,000 preferred shares outstanding, of which 289,450 were in the hands of the public. A basic objection to the above plan was the income loss of 2%, without adequate compensation.

The company subsequently proposed a revised plan providing for a similar exchange of shares but adding $4 per share in cash. The revised plan also contained expanded sinking-fund provisions.

The following comparative table shows the chief characteristics of the old and new preferred stock.

	Old Preferred	New Preferred
Par value	$100	$50 (each share of the old being changed into 2 shares of the new, plus $4 in cash)
Dividend rights	7% noncumulative (but has certain vested rights in annual earnings)	5%, fully cumulative
Redemption	Not redeemable	Redeemable at par, plus accumulated dividends and 10% premium, at the option of the company or through the sinking fund.
Conversion	Not convertible	Convertible into 1 1/8
Voting rights	Full 1 vote per share	Full 1 vote per share
Rights on liquidation	Par value	Par value, plus accrued dividends
Sinking fund	None	Earnings applied to sinking fund

The Profit

When the revised plan was announced the preferred was priced around 100. The approval of the plan by the stockholders was reflected in the market price of the preferred, which moved to 106. This was the final price for that issue. The new preferred ranged between 51 and 51 7/8, which was equal to a price of 107 including the $4 cash payment. In addition to the $4 payment, two unpaid dividends of $1.75 each would be payable to holders as of the effective date of the plan. (Thus the old preferred holder would receive two new shares plus $7.50, bringing the total value to $111.24) The profit of $11.24 per share could have been obtained by any special-situation investor who had followed the situation from the inception. He would have gleaned from the reports of the voting of the first plan that a subsequent plan to meet objections would be presented and probably adopted. Thus he could have participated in the recapitalization by merely reading the notices from the company, which contained comprehensive information and statistical data.

The Importance of Voting on a Plan

The disposition of a plan is determined by the vote of the security holders. Therefore, as in other investigations, locating the strength and intentions of the voting securities is essential. The percentage of outstanding securities needed for assent to the plan, in relation to the number of votes controlled by the proponents of the plan, is significant. Generally, security holders give greater attention to voting in a recapitalization than in other corporate activities. This is understandable since it affects the security holders directly in the pocketbook. Voting power has been lost through the erroneous belief that the absence of a market value for the securities also eliminated the voting rights. Valuable rights existing in outstanding securities can be lost through supersedence by a new issue. American Woolen Co.'s recapitalization created a prior preferred stock which took precedence over the then existing preferred stock. When such action occurs, the stockholder would do well to investigate the pertinent "rights of appraisal." Where appraisal rights exist, the analytical approach to security evaluations described in Chapter 11 on Appraisals should be followed.

Also keep in mind that a corporation's recapitalized structure should permit the benefits of improving conditions to flow to the securities entitled to them.

Symptoms of a Recapitalization

Generally, the need for a capital adjustment is as obvious as a bandaged thumb, and the likelihood of a recapitalization may appear long before the corporation has conceived a plan. Participation in a recapitalization can occur at various stages and offers a wide range.

The signs leading to a recapitalization are highlighted by the following: (1) improving earning power, and (2) capitalization burdened with arrears in bond interest and/or preferred dividends.

What to Look For before You Buy

A recapitalization-investment position would be established only when a plan is under consideration. The analytical procedure to be followed is that used in mergers/acquisitions and reorganizations. The following questions can help point out the important steps to be taken.

1. Who proposed the plan? Was it offered by any of the following groups:

   a. The opposition to the present management?
   b. The management?
   c. The protective committee?
   d. The banking group?

The origin of the recapitalization plan frequently can give a clue to the probability of its consummation. If new management is contemplated in the recapitalization, then their competency and experience must be included in the evaluation of the securities. Likewise, when no management change is indicated, the question as to continuing with an unsuccessful management may exist, which also has pertinent implications, particularly where the management controls substantial voting interests.

The following questions can be answered by applying our basic procedures, particularly to the notice of meeting and proxy statement.

2. What voting strength is represented by those who proposed the plan?

3. What percentage of the voting securities is needed to declare the plan effective?

4. How much time will elapse until voting occurs?

5. Who is the opposition? Why are they opposed? What do they suggest?

6. Who are the various committees and what do they represent?

7. What has been the recent market action of the securities? This research may disclose anticipatory purchases or sales which may influence the proposed plan. Check SEC reports for changes in security holdings of officers and substantially large holders.

8. Has the corporate action been discounted the market? Has this activity brought the securities to their indicated investment level?

9. Will it be possible to arbitrage or hedge the investment position? Consider the possibility of establishing an offsetting position, the procedure for which as well as the financial approach, is discussed in Chapter 2.

Working Aides

The latest available balance sheet and earnings report will be most useful when working out the relationship of the "old" and "new" capital structure. Pro forma statements of previous and future years are good guides. The benefits and costs to the corporation can be seen graphically in a pro forma balance sheet and earnings statement. The fairness of the plan to all classes of securities is to be considered since people will not knowingly vote against their own interest, particularly in money matters. If the plan appears inequitable, stay on the observation sideline until the condition has been corrected. If the plan appears reasonable, the profit possibilities should then be determined.

Types of Recapitalizations

Recapitalization proposals that offer profit possibilities can be divided into the following types:

1. Payment of arrears in cash. This would probably not have a substantial profit potential as the securities would tend to seek their investment level directly in response to the announcement of a plan. The combination of anticipatory purchases and response to the public announcement might consume the profit possibilities.

2. Payment of arrears in securities issuable under the existing capitalization. Where the payment of arrears is to be made in authorized but not outstanding stock, the amount of additional common stock would dilute the then outstanding shares. For example, a corporation paid the accrued interest on its bond by issuance of 100,000 shares of common stock. The total amount of common stock outstanding was 1 million shares. Therefore the dilution would be 10%. Consequently, the common stock would be worth 10% less than the market price prior to the issuance of the 100,000 shares. If the market price of the common stock had been $10 per share, it would be worth $9 per share reflecting the dilution. The Penn Dixie recapitalization case which follows illustrates this procedure.

3. Creation of new securities to meet a specific condition such as payment of interest arrears on a bond, or dividend accumulations on preferred stock. Where a recapitalization creates a new class of security to pay off arrears, this security must be valued on its own merit. One type of special-purpose security is known as dividend- or interest-arrears certificates. Frequently the provisions of the special-purpose security stipulate a termination date and an automatic procedure for eventual elimination of the security. Such securities might qualify as a special-situation investment. The R. Hoe & Co. Class B stock, described on page 142, presents this type of investment opportunity in step-by-step detail.

4. Creation of one or more class of new securities to be exchanged for one or more class of old securities. A new capital structure involving an exchange of outstanding securities for new securities, may harbor more opportunities for profit than

other recapitalizations. The point is to estimate values for securities to be issued. The profit potential exists in the "when-issued securities," that is, securities which come into existence upon consummation of the plan.

If the "old" securities can be purchased for less than the estimated value of the new, then a profit should accrue when the recapitalization is completed. This type of situation would be recognized by the proposed issuance of the following securities: new bonds and preferred and common stock in exchange for the outstanding security issues.

Since this type of recapitalization closely resembles a reorganization, the illustrations discussed in Chapter 8 under Denver and Rio Grande Railroad and Missouri Pacific Railroad show the procedure.

PENN DIXIE CEMENT CO.
(Payment of Arrears in Securities)

The Penn Dixie Cement Corporation consummated a recapitalization that eliminated a $7 convertible cumulative preferred stock on which dividend arrears in excess of $90 per share had accrued. To accomplish elimination of arrears the stockholders approved an increase in the amount of common stock. The table shows the comparative capitalization:

Old Capitalization		New Capitalization
Debt: Mtg. Bd. 3 1/4%	$3,250,000	Same
$7 Class A pfd. no. of shares	125,000	Eliminated
Common, no. of shares	400,000	750,000

The exchange of shares established a more realistic status for the new capitalization. The heavy burden of debt and pressure of the high 7% rate for the use of the (Class A pfd.) money was eliminated. In return, the preferred shares received two-thirds of the new equity stock and retained their preferential position, no other securities being created. First call on net earnings would continue in effect to accrue to the old preferred shares though now shared with the common.

The old common stock received but one new share for each 10 held, plus a warrant to purchase two additional shares at $20 per share for each ten shared owned. Thus the opportunity to participate in the future of the company was preserved for the common. This position was all they had before, but with little probability of receiving dividends. The profit opportunities existed in the Class A shares on which the dividends had accrued.

R. HOE & CO. SPECIAL-PURPOSE STOCK
(Creation of New Securities)

The fact that R. Hoe & Co. participated in various capital readjustments permits uese of this corporation for more than one illustrative purpose. It is further helpful to the reader since it familiarizes him with a single corporation and provides a continuous line for tracing capitalization activities. The following is a detailed description of the profit opportunities in "special-purpose shares," sometimes known as "dividend-arrears shares."

R. Hoe & Co.'s origin dates back to the early 1800's. The corporation is one of the largest printing-press manufacturers in the country. It is also a large-scale manufacturer of saws. Second World War military-production activities restricted the company's normal business. However, by 1946, the corporation had a record backlog of commercial orders.

Origin of the Class B Stock

Revenues and profits were increasing substantially, but the lost business had left a burden of $83 per share of accumulated dividends on the Class A stock. The improving income gave rise to the idea of segregating these accumulations and putting the Class A stock on a current-dividend basis. Thus a plan was created, the effects of which are shown in the following tabulation:

	"Old" Capitalization	New Capitalization
Funded Debt	None	None
Class A stock outstanding	95,997 shares	95,997 shares
Common stock outstanding	160,000 shares	160,000 shares
Class B stock	None	383,988 shares

The Corporate Action in the Recapitalization Plan

The approved plan provided for the creation of a new class of stock identified as B stock, or "special-purpose" stock. It had no voting power. However, the stock was entitled to participate in a redemption fund at a maximum price of $20 per share. This type of fund created the corporate action and the special-situation investment opportunity. The terms of the redemption fund required, after paying the Class A dividend, that 50% of the net earnings in excess of $200,000 be placed in a "redemption and dividend fund" for Class B shares. Out of this fund dividends of $0.10 per share were payable on the Class B stock. Such distributions would be meaningless except that they would reduce the redemption price by the amount of the distribution.

The terms of the redemption fund required, after paying the Class A dividend, that 50% of the net earnings in excess of $200,000 be placed in a "redemption and dividend fund" for Class B shares. Out of this fund dividends of $0.10 per shares were payable on the Class B stock. Such distributions would be meaningless except that they would reduce the redemption price by the amount of the distribution.

Dividend requirements on the Class A shares plus the $200,000 amounted to $583,988, which was the required earnings before which the B redemption fund shared on a 50% basis.

The corporation was required to use the redemption-fund money to purchase Class B stock in the open market, or redeem at $20 per share a sufficient number of shares to exhaust the fund.

To satisfy the claim of the Class A stock in regard to the accumulated dividends the company distributed $3 in cash and four shares of Class B stock for each Class A share held. 383,988 shares of B stock were issued.

Practical Application

The B shares were priced around the $7 to $8 level at the time of issue. Earnings, at that time, fell short by a slight margin of any required contribution to the redemption fund. However, increasing order-backlog indicated that earnings would mount in the immediate future and that the redemption fund would become operative. This belief was further supported by the unique financial operations of the business, which would permit a large flow of cash to accrue. The huge volume of orders would not call upon large amounts of working capital since orders required progress payments by customers.

Discussion:

The improving earnings were reflected in the first quarterly report, which indicated that a sum of $450,000 might be available for the redemption fund within the year. This amount of money could purchase about 60,000 shares of the B stock at the current $7-8 level. This would equal 16% of the issue. If the above earnings were available for the ensuing few years, then over 50% of the B stock could be eliminated through open-market purchases by the company.

Accordingly, based on the indicated earnings, supported by substantial backlog of orders and the operations of the redemption fund, the B stock appeared attractive. However, the potential profit could only be conjectured. As a starting point for estimating, we could assume it would take seven to ten years for full redemption of the shares based on the indicated earnings. A maximum profit of $12-$13 per share could be established if the B shares were purchased at the $7-$8 level and if the shares were redeemed at the redemption price of $20. Keep in mind that this conjecture was not an expectation but merely a base for calculating. The calculable profit then equals 150% to 180% on a ten-year and seven-year basis, respectively. On an annual basis this would approximate 15% to 27%, while an average would be

21%. By taking 21% of $7 and $8 we arrive at $1.47 and $1.68, respectively. In such wise we could estimate an expected profit of 1 1/2 points, or $1.50 per share per annum.

Related Elements

The above return could be enhanced by the following factors:

1. The stock-scarcity factor. As fewer B shares remained outstanding the price would tend to stabilize at higher levels.

2. A compelling force for retirement of the B shares was the influence of the restrictive provision on dividend payments to the common holders while any B shares were in existence. This gave support to the probability that all efforts would be made to eliminate the B stock, a strengthening element indeed.

3. The activity of the redemption fund would also tend to give support to the market price of the B shares as the corporation was permitted to make open-market purchases.

4. The mere existence of the redemption fund would act as a support to the market price, though no purchases were made.

5. Consideration must be given to the fact that as shares would be purchased or redeemed the price would advance in response to the law of supply and demand. However, offsetting this would be the fact that more monwy would be required to obtain fewer shares.

Summation:

The situation offered (1) capital appreciation equal to a return of approximately 20% on a per annum basis, (2) marketability, (3) a minor risk factor, and (4) the possibility of even greater profit percentagewise than estimated. Those items add up to a fully qualified special-situation.

Progress Report

The B shares were influenced by the operations of the redemption fund through open-market purchases and through the use of "tenders." This procedure is described in the chapter on Tenders. The effects of these purchases brought the price of the B shares to the $10 level. Thus a profit of $2 to $3 or 25% to 43%, could have been obtained within one year. Taking an average, this would equal 33% on the money invested. Subsequent market action saw the shares return to the $8 level.

It was thus possible for those who had completed a transaction at the earlier and higher level to reenter the situation; while other investors were offered the opportunity of initiating an investment position at that attractive level.

From this point the shares moved steadily up to the $14 level, a 100% rise from our original purchase. This profit by far exceeded our conjecture of 1 1/2 points per year.

This favorable market action was sparked, no doubt, by the earnings, which permitted the sum of $707,000 to be applied to the redemption fund; while the three-year average amounted to $626,000. During this period the number of B shares outstanding was reduced by 50%.

Another factor which may have been reflected in the price advance of the B shares was the proposal of a recapitalization to eliminate the B shares entirely. This was proposed for the purpose of freeing the common shares for dividends. Details of this plan are discussed in Chapter 11 on Appraisals.

By-product Beneficiaries of a Recapitalization

The nonparticipating securities of a corporation under recapitalization proceedings generally offer few opportunities for special-situation profit. However, the benefits of the recapitalization may redound to all the securities of the company. This condition is best observed where a recapitalization has removed restrictions on payment of dividends on the common stock. The R. Hoe & Co. recapitalization described here accomplished this. As a result, the equity shares were placed in a position to receive dividends. This, in turn, would be reflected in a better price for the shares. Then, too, an improved market price for the shares could create a better credit rating for the corporation.

Summary of Important Points to Be Considered in a Recapitalization Situation

1. Is the plan fair and equitable to all classes of securities and creditors? More often than not each security or creditor group proposes a plan oriented to that group's particular benefit.

2. Does the plan relieve the pressure on the financial structure of the company?

3. Does the plan remove the adverse factors which contributed to the company's difficulties?

4. Is the recapitalization necessary or is it a subterfuge?

5. What position has been taken by the various committees representing securities holders?

6. Is the recapitalization a result of unfavorable business conditions?

7. Is a change in management contemplated?

7. Is a change in management contemplated?

8. Is a fight for control of the company in progress?

9. Do prospective earnings for a few years hence give adequate support to the plan?

10. Will effective operation of the recapitalized company benefit the securities issues purchased as a special situation?

11. Can the plan succeed?

CHAPTER 11

Appraisals

This chapter discusses requests for appraisals, a procedure used to obtain calculated values for securities. The purpose is to secure a better price for the security than that which results from a corporate action. For example, after a merger of two companies, a stockholder of one believes his shares to be worth more than the value placed on them in the merger agreement and invokes his right to request a "fair value" for his shares through having them "appraised."

We have already discussed the profit opportunities which come into being with a pending corporate action, and again, when security holders assent to a proposed corporate action. However, we have not considered the position of security holders who do not wish to participate. They have varied rights under stipulated conditions, one of which is to ask for a "fair and reasonable price" for the security in question. This is known as requesting an appraisal.*

The placing of an estimated value on an asset is known as appraising. A familiar example is the jeweler who estimates a value for a gem.

---

*Recent court decisions have followed a pattern of basing appraisal suit settlements on market prices of the shares around the time of consummation of the corporate action. Consequently, appraisals are now unsatisfactory means for obtaining a calculated value for a security. However, customs change, and the appraisal procedure may again take its place as a calculated investment method.

Who Creates an Appraisal

Requests for a "fair value" for a security originate from its loss of position in the corporate structure resulting from the changed status of the corporation. Stockholders who object to a corporate change and also request the fair value for their securities have created an "appraisal situation." Thus it is not the company but the stockholder who, through opposing a proposed plan, creates the special-situation opportunities.

How to Profit from an Appraisal

The profit possibilities lie in the methods used to expedite the procedure and in the estimated worth of the security. Therefore it follows that the success of an appraisal venture is dependent upon (1) the skill in evaluating a security, and (2) the methods used to obtain the calculated value.

An appraisal contains the germ of a special situation, when the securities are undervalued. Through an appraisal you can establish the undervalue. The opportunity to request an appraisal arises in such corporate changes as mergers/acquisitions, reorganizations, and recapitalizations. The appraisal status does not come into being until after the corporate change has been consummated.

You can create profits through the exercise of your right to oppose a proposed corporate change. Your profit potentiality will be determined largely by your knowledge of security holders' privileges, along with your ability to evaluate the worth of the security. The procedure for analyzing an appraisal situation is outlined on page 155.

How to Anticipate an Appraisal Situation

A profitable investment can be developed by anticipating a corporate action which would give the security holder the right to request an appraisal. Clues to such actions are found in the following:

1. Acquisition of shares of one corporation by another, detectable in unusual trading activity in the shares.

2. Interrelated officers and members of the boards of directors, detectable in news items and SEC reports.

3. Joint use of facilities and close business arrangements, detectable in company progress reports and news items.

4. The financial statement. A good cash position and high book value, combined with a carry-forward tax loss is a pertinent clue to a merger.

Such signs would alert you to further examination of the corporation. Should the security issue then offer a satisfactory investment base, you would consider entering the situation for the possibilities inherent in an appraisal.

The Importance of Placing the Right Value on a Security

Estimating the proper value of a security is more significant in an appraisal situation than anywhere else because, when you request an appraisal, you must be able to justify the accuracy of your calculated values. The proof supporting your values may have to be presented to experts, judges, juries, or appointed appraisers.*

The thinking of the appointed appraisers in relation to security values may differ from that of investors closely associated with markets and security values. Those whom you may have to convince include:

1. The corporation with whom the dispute has arisen and which knows the value of the security and, also, to what limit it will go in compromising or defending its position

2. The selected appraisers, arbitrators, or court

The first skirmish generally is with the corporation. If after a specified period of time, agreement between the corporation and dissenting shareholders is not reached, the latter may have the right to petition the court (in the county in which the principal office of the corporation is located) to have the value of their shares determined by appraisal, subject to confirmation or determination by the court.

It is one thing to convince a fellow investor of the worth of a security since you and he would use similar criteria. It is quite another thing to prove the worth of a security to those who are judging by use of values other than yours. An experienced investor places strong emphasis on cash, fixed assets, earning power, and relative position in the industry. His case could be established without reference to the market price of the security. The omission of the market prices from the investor's proof would be an indication that the security was undervalued.

On the other hand, a referee, judge, or jury not experienced with the professional investors' techniques would find merit to the argument that a security's worth should approximate (1) the market prices for said security over a reasonable period of time, or (2) the market price on the date of consummation of the corporate action. The Hudson Motor case described in this chapter furnishes a good example. The company announced that the price to be paid for shares, not exchanged, would be

---

*In the Hudson Motor merger, the Circuit Court appointed as appraisers, a lawyer, a business man and an investment banker, to determine the "fair cash value" for the shares.

9 5/8, the closing price on Mar. 23, 1954. This created the setting for a protracted appraisal case.

Market-price evaluation of a security would not be looked upon with favor by the investor who has been a holder for a protracted period. If the corporation had reinvested its profits, this would have created an increased worth for the security, although this might not have been reflected in the market prices. Consequently, the reinvestment of earnings would not receive fair consideration in establishing a reasonable worth for the security.

Types of Appraisals

The origin of the request for an appraisal has definite significance. This can be seen in the different approach one would make when asking for a fair value in a merger/acquisition and in a reorganization or recapitalization. In the former, the foundation for the appraisal request would be the difference of opinion as to price, while in the latter it could be the relationship of the subject security to the whole corporate capitalization. Examples of both types are given in this chapter.

What Every Dissenter Should Know: Your Rights and Obligations

The right to request an appraisal is not inherent in all securities. Where it does exist and it is invoked, it creates an obligation on the part of the security holder to sell at the appraised or agreed-upon value to the corporation upon whom the demand was made. In turn, the corporation is obligated to pay the appraised price. The appraisal claim established in a merger/acquisition would be a liability of the acquiring corporation; in a reorganization or recapitalization the corporation that issued the security would be responsible.

Who Creates the Stockholder's Rights

There are two authorities which give a security holder "rights and privileges." One is in the corporate charter, the other the laws of the state in which the company is incorporated. State laws differ in regard to security holders' perogatives in event of mergers/acquisitions, reorganizations, and recapitalizations. Some states require of those requesting an appraisal that ownership of the security must date prior to the record date for the meeting pertaining to the proposed plan; other states specify ownership of the securities prior to the date of the public announcement of the proposed plan.

Fortunately, the data defining the laws and charter provisions for those requesting appraisals are readily available. The corporation's notice of meeting, sent to all security holders, usually contains a summary of the corporate charter as well as the state laws governing security holders' rights.

Charter rights are stated in the by-laws and security provisions of the corporation. They define the obligations as well as the privileges of each security classification. Each security issue has its own "rights and privileges."

Since rights and privileges of various classes of securities determine profit possibilities, it would be useful to know the structure of securities as they apply under appraisal conditions.

A bond or debenture is a fixed debt. The context of the bond indenture states the conditions to be met and the penalty for failure. The indenture also contains the provisions which give voting rights to bondholders. It further discloses bondholders' rights and responsibilities when a corporate change affects the position of the bond.

Preferred shares have a fixed principal and stated dividend rate. The rights of the issue are explicitly noted in the charter provisions. These usually apply to (1) dividend rate, (2) stated value, (3) sinking-fund prices, (4) redemption price, (5) maximum value under liquidation, (6) voting rights, and (7) rights under merger, sale of assets, and reorganization conditions.

Common stock represents the ownership of the property. It is unlimited as to principal participation. However, voting privileges and rights under corporate changes as indicated above are specified.

Along with the prescribed privileges a security holder has a responsibility which must be performed to preserve his authority. This is the exercise of the right to vote. One penalty for not voting may be the forfeiture of the privilege to request an appraisal. A point to keep in mind is that a usual requirement, when establishing demand for an appraisal, is the submission to the corporation of a written objection to the proposed corporate action.

The right to vote is a privilege most often exercised by investors. While, generally, the voting privilege is used for the election of officers, it frequently is effective when expressing objection to a corporate action involving:

1. Sale of assets in part or full
2. Change in the nature of the corporate activities
3. Merger/acquisition terms
4. Increase in capitalization
5. Creation of pension funds and stock-option plans

Importance of Knowing Your Rights

Awareness of your rights can have financial value in special situations. This is demonstrated in the accompanying merger case where lack of knowledge of the rights of a security holder proved costly to many stockholders of Hudson Motor Car Co., in its merger with Nash Kelvinator.

The merger was approved by Hudson's stockholders by a vote of 1,419,268 shares versus 245,870 and by Nash Kelvinator stockholders by a vote of 3,277,754 versus 238,115. A new company, the American Motor Corporation, was formed to implement the merger.

The merger terms gave Nash Kelvinator stockholders one share of the new corporation for each share held. The Hudson Motor stockholders received two shares of the new corporation for each three shares held. Nash Kelvinator was priced around 16-18 and Hudson Motor around 10-13 on the NYSE.

Since Nash stockholders would retain their holdings, Hudson stock could be valued in relation to Nash, at two-thirds of a share, or 10 5/8 to 12 per share.

However, from the beginning, the terms of the merger did not satisfy many stockholders. The accompanying table shows the financial comparison of the two corporations.

	Hudson Motor		Nash Kelvinator
Book value,	$34.32 per share		$32.25 per share
Year	Earnings	Year	Earnings
1949	$5.05 per share		6.04
1950	6.00	1950	6.64
1951	(.56)	1951	3.73
1952	4.15	1952	2.90
9 months to Sept. 30, 1953	(3.23)	1953	3.25
Year	Dividends	Years	Dividends
1949	$1.43	1949	$1.40
1950	2.38	1950	2.95
1951	0.95	1951	2.50
1952	0.96	1952	2.00
1953	0.50	1953	2.00

( ) deficit.

The directors of both corporations were aware of the possibility of dissents and had provided for that contingency by an escape clause permitting abandonment of the proposed merger in the event 40,000 or more shares of Hudson demanded fair cash value for their shares. The Hudson dissenting vote was 18% of the issue, while the Nash negative vote amounted to only 7%. The statistical comparison of the two corporations disclosed inequities in the two-thirds share relationship of Hudson to Nash.

The 140,000 Hudson shares that voted against the merger exercised their right to request the fair cash value for the shares. The rights of dissenting stockholders are clearly defined in the "Notice of Meeting" which was sent to stockholders. (See below).

RIGHTS OF DISSENTING STOCKHOLDERS

In the event that the merger shall become effective, stockholders of Hudson who shall have voted against the merger will have the rights as set forth in Section 54 of the Michigan General Corporation Act, which reads as follows:

"1. Any shareholder in any corporation of this state consolidating or merging as aforesaid, who was such shareholder at the time such consolidation or merger was authorized by the shareholders of such corporation and who voted against such consolidation or merger, may within 20 days after such consolidation or merger was so authorized object thereto in writing and demand from said resulting corporation payment of the fair cash value of his shares in the constituent corporation as of the day preceding the day such consolidation or merger was authorized by the shareholders of such constituent corporation, excluding from such fair cash value any appreciation or depreciation in consequence of the action authorized, and surrender at such time to the resulting corporation the certificate or certificates for his shares as to which he is demanding payment. If within 30 days after receipt by said resulting corporation of such written demand said resulting corporation and such shareholder cannot agree upon such fair cash value of the shares, such shareholder or said resulting corporation may secure an appraisal of such shareholder's shares in the same manner and with the same effect as is provided in paragraph 1 of section 44 of this act. If such fair cash value shall be determined by agreement, such agreed fair cash value shall be final and conclusive. If such awarded or such agreed fair cash value of such shares is not paid by said resulting corporation within 60 days after the entry of such order or after such agreement, such fair cash value may be collected as other debts are by law collectible. Upon payment by said resulting corporation of such awarded or agreed fair cash value, such shareholder shall forthwith transfer and assign such shares at, and in accordance with, the request of said resulting corporation. Objection by any such shareholder to any action of the constituent corporation, of which he is a shareholder, or of the resulting corporation provided in this section and his rights thereafter under this section shall be his exclusive remedy.

"2. The right of any dissenting shareholder to be paid the fair cash value of his shares shall cease if and when the constituent corporation, of which he is a shareholder, shall, within 6 months after such demand for payment, abandon such action or the shareholders of such corporation shall revoke such action taken, entitling such dissenting shareholder to payment as in this act provided.

"3. No demand for payment of such fair cash value may be withdrawn by the shareholder making the same unless a majority of the board of directors of the resulting corporation shall consent thereto.

"4. Any shareholder who so demands payment for his shares shall not be entitled to vote such shares or to receive any dividends or distributions thereon, or to exercise any rights respecting such

---

The consummation of the merger was deferred pending decision in regard to invoking the escape clause in view of the substantial number of requests for fair cash value. A press release on Apr. 9, 1954, stated that Hudson Motor Car Co. had informed those "stockholders who voted against the merger and who seek cash for their shares" that the price will be based on the market value on the New York Stock Exchange, as of Mar. 23, 1954. This was 9 5/8. The letter went to each stockholder who requested a fair cash value for his Hudson shares.

As indicated in the excerpt from the "Rights of Dissenting Stockholders," the objecting stockholders were not required to accept this offer. They could, if they desired, file suit. The demands for appraisal aimed at the value for Hudson's shares up to the book value of $30 per share.

Nevertheless, on April 22, the merger of the two companies into American Motors Corporation was declared effective as of May 1, Hudson, selling at $9 on April 26, dropped to 8 1/4 on April 30. It was then that the uninformed investing public learned that, through ignorance, they had dissipated a valuable right.

Directly after the merger was declared effective, suits were filed in the Circuit Court, Detroit, Mich., by 17 stockholders of Hudson Motors for appraisal. After a lapse of four months, the Court appointed three appraisers to determine the fair cash value of Hudson Motor Car Co. stock that had not been exchanged. About 125,000 Hudson shares were involved in the appraisal request. Thus 15,000 shares apparently had settled with the company.

Generally, the investing public is not informed of the offer to settle requests for fair cash value since this procedure is usually a private transaction.* Here we wish to point out that the public announcement of the offer of $9.62 per share for Hudson stock, to qualified holders, was higher than the value of two-thirds of a share of American Motor Corporation, which at the first day's trading on the New York Stock Exchange was 11 1/2 to 11 7/8 per share, equal to a little less than $8 per share of Hudson.

Many stockholders of Hudson thought they were entitled to $9.62 by merely offering their shares to the corporation. Many stockholders who had voted against the merger thought they were entitled to the $9.62 offered by Hudson (or the new corporation). Frequent references to the legal "rights of stockholders" were required to convince many stockholders that they had not performed the necessary step of making the demand for a fair cash value within 20 days after the voting in order to establish a position entitling them to negotiate a fair value for their holdings.

The point stressed here is the importance of knowing one's rights.

Birthplace of an Appraisal

The opportunity to exercise the privilege to request an appraisal may arise through circumstance or intent. The unanticipated resort to the use of the appraisal medium would occur where an investor did not make the original purchase with intent to request a fair value for his securities. However, at some time during his ownership of the security, the company proposes a corporate action. At that time the investor is opposed to the specific action and concludes that he wants the company to pay him a fair value for his securities. In this case the appraisal request is an afterthought.

---

*See example at close of this chapter.

In the premeditated use of the appraisal the investor would have considered using this medium to take an investment position in the situation. This could be achieved where merger or recapitalization possibilities are evident.

In our approach to appraisals we concentrate on the use of the "right to dissent" as a means to profitable investment, since such action must be preconceived.

How to Evaluate a Security for Appraisal

In an appraisal the financial analysis of the corporation is fundamental. Therefore, the first step is our standard financial analysis described in Chapter 2. Particular reference should be made to the following:

1. <u>What is the earnings record of the corporation</u>, both present and projected for the immediate future?

2. <u>What is the worth of the security</u> based on a recent balance sheet?

3. <u>What is the value of the inventory</u>? This may be pertinent in a sale of assets while in a merger the inventory value might be unimportant. On the other hand, the company's good will, patents, and advertising may have great significance.

4. What voting rights are given the security under the new conditions?

5. What is the relative position of the specific security in relation to other participating securities?

6. Are all securities given full recognition of their respective asset values?

7. Does the security receive any preferential treatment in respect to allocation of assets and/or income?

8. How does the specific security compare with similar securities of other corporations? This can also be used in presenting one's case for valuation during the legal proceedings.

Pitfalls

There are hazards associated with appraisals which must be recognized when establishing an appraisal investment position. These are mainly:

1. The registration of legal objection for an appraisal incurs the risk of loss of control over the securities. This means that the holder of the security may not sell until the securities are released by (a) settlement of the claim, (b) permission of the defending company to withdraw the request for the appraisal.

2. The locked-in position can be costly through delays due to (a) slow court procedure, (b) tactics of the company. These may result in erosion of the profit or even a loss of part of the money invested in the situation.

3. The court appraisers' verdict may compel settlement at less than the "plan" offer.

4. Dissenters must be prepared to press their claim through litigation which can be costly.

A point to bear in mind is that it may be possible to combine forces with other dissenters. This would reduce the costs and perhaps strengthen one's case. On the other hand, many appraisal requests are compromised prior to court action.

A common characteristic of an appraisal is the procedure of settlement out of court. Since such proceedings are confidential, there is a sparsity of statistical data on compromises. Thus it is difficult for an investor to know the price another security holder received for his stock.

The "Lone Wolf" Approach

An appraisal situation is primarily a "lone wolf" transaction. Here the investors' role has direct influence on the outcome, creating the possibility for profits by the determination to request an appraisal. This action may create the feeling that he is alone in his demand for a fair value. Since each appraisal request must be made individually, cooperative action is difficult to achieve. Furthermore, such action might not be favorable to the investor in cases where the corporation prefers to treat with each demand as a separate claim, as in the following example.

Example of Appraisal through Individual Action

In the case of Maxson Food System Corp.-Foremost Dairy Co. merger, dissenters who were prepared to litigate obtained their appraised values for the shares via individual settlements. The entire transaction required less than two months.

The proposed acquisition of Maxson through an exchange for Foremost shares was made public in February. The preferred shares of Maxson were then priced around $2 per share. Our basic analysis disclosed that the preferred appeared to have a value of $3 to $3.25 per share. This valuation was considerably greater than the price to be received in shares of Foremost.

How to Establish the Right to Request an Appraisal

The stockholders meeting was scheduled for March 21. To establish the right to request an appraisal, stockholders were required to vote against the merger and at the same time present, in writing, a petition for appraisal. Since procedures for establishing the right to an appraisal differ in state laws, it is advisable to know in what state the company is incorporated and its regulations pertaining to appraisals. This can be obtained from the notice of meeting and from the company directly.

The merger was approved, and the plan declared effective. Shareholders who had established their opposition then could legally request an appraisal.

Subsequent action was quick. Through compromise, Foremost satisfied the dissenters individually within a period of a few weeks. While all settlements were not released to the public, it was generally understood that a price around $3 was accepted by most of the objectors. A profit of 50% was obtained in less than three months.

A recent pending request for appraisal is that of Climax Molybdenum Co. American Metal Climax, Inc., announced that three stockholders, holding a total of 310 shares of Climax Molybdenum Co., have filed for appraisal of their shares. The two companies have merged. The ratio of exchange was three shares of American Metal for each share of Climax. Originally the holders of nearly 200,000 shares of Climax had objected.

CHAPTER **12**

Oversubscriptions

This chapter deals with oversubscription--a recent addition to the special-situation investment field. To obtain substantial profits, it is advisable to participate in as many "oversubscription" situations as possible. An oversubscription is the third and final phase in an offering to stockholders of a specific number of additional shares.

The Three Phases of Subscription "Rights"

1. A corporation offers to its stockholders the privilege of purchasing additional shares. This privilege is called a right. Each share of stock is entitled to subscribe to the additional shares on a pro rata basis. Thus each share of stock carries one "right" (See following page). A printed legend on the "right" certificate gives the pertinent data.

2. The second phase is the offer by the corporation to permit the stockholder to subscribe to a full share in instances where the number of rights held would entitle holders to a fraction of a share. This phase is not significant and is only mentioned to clarify the important final step.

3. To those holders of shares who have exercised their privilege of subscribing to additional shares, the company offers the opportunity to purchase at the subscription price, on a pro rata basis, any remaining shares unsubscribed for by holders of rights.

An "oversubscription," then, is the optional privilege of a shareholder to participate in the residual portion of a corporation's offering of shares to its stockholders. Such an offering generally has a duration period of about two weeks. Allotment of the remaining shares seldom requires more than a few days after the expiration of the rights.

It is worth noting that the exercise of the oversubscription privilege is optional with the shareholder. In no way does it affect the holders' basic privilege outlined in steps 1 and 2.

Since loose usage has led to a frequently confusing interchange of the terms, it would be helpful, at this point, to distinguish warrants from rights.

What Are Rights and Warrants?

A "warrant" is a transferable instrument entitling the holder to subscribe to capital stock of the issuing corporation at a fixed price. It has privileges similar to rights, in that it is an option to purchase. It differs in respect to longevity since a warrant may have a protracted or unlimited existence. At the time of a warrant's creation, it may not have real value because the price at which shares may be purchased (under the privilege) may be too far away from the market price of the stock.

A "right" is a perishable option to purchase securities at a fixed price below the market level. It requires prompt attention since it has a short though valuable life. Its market value and negotiability contribute to its usefulness in processing oversubscription situations.

The following example shows where rights are born.

The Preemptive Privilege

Corporation X seeks additional money for expansion and decides to sell additional shares. Since equity shares, in this instance, have preemptive rights, the additional shares to be sold must first be offered to the shareholders. In this way the shareholder retains his pro rata stock position in the corporation. When the preemptive privilege clause is effective, then the shareholder receives first opportunity to purchase an amount of shares so that his stock position in the company will be the same as before issuance of the additional shares.

Example: A corporation with 1,000,000 shares outstanding, having decided to sell 100,000 additional shares, would, in the above instance, give each outstanding share the right to purchase one-tenth of the new shares. Thus, for each 10 shares, the stockholder could buy 1 new share. A stockholder with 100 shares would be entitled to purchase 10 shares. Should he exercise his right, he would have 110 shares of the 1,100,000 as against 100 shares out of 1,000,000. In each case his interest would be the same, 1/10,000.

How to Locate the Profit

An oversubscription transaction is a discount situation since the profit arises from the purchase of shares for less than the market price.

Calculating the profit potential of an oversubscription situation requires simple arithmetic applied to finding the difference between the cost, which is the subscription price of the shares, and the market price. A stock priced around 12 5/8 would show a 5% profit if the corporation offered shares to the stockholders at $12 per share. The quality of the security would determine the size of profit since a high-quality company could command a better price for its shares than, let us say, an unseasoned company.

Wherein Lies the Profit?

The subscription price generally is sufficiently below the market level to be attractive. However, it can happen that the price spread (the difference between the subscription price and the market price) could be lost through a decline in the market. On the other hand, the shares of a favored corporation could command a premium, in which event value of the rights would correspond to the size of the premium. The premium is the difference between the market price of the shares and the subscription price. It is in the latter cases that a profit can be made through oversubscription.

Experience has shown that the number of unsold shares available for oversubscription varies from negligible amounts to as much as 60% allotments. The latter high oversubscription allotment occurred in the Central Hudson Gas & Electric Corporation's offering of common shares to the stockholders. This 60% allotment does not imply that 60% of the issue remained unsold. It means, that stockholders who applied for the oversubscription participation received 60% of their primary subscription. The oversubscription allotments are based on the primary subscription. Thus a stockholder who subscribed for 1,000 shares on his primary subscription and requested 1,000 shares on his oversubscription participation would have received 600 shares on a 60% allotment basis. An absence of interest in the subscription offering is beneficial to the special-situation investor since the fewer shares purchased by stockholders exercising rights leaves more to be divided amont the oversubscription participants.

An oversubscription is the cautious investor's delight since the risk involved can be negligible. The spread, which is the profit, is in existence and available. The time needed to establish the profit is short because you need not indicate your intent to participate in the oversubscription until the day the rights expire. Thus, at the most, just a few days intervene while awaiting the allotment distribution in the oversubscription pool.

The Procedure

Your objective in oversubscription transactions is to create a stock position which will entitle you to participate in the oversubscription privilege. This is extended only to holders whose shares have exercised the primary subscription rights. Therefore you must purchase rights to establish this transaction. A desirable price level for the rights would be where the cost of the rights, when added to the subscription price, would amount to no more than the market price of the stock.

How to Calculate the Value of a Right

The concept of rights and their relationship to the market price of the shares can be seen in the following (keep in mind that each share is entitled to one right):

If 10 rights are required to purchase one share of stock at $20 per share and the stock is selling around $22 per share, then the value of the right is 20¢. This is arrived at by subtracting 20, the subscription price, from 22, the market price, then dividing the remainder of $2 by 10, the number of rights needed to purchase one share. This would be a parity price for the rights. If the rights were selling at 30¢ per right, then 10 rights would cost $3, which, added to $20 (the subscription price), amounts to $23. That would create a premium for the rights of $1 per share, as purchase of shares through rights would cost $23, against $22 in the market.

Sometimes the combined costs of the rights and the subscription price amounts to less than the market price of the shares. This is known as a discount. When this condition prevails it is possible for brokers and investors to step into the situation by purchasing the rights and simultaneously selling the aliquot shares (equal number of shares), thus establishing and instantaneous profit. An example can be drawn by using our previous illustration but substituting a condition where the rights could be purchased at 15¢ per right, which would bring the total cost to $21.50 (20 plus 1.50, the cost of the rights), while the shares would be selling at 22. A spread or profit of 50¢ per share before taxes and costs would thus be established.

Quality Analysis

A good approach to an oversubscription situation is first to do a financial analysis of the shares to establish a quality rating. The prospectus issued with each offer of rights will have most of the needed data. This will offer a clue to the status of the shares in relation to market stability. It has been found practical to participate in oversubscription situations only when the quality of the shares indicates a price stability for the period immediately following expiration of the rights.

Next step is to purchase the rights. This will establish the privilege to subscribe to shares, plus additional shares at the termination of the offering. It is helpful to keep in mind the objective, which is to establish a position entitling one to participate in the oversubscription allotment. However, we do not want to own shares permanently, but merely to subscribe to shares to establish the oversubscription participation. Therefore, the rights are used to subscribe to shares. However, those shares should be sold at the time the rights are purchased. In this way we have purchased rights, to be used to subscribe to new shares, and will have established our privilege to participate in an oversubscription. Nevertheless, we do not have a long* position in the shares. On balance we are even, having sold as many shares as we have rights to buy. Then, on the date the rights expire, we can decide whether to use this participation privilege which we have created. If the spread between the subscription price and the market is adequate, we would exercise our privilege. Should the spread be insufficient, we are not required to do anything.

The following case illustrates the step-by-step action.

South Carolina Electric & Gas Co. offered rights to the stockholders to subscribe to shares at $12 per share in the ratio of one new share for each seven shares held, plus an oversubscription privilege. The shares were selling around 12 3/4 at that time.

A purchase of 3,500 rights at 3/32, which cost $347.55 including commission, assured the buyer of 500 shares (3,500 ÷ 7 = 500) plus the privilege of participating in the oversubscription. The total cost for the 500 shares, based on the subscription

---

*A long position is one where the investor is a holder of a security; a short position is one where an investor has sold and owes the securities.

- 162 -

price of $12, amounted to $6,347.55, equivalent to $12.69 per share. This was around the market price at that time.

It was possible to purchase rights and sell the equivalent number of shares at 12 3/4. This resulted in a small profit since the cost was $12.69 per share. However, the real profit was in the 75¢ per share spread between the subscription price of $12 and the current market price of 12 3/4. Therefore, it would be profitable to establish the right to buy as many shares as possible at $12.

You could do this to the extent the market and your money would permit. Bear in mind that your market position of "long" the rights and "short" the stock would be margined; also that the technical market problems of buying and selling could limit the number of shares you would be able to process at your specified prices. Of course, you could continue buying rights at a higher level and selling the shares at the equivalent higher level at no greater cost than at the previous levels. In most instances financing the foregoing positions requires funds for a few days. Thus large positions may be assumed.

We know that every 700 rights purchased created the privilege to subscribe to 100 new shares, and that this subscription entitled you to participate in the distribution of any unsubscribed shares at the price of $12 per share. After having established your position, you wait until the day the rights expire. At that time, if the shares still offer a profit, as prevailed in South Carolina Electric & Gas, which then were priced around 12 3/4, you would request participation in the oversubscription to the full extent of your primary subscription privilege.

Our purchaser of 3,500 rights exercised the subscription for 500 shares which had been sold at 12 3/4. The request for oversubscription for the full amount required a deposit of funds for good faith. Two days hence the purchaser received his pro rata distribution of 131 shares at a cost of $12 per share. This amounted to a 26% allotment. These shares were sold at 12 3/4, and a gross profit of $98.25 was established.

The _Barium Steel_ illustration follows:

Subscription price	$4 per share
Ratio	1 share for each 4 shares held
Record date	November 4
Expiration	November 26

During the life of the rights the shares sold around 4 3/4-7/8, while the rights were priced at 5/32. Purchase of 4,000 rights entitled the holder to subscribe to 1,000 shares of stock on his primary subscription and carried with it the privilege of participating in the oversubscription. The cost of 4,000 rights including commission was $644.80. This amount, when added to the subscription price of $4 per share, brought the cost of the 1,000 shares to $4,644.80, just about parity with the market. Therefore it was advisable to subscribe to the primary number, 1,000 shares, and also request an equal amount in the oversubscription to obtain full participation.

The day following the expiration of the rights the allotment ratio for the oversubscription was made public. This could be obtained from the bank which was processing the rights offering. The oversubscription percentage was 16%. This meant that the 1,000-share investor received 160 shares at $4 per share. The account when balanced would appear as follows:

Purchased		Sold	
4,000 rights, cost	$ 624.80	1,160 shares at 4 7/8	$5,645.00
Commission on rights	20.00	Less commission and taxes	$ 126.00
1,000 shares on subscription at $4 per share	4,000.00	Proceeds	$5,519.00
160 shares on oversubscription at $4 per share	640.00	Less cost	5,286.80
Cost of 1,1160 shares	$5,284.80	Net profit	$ 232.20

The transaction required but a few days, which made the oversubscription investment a satisfactory one.

Information and Publicity Sources

You can find out about oversubscription opportunities through newspapers, financial publications, and your investment dealer. Of course, if you are a registered stockholder, you will be notified by the company through a prospectus, notice of a meeting, or letter of information. See following page for an excerpt from a prospectus demonstrating the oversubscription privilege. Finding oversubscription opportunities is as simple as "if you know what you are looking for, you will find it." A point to bear in mind is that companies which have previously offered oversubscription privileges generally extend similar opportunities at subsequent times when resorting to financing through rights.

Summary of Important Points in Oversubscriptions

1. A company offers stockholders rights to subscribe to additional shares. This option includes the privilege of participating in any unsubscribed shares.

2. Important data includes: (a) the market price of the shares, (b) the subcription price, (c) the ratio for subscription, and (d) terms of oversubscription.

3. The indicated profit is the difference between the market price and the subscription price.

> **599,215 Shares**
> **BARIUM STEEL CORPORATION**
> **Common Stock**
> ($1 Par Value)
>
> *Transfer Agent:*   *Registrar:*
> GUARANTY TRUST COMPANY OF NEW YORK   BANKERS TRUST COMPANY
>
> SUBSCRIPTION OFFER
>
> The Company hereby offers to the holders of its outstanding Common Stock rights to subscribe (herein called "Rights"), at the Subscription Price per share set forth on the cover page of this Prospectus, for a total of 599,215 shares of Common Stock (herein called the "Additional Stock") at the rate of one share of Additional Stock for each 4 shares of Common Stock held of record at the close of business on November 4, 1954. The Company also offers to persons exercising such Rights the privilege of subscribing (herein called the "Additional Subscription Privilege"), at the Subscription Price, for any shares of the Additional Stock not subscribed for through the exercise of Rights, subject to allotment as set forth below.
>
> **Expiration Date:** The Subscription Offer will expire at 3:30 P.M., New York City Time, on November 26, 1954.
>
> **Warrants:** Rights and the accompanying Additional Subscription Privilege will be evidenced by a single form of fully transferable Warrant in registered form.
>
> **Exercise of Rights:** Rights may be exercised by filling out and signing the subscription form on the Warrant and sending or delivering it to the Warrant Agent, Guaranty Trust Company of New York, 140 Broadway, New York 15, N. Y. Four Rights plus the full Subscription Price are required to subscribe for each share of Additional Stock through the exercise of Rights. No fractional shares will be issued.
>
> **Exercise of Additional Subscription Privilege:** The Additional Subscription Privilege may be exercised by appropriate indication on the subscription form on the Warrant if Rights evidenced thereby are exercised at the same time.
>
> **Payment for Shares Subscribed For:** Subscriptions through the exercise of Rights or the Additional Subscription Privilege must be accompanied by full payment for all shares subscribed for. Payment of the Subscription Price may be made in cash or by check, bank draft or postal or express money order payable to the order of Guaranty Trust Company, Agent.
>
> **Allotment Under Additional Subscription Privilege:** The only shares available for subscription pursuant to the Additional Subscription Privilege will be such of the shares of Additional Stock as shall not be required to satisfy all subscriptions pursuant to the exercise of the Rights. If the shares so available are insufficient to satisfy all subscriptions pursuant to the Additional

    4. Rights move in close relation with the stock. They also are generally priced around the parity level, that is, the subscription price plus the cost of the rights equal the market price.

    5. To participate in an oversubscription, you must be a primary subscriber. Therefore it is essential to purchase rights to obtain the oversubscription privilege.

    6. Since this is not an investment situation, dispose of the shares purchased on subscription at the time the rights were purchased.

    7. The foregoing procedure establishes the privilege to subscribe to the oversubscription without having a long position in the shares.

8. If a spread exists at the expiration date, then the oversubscription privilege is exercised.

9. A day or so hence, when advised of the allotment on the oversubscription, these shares are sold, thus establishing a profit.

A few of the recent oversubscription opportunities follow:

General Public Service Corp. Listed on the NYSE. The subscription price was $5, while the shares were priced around 5 3/8 to 5 1/2. The oversubscription participation averaged around 16% of your primary subscription. The net result was that you could have made close to $6 through the oversubscription on each 100 shares of your original purchase.

Southwestern Public Service. Listed on the NYSE. The subscription price was $24.50 per share while the market price was around 27. The oversubscription participation amounted to about 10%. However, the profits are greater than in a low-priced issue since the spread between the subscription price and the market value equaled $2.50 per share.

CHAPTER 13

"Something Doing" Situations

Now that you have absorbed the methods for recognizing and processing special situations, you no doubt realize that this knowledge has byway applications to other profitable investments. Significant profit possibilities exist wherever activity occurs. This brings us to an area which is a bit afield from special situations yet closely related since, generally, all but one of the basic characteristics of a special situation are present. Besides, these situations offer opportunities for substantial profits through the application of your special-situation "know-how." These situations are first recognized by market activity which warrants investigation in any case.

In the situations to which we refer "something is doing" in a certain stock, bond, or company. These situations have what "Wall Street" calls "a kicker," that is, something which gives it romance. And, you rightfully inquire, what can be doing? An early identifying characteristic is that the "something doing" centers around certain securities of a company in order to accomplish an objective. Behind the "something doing" you will find the activities of an individual, a corporation, or a group.

Characteristics

It is sponsorship that makes "something doing" situations. A force opposing the existing status is behind a movement in which a corporation's securities are the focal point. Increased activity could indicate planned "buying." Sponsorship can also be present in the activities of opposing groups, readily identified by a proxy battle for management control; and, in a corporation management's action. Through use of tenders the management may be attempting corporate moves which might substantially raise the market value of a security issue. When a company buys shares of another corporation, sponsorship is present whatever the size of the purchase. The ultimate end may be marriage. "Something doing" situations may be considered currently active if a major part of the objective is to be achieved in the near future.

Where Can "Something Doing" Situations Be Found?

The following is an outline of the areas where "something doing" situations are created, along with a typical example in each. Since most of the examples are currently active they offer opportunities for investigation of profit possibilities.

1. The Business Baron. A "something doing" situation can occur where control of a company is being sought by a business entrepreneur sometimes called "business baron." Merritt, Chapman & Scott's expansion (see Chapter 2) is an example and, today, Burlington Industries is another in their continuing move to further the acquisitions of Pacific Mills and Sidney Blumenthal Co. American Hardware's bid for control of Savage Arms Corp. is seen in their recently announced holdings of more than 50% of the outstanding stock.

2. Holding Companies. "Something doing," akin to the foregoing and also overlapping some classifications of special situations, is the pyramid builders. These are the financiers who construct industrial-commercial holding companies. In character these are similar to the public utility holding companies of the past. However, unlike the latter, the activity is based on partially liquidated enterprises whose cash is used to purchase other concerns and the procedure is repeated as frequently as possible. Another difference is that no product or business relationship exists between the parent and subsidiary companies.

The holding company procedure seeks to obtain control of companies that can be reduced to sizable cash positions. Therefore the first place to look for likely investments is in companies where liquidation seems inevitable. Typical of this condition is Electric-Auto-Lite Co. While it has a strong financial position of about $50 per share in working capital the company is faced with the loss, by 1960, of its main source of revenues - the Chrysler business. Partial liquidation to dispose of excess facilities and build cash for diversification is an apparent step.

The common stock of Electric-Auto-Lite has a book value of $68, while the market price for the shares is around 37. Because this has been a perfect situation for a "control" operation, it now is a component in a pyramid holding company group through the Mergenthaler Lynotype Corp. which owns in excess of 11% of its stock, Mergenthaler, in turn, is controlled by another corporation. However, this factor may not deter other operators or companies from attempting to gain control of Electric-Auto-Lite. In that event a proxy fight might result which could have sharp influence, marketwise, on the shares.

Profit possibilities in holding company situations arise first in the shares of companies being acquired since these shares will be in demand. The secondary beneficiary may be the company sponsoring the activity, though this might not be effective until later. Bear in mind that when shares are being accumulated the purchaser may make successive public-tender offers at higher prices in order to obtain the needed amount for control. This practice may give you a second chance to "get in" if you were not aware of the original purchasing.

An example is Houdaille Industries, which recently acquired a "majority" of the stock of Buffalo Eclipse Corp. through two offers to purchase. The first offer brought in approximately 20% of the outstanding shares, while the second offer completed the required amount.

A typical pyramid holding company is Century Investors. Through its own holdings and control of Webster Investors, Inc., it controls American Mfg. The latter company controls Mergenthaler Linotype Co., which has important holdings of Electric-Auto-Lite Co., which recently acquired a 10% interest in Crane Co. This shows how the cash of one company has been used to acquire control of another, while the top company in the pyramid just pulls the strings.

3. <u>Forced Change of Management</u>. A "something doing" situation may be detected <u>where a new group</u> desires to depose the incumbent management in order to obtain control for themselves. The Bullard Company is a good example since a publicized proxy fight, last year, indicated continued buying by the opposition to strengthen their position. In such cases the proxy fight, combined with the purchasing pressure of both management and opposition, tends to give the shares a floor as well as appreciation possibilities. An identifying characteristic of this type is a poor business record which makes the company vulnerable to "change of management." Nevertheless, Bullard shares have enjoyed a range in price from a low of 10 to a recent high of 18. Of course, the famous proxy fight by Wolfson for control of Montgomery Ward brought substantial profits to the stockholders during that fray.

4. <u>Carry-Forward Tax Loss</u>. "Something doing" is quite likely to be the case where a company has a sizable "tax loss." The Revenue Act permits a corporation the following leeway: (a) to carry back an operating loss to each of the three taxable years preceding the year such loss was established; (b) to carry such loss forward to each of the five following years. This extends the loss period to nine years.

Thus a company with losses can have tax-free years while its profits offset the losses. If a company finds itself unable to make use of the tax loss, it can search for a profitable corporation to acquire it or merge. In this way the profits will be doubly swelled because of freedom from taxes. Thus a company with $2 million tax-loss credit could earn $2 million without becoming subject to taxes. Without the tax credit, taxes would reduce its net to $960,000. A recent example of the use of tax credits is Food Giant Markets, to which the unprofitable Magic Chef Co. sold out. Using the tax credit, the new organization showed a profit of 45¢ per share in 1957, while 1958 is expected to net about $2.25 per share. The stock, of course, enjoyed a substantial rise.

The Studebaker-Packard situation is of current interest since large potentials are present in the $134 million tax credit. New management has taken over, and its use of the tax credit could create opportunities for profit from acquisitions as well as its own development.

The field of carry-forward tax credits is broad, with new situations developing daily. To give you an idea of the types of companies involved, we have prepared the following table, which presents a few companies currently have substantial tax credits.

CARRY-FORWARD TAX CREDITS

Company	Amount	Per Share	Earnings 1957	Approx. Price
American Motors	$47,000,000	8.41	d. 2.12	33
Blumenthal (Sidney)	3,800,000	6.50	0.27	6
Duplan Corp.	4,350,000	4.45	0.07	11
Elgin Natl. Watch	6,000,000	6.57	d. 2.68	10
Glen Alden	14,000,000	8.00	d. 1.64	10
Jacobs (F. L.)	7,000,000	7.29	d. 1.12	9
Kaiser Industries	23,000,000	1.01	0.70	14
Mohasco Industries	10,500,000	3.42	0.96	12
Servel, Inc.	18,000,000	9.90	d. 0.22	9
Studebaker-Packard	134,000,000	20.81	d. 1.73	15
Textron, Inc.	31,600,000	7.40	2.25	18
Underwood Corp.	13,000,000	17.15	d. 2.13	20

d = deficit.

5. "Worth More Dead Than Alive." "Something is doing" when an operator or group seeks to liquidate or change a company which apparently is worth more dead than alive, as in Motor Products at the earliest stage of its development. (See following page). It was also believed to be present in Loew's, Inc., recently in a management battle for life or liquidation. The analytical study of Motor Products Corp. was used to acquaint the author's clients with the company's changing conditions. It shows the working procedure used to locate and follow through a "something doing" investment. In this discussion you see the pertinent factors, (the Motor Products Corp. illustration is lettered alphabetically for corellation), which create this type of investment:

    a. Business reverses and losses
    b. New program and sale of property
    c. Strong financial position
    d. Merger-offer germ planted
    e. Calculations of potentials
    f. New directors
    g. Additional sales of properties

Over the past few years this situation developed from a liquidation possibility to the present revamped organization, with the stock now around 33 after having been split two for one.

MOTOR PRODUCTS CORP.

Price: 24 1/2 - N.Y.S.E.

An old time company that apparently has turned the corner to better times is Motor Products Corp. The company's principal business is that of a supplier of original automotive equipment, such as window vents, instrument panels and automotive hardware, while other products include freezers and refrigerators.

(a) The company had been confronted with a series of unfortunate business reverses which required strong corrective measures. The recent difficulties consisted of an industry-wide decline in sales directly affecting the Deepfreeze division, coupled with a decline in atuomotive profit margins. The latter was due to unexpected retooling costs and a strike in the Canadian division. Readjustments, which have been substantially completed, brought sales, volume, costs and production capacity into earning power line.

(b) The annual report recently released discloses a fiscal program which is now in effect. A summary of the program, as stated, follows: "Operating profits in the automotive parts divisions if automotive sales continue at anticipated levels; Deepfreeze losses eliminated after the sale of one plant; the financial atmosphere cleared with the elimination of bank indebtedness; working capital returned to about $15,000,000. These plans, if completed by December 31, 1955, should permit the company to consider the resumption of dividend payments, the objective which is for the benefit of all the shareholders."

(c) Despite the recent difficulties, the company has been able to maintain a strong current asset position, which at June 30, 1955, amounted to $26.58, while book value stood at $46.59. A factor of significance is the company's small capitalization, which consists of only 468,304 common shares and the aforementioned bank loans of $4,900,000, available under a revolving credit arrangement.

(d) This compact capitalization creates a favorable base for a merger or acquisition. In this category it is interesting to note that last December the General Tire Corp. offered approximately $23.50 per share for 315,000 shares (being a majority interest in the company). However, the offer failed to be consummated due to strong opposition. An interesting new influence presented itself in merger tactics at this juncture, when the Union actively opposed the acquisition.

(e) Despite this opposition, the present trend of mergers and acquisitions, particularly in the field of suppliers of components, leads us to believe that one of these developments will take place. Thus the shares at $24.50 would appear to be greatly undervalued in relation to the current assets and book value. In this respect it would seem reasonable to estimate a minimum price of midway between the current assets and book value as the price objective. This would be equal to an appreciation of approximately 50% above the present price of the stock.

(f) As a merger or acquisition plan is not known to be in the offing, a purchaser of shares at this time would be faced with a waiting period. During this time the stockholder should, as indicated, receive some dividends. He would also participate in the benefits resulting from the influence of the upper echelon's new blood. Here it is interesting to note the several changes that have been made in both the

continued

MOTOR PRODUCTS CORP. (CONTINUED)   Page - 2 -

management and the Board of Directors. Mr. William Golden, Chairman of the Executive Committee of National U.S. Radiator Corp., Mr. Fred M. Kaufman, a partner in an investment banking firm, and Mr. David A. Wallace, former President of the Chrysler Division of Chrysler Corporation, have been added to the Board.

(g) Recent activities include the sale and offering for sale of inefficient manufacturing plants, while production has been expanded in retained factories. This, plus modernization of facilities, and the relief from untimely retooling by customers, which previously had increased costs, portend profitable operations for the ensuing fiscal year.

It is interesting to note that the company has operated profitably in every year but two of the past 15 years and that some dividends have been paid in all but the past year. Earnings reached $9.73 per share in 1950, while the ten-year average amounts to $4.75, despite the past two years of deficit operations. The accompanying table shows the ten-year sales, earnings, dividends and price range.

Year	Net Sales*	Earnings*	Dividends	Price Range High	Low
1955	$83.4 +	$3.73(d)		26 1/8	20
1954	87.0	2.41(d)	$1.50	23 7/8	16 1/4
1953	101.6	6.62	2.00	34 3/8	21
1952	74.3	6.11	2.00	32	22 1/2
1951	104.3	3.20	2.67	31 3/4	23 1/2
1950	65.7	9.75	1.67	39 1/4	22 1/4
1949	59.1	5.81	1.67	22 7/8	13 3/4
1948	46.2	6.11	1.67	24 5/8	17 1/4
1947	36.7	3.98	1.25	22 3/4	14 1/8
1946	16.8	1.01	0.42	28 1/2	13 1/4
1945	24.0	2.16	0.83	28 1/8	18 1/8

* Fiscal year ended June 30.
+ Millions.
(d)=Deficit.

6. <u>Declining Business Trend.</u> "Something is doing" can be found in a company which is in a declining business trend, making it vulnerable to acquisition by another. The company can try to strengthen itself through acquisition of other companies. Electric-Auto-Lite, whose business has been receding, offers an example of both conditions. Recently it acquired a block of Crane Co. for just under $7 million. Over the recent years Electric-Auto-Lite has disposed of certain properties and is seeking other sources of income. In the interim it is exceedingly strong in cash. For other information about this company, see page 168. Underwood Corp., which failed to consummate proposed mergers, falls into the category of a high-asset-value company, ripe for "something doing" in a merger or acquisitions. Besides, the company has a substantial tax credit (see table, page 170).

7. _A Tender_. A clue to "something doing" may be found in a tender. Parmelee Transportation Co.'s recent tender offer (see Chapter 4, Tenders) has led to the disclosure of sales of certain assets. Because of this and the company's close relationship with Checker Motors and Chicago Yellow Cab, where things may be brewing, the situation warrants investigation.

8. _Holdout Opportunities_. The accompanying discussion and work-out procedure of a "holdout" situation deals with another type of "something doing" situations. Burlington Industries' bid for Sidney Blumenthal & Co., in the course of which it acquired 77% of the Blumenthal stock, offered an opportunity for a holdout situation. A condition of the acquisition stated that Burlington would purchase the remaining stock at $6.50 per share from other stockholders. S. Blumenthal & Co. stock had been priced around 7 3/8 at the time of the offer, thus indicating a difference in opinion as to the value of the security. The holdout procedure follows:

A holdout is a security holder who declines to sell at a proferred price. Unlike a dissenter seeking an appraisal, the holdout is a passive objector while the dissenter is an aggressive contender for a better price. A holdout has not established the right to demand a fair value for his securities, nor has he any intention of doing anything about getting a better price other than "sit and wait."

Opportunities for holdout positions arise from mergers, recapitalizations, reorganizations, and instances where control of a corporation is being furthered. A holdout has basis for his negative position in that, he has reason to believe that a better offer will be forthcoming. This is the essence of the holdout's investment position. His confidence in an ultimately higher price for the security rests on the following:

    a. The security issue gives control to the buyer.
    b. It gives the buyer accounting benefits.
    c. It gives the buyer substantial tax benefits.
    d. It permits consolidation of a security position.
    e. It cleans up an outstanding minority stock interest.

If your holdout position is based on the presence of any of the above factors, then proceed with the following investigation.

Analytical Procedure

1. A financial evaluation of the security. This will establish:

    a. Whether the security is worth holding over a protracted period.
    b. Whether the potential profit is satisfactory.

2. An investigation of the company which has made the offer. This may be the company which issued the security, or an outside source. The

investigation may produce a clue as to possibilities for subsequent offers. When a company has established a precedent of making offers for securities, you may assume that it will continue to do so.

This has occurred in innumerable instances, particularly where a large corporation is desirous of buying securities of subsidiaries or affiliated companies. Standard Oil of New Jersey, New York Central RR, and Western Union are classic examples.

The following case history shows how a hidden tax credit was turned into a holdout situation that resulted in substantial profits.

RKO Pictures Corporation sold its assets to Howard Hughes for $23,489,478. Stockholders were offered $6 for every share turned in to the corporation. The shares reflected this offer and were priced at the $6 level. However, examination of the facts behind the offer disclosed reasons against selling one's shares to the corporation.

The initial reports stated that all of RKO's assets and properties had been sold and that stockholders had the right to get $6 a share for all shares submitted. In fact this was a tender offer. Further information stated that Mr. Hughes would retire all outstanding shares (at the rate of $6 a share), except his own, and thus become the sole owner of RKO Pictures Corporation. Mr. Hughes owned 1,262,120 of the 3,914,913 shares outstanding.

Disclosure of the Shell Game

The point that many stockholders did not realize was that, while the $6 per share appeared to be a minimum price (though limited to 60 days), as stated in the terms of "liquidation" of assets, the corporate shell remained in existence and had a value. If all stock were turned in, then Mr. Hughes as the sole stockholder would have complete ownership. However, some investors realized the value of the RKO shell, and the situation became stalemated. Nevertheless, about one million shares had been redeemed. Subsequently, a NYSE report disclosed that Atlas Corporation had purchased nearly 17% of the outstanding shares. The price on the exchange had moved to 6 1/8, which was understood to be Atlas' bid. There was no public comment from Atlas regarding the purchase.

The shares continued to reflect the purchasing influence and advanced to $7.37. Atlas Corporation's interest grew to 884,900 as compared with Mr. Hughes' 1,262,120. News releases revealed that negotiations were pending for the sale of Mr. Hughes' holdings to the corporation at $6 per share. This was a reversal of the original plan.

A report from the company disclosed the expiration of the $6 tender offer. It further disclosed that neither Mr. Hughes nor Atlas Corporation had tendered any shares and that between 700,000 and 800,000 shares of stock exclusive of the aforementioned were outstanding. The more important item contained in that report stated:

"Your Company has been advised by its tax counsel that, under the recently enacted new federal tax code, its substantial capital loss presently continues to be a capital-loss carry-forward available under appropriate circumstances as a set-off against capital gains (if any) that might be realized by your Company in the future; which capital-loss carry-forward, based upon preliminary study, may be as much as approximately $30,000,000."

Thus, stockholders who held out fared better by 23% if they sold at the $7.37 price, while others eventually did even better as the shares moved higher.

How to Get the Profit -- The Procedure in "Something Doing"

Your making a profit depends in the first place upon your ability to place a situation within a category. This is an important aid to your analysis since proper classification will clarify the objective of your search. Through classification you will know whether you seek asset value, new management's aggressive influence, or whether you are merely riding along in a proxy battle.

You will note that the foregoing "something doing" situations are unlike our special situations because the profit is not in existence. The profit is often dependent upon the market appreciation of the security. The appreciation possibilities in most instances reflects such influences as the success of the sponsor's activity, the general market's evaluation along with the calculated worth of the situation. This latter factor will vary widely since in many instances it may be an evaluation of management's potentials.

The profit, then, is partly in your appraisal of the situation and in the achievement of the sponsor's objective. Since you do nothing directly toward the success of the movement, then your scope of analysis lies mainly within the security. The approach, therefore, is to establish a value for the security (on its own) in relation to the market. This will be determined by the type of situation with which you are working. Evaluation for a liquidation is different than for a merger or proxy battle, since the former is an asset-value situation while the latter will reflect market movement. Don't lose sight of dividends or interest that accrue to you.

It is advisable to note whether the security has discounted any portion of the potential. This, of course, would be the difference between your evaluation of the security on its own and the market price. Should the market price be lower than your evaluation, so much the better for your prospects.

The next step is to examine the situation for duration. Always be ready to sell the security should the "movement" lose momentum or fail to achieve the objective.

Since the main reason for considering the situation is to participate in the "something doing," an important part of the procedure is to endeavor to know the people behind the move. Helpful information channels, open to the public, include:

company meetings, protective committees, officers and directors of the company, and conversations with important or large security holders.

Where are the sources of information about these situations?

Awareness about a "something doing" situation can be acquired from talking with people in financial circles. Reading newspapers, trade journals, and financial publications will turn up useful information. Observing the market activity of the security provides clues.

"Something doing" situations fall within two classes in regard to information. Where the "something doing" is currently in progress, the information has become widespread. Where you are anticipating an action you can combine the clues you have picked up with the know-how you have gathered from this book to piece together sufficient information to act upon your own judgment. Bear in mind that "something doing" situations are created by people, either individuals, groups, or a corporation acting as people. "Something doing" could not come into being without sponsorship. Therefore the situations often generate dynamic, aggressive security market momentum.

This brings to a close the journey through special situations. You are now well equipped to practice the art of making money through special-situation investments.

For you, therefore, the end of this book is

THE BEGINNING.

INDEX

A

ACF Brill Motors, Inc., 62, 63, 64
Allied Paper Co., 49
American Bank Note Co., 82, 83
American Can, 41
American Car & Foundry Corp., 133, 136
American Cyanamid, 39
American Hardware Co., 168
American-Hawaiian S.S. Co., 59
American Mfg. Co., 169
American Metal Climax, Inc., 157
American Motor Corp., 152, 154, 170
American Power & Light, 66, 72, 75, 116, 117
American Republics Corp., 45, 46
American Screw Co., 39, 77
American Woolen Corp., 13, 14, 37, 38, 138
Arkansas Fuel Corp., 39
Associated General Public Utilities Corp., 54, 55
Atlantic Coast Line Railroad, 40
Atlanta & West Point R.R., 66, 69, 70
Atlas Corp., 39, 174
Austin Nichols, 41

B

Backmann Uxbridge Co., 38
Bangor & Aroostook Railroad, 40
Barium Steel, 163, 165
Basic Products, 41
Blaw-Knox & Co., 43
Sidney Blumenthal & Co., 168, 170, 173
Boston Elevated Ry. Co., 50
Boston & Maine Railroad, 40
Boston & Providence R.R., 73
Briggs Mfg. Co., 34, 35, 36, 46
Buffalo Eclipse Corp., 169
Bullard Co., 169
Burlington Industries, 168, 173
Bush Terminal Co., 41
H. M. Byllesby & Co., 125, 126, 127

C

Celotex Corp., 41
Central Hudson Gas & Electric Corp., 161
Central Illinois Light, 119
Century Investors, 169
Checker Motors Corp., 78, 80, 173
Chicago Eastern Illinois R.R., 133
Chicago Yellow Cab., 173
Chrysler Corp., 34, 168
Cities Service, 39
City Investing Co., 97
Climax Molybdenum Co., 157
Commodore Hotel, Inc., 86
Commonwealth & Southern Corp., 119
Consolidated Paper Co., 25
Consolidated Retail Stores, Inc., 66, 68, 91, 92, 94
Consumer Power Co., 119
Continental Foundry & Machine Co., 43
Crane Co., 169, 172
Creole Petroleum, 79

D

De Voe & Raynolds Co., 14, 16
Denver & Rio Grande, Western Ry., 75, 99, 100, 101, 102, 103, 104, 141, 145
Duplan Corp., 170
du Pont de Nemours, 41, 64, 92
Duquesne Light Co., 114, 126, 127, 128

E

Eastern Corp., 41
Eastern N.Y. Power Corp., 120, 122, 123, 124
Eastern Steamship Lines, Inc., 83, 84, 85
Electric Auto Lite Co., 46, 168, 169, 172
Electric Bond & Share Co., 117
Elgin Natl. Watch, 170
Equitable Office Bldg., 95-96

F

Firstamerica Corp., 60, 61, 62
Follansbee Steel Corp., 38
Food Giant Markets, 169
Foremost Dairies, Inc., 20, 156

G

Gatineau Power Corp., 120, 122, 123, 124
General Bancshares, Inc., 64
General Cigar Co., 41
General Contract Co., 64, 92
General Dynamics Corp., 33, 34
General Motors Corp., 64, 92
General Public Service Corp., 166
General Public Utilities Corp., 54, 55
General Realty & Utilities Corp., 59
Georgia Railroad & Banking Co., 69
Glen Alden Co., 170
Gold & Stock Telegraph Co., 74, 75
Golden State Co. Ltd., 20
Graham-Paige, 63

H

Hall Scott Motors, 62, 63
Hevi-Duty Electric, 41
Hickock Oil Corp., 36
Hilton-Davis Chemical Co., 27, 28, 29, 30, 31, 32
R. Hoe & Co., 75, 140, 142
Houdaille Industries, 169
Hudson & Manhattan R.R. Co., 97, 105, 106, 107
Hudson Motors, Inc., 23, 24, 26, 149, 151, 152, 153, 154

I

Internat'l Hydro Electric Corp., 116, 120, 121, 122, 123, 124
Internat'l Paper Co., 66, 71, 120
International Railways of Central America, 41, 59

J

Jacobs (F. L.), 170

K

Kaiser Industries, 170
Kalamazoo Stove & Furnace Co., 55, 56, 57

L

Liquid Carbonic Corp., 33, 34
Loew's, Inc., 64, 170
Louisville Gas & Electric Co., 126

M

Magic Chef Co., 169
Maine Central R.R., 40
Manufacturers Trust Co., 97
Maremount Automotive Products Co., 57
Marion Power Shovel Co., 14, 16, 24, 25, 26
Marquardt Motors, 41
Maxson Food System Corp., 156
McCrory Stores, Inc., 18
McLellan Stores, Inc., 18
Merck & Co., 12, 33
Mergenthaler Lynotype Corp., 168, 169
Merritt, Chapman & Scott Corp., 14, 15, 24, 25, 26, 168
Metal & Thermite Co., 41
Middle South Co., 113
Middle South Utilities Inc., 159
Missouri Pacific R.R., 88, 90, 91, 109, 110, 111, 112, 141
Mohasco Industries, 170
Montgomery Ward, 169
Motor Products Corp., 170, 171
Mt. States Power Co., 126
Mt. Vernon Mills, 39

N

Nash Kelvinator Corp., 23, 26, 57, 151, 152
New England Electric System, 120, 122, 123
New York Central R.R., 40, 174
New York, New Haven & Hartford R.R., 31, 40, 66, 67, 73
New York, New Haven & Hartford Railroad CBI's, 73
New York Shipbuilding Co., 15, 16
Newport Steel Corp., 14, 16, 24
Niagara Mohawk Power Corp., 124
Noma Lites, Inc., 39
Norfolk & Western Ry, 40
Norwich Pharmacal, 39

O

Occidental Life Insurance Co. of California, 60, 61
Ohio Edison Co., 113, 119
Oklahoma Gas & Electric Co., 114, 126, 128
Olin Mathison Chemical, 41
Oliver Corp., 41
Osgood Co., 15, 16, 24
Overland Corp., 47
Owens-Illinois Glass, 66, 68

P

Pacific Mills, 168
Parmelee Transportation Co., 78, 79, 80, 173
Penn Dixie Cement Co., 140, 141
Pennsylvania R.R., 40
Philadelphia Co., 114, 125, 127, 128
Philadelphia Reading Co., 49
Pittsburgh Railway Co., 126, 127, 128
Porter Co., 40
Portland Gas & Coke, 72
Pure Oil, 36

R

Radio Corp. of America, 41
Rayonier, Inc., 41
Reaction Motors, 41

Remington Arms, 41
Republic Steel Corp., 38
Revlon, Inc., 41
Richfield Oil, 41
Ridgeway Co., 66, 71
Rio de Oro Uranium Mines, Inc., 39
RKO Pictures Corp., 174
Robbins Mills Co., 13, 14, 38
Royal American Corp., 63
Rutland Ry., 40

S

Savage Arms Corp., 168
Schenley, Inc., 41
Schick, Inc., 41
Seaboard Air Line R.R., 40
Servel Corp., 48, 49, 170
Sharp & Dohme Co., 12, 33
Sinclair Oil, 41, 43
South Carolina Electric & Gas Co., 162, 163
South Coast Corp., 41
So. Colo. Pwr. Co., 126
Southern Co., 113, 119
Southern Natural Gas, 43
Southern Production, 42, 43
Southwestern Public Service, 166
Standard Gas & Elec., 66, 67, 70, 114, 116, 124 thru 130
Standard Oil Co. of N.J., 79, 174
Standard Power & Light Corp., 114, 124, 125, 126, 127, 128, 130
Sterling Drug, Inc., 27, 30, 31, 32
Studebaker-Packard, 170
Susquehanna Corp., 39

T

Tennessee Products & Chemical Corp., 15, 16
Texas Pac. Coal & Oil, 41
Textron, Inc., 13, 14, 37, 38, 39, 77, 170
Thermoid Corp., 40
Thor Corp., 49
Transamerica Corp., 60, 61, 62, 64, 92

U

Underwood Corp., 170, 172
Union Chemical & Materials Corp., 39
Union Electric Co., 113
United Corporation, 127
United Fruit Corp., 41, 59
Utah Fuel Co., 75, 103

V

Virginian Ry., 40
Vitro Minerals Corp., 39

W

Warner Bros. Pictures, Inc., 80, 81
Waukesha Motors, 41
Webster Investors, Inc., 169
Western Ry of Alabama, 66, 69
Western Union Telegraph Co., 74, 75, 174
Whirlpool Corp., 41
Willys Overland Motors Co., 26, 47
Wisconsin Public Service Co., 114, 126, 128

The information in this Report is based on sources and computations believed to be reliable. It has been carefully checked for completeness and accuracy but cannot, of course, be guaranteed. Nothing in this Report is to be taken as advice to buy or sell specific securities.